658.8

Macmillan Business Masters

Marketing

Macmillan Business Masters

Company Accounts Roger Oldcorn
Economics S. F. Goodman
Financial Management Geoffrey Knott
Management Roger Oldcorn
Marketing Geoff Lancaster and Paul Reynolds
Operations Management Howard Barnett
Personnel Management Margaret Attwood and Stuart Dimmock

Marketing

Geoff Lancaster
and
Paul Reynolds

First published 1998 by
MACMILLAN PRESS LTD
Houndmills, Basingstoke, Hampshire RG21 6XS
and London
Companies and representatives throughout the world

ISBN 0–333–65847–7

A catalogue record for this book is available from the British Library.

This book is printed on paper suitable for recycling and made from
fully managed and sustained forest sources.

10   9   8   7   6   5   4   3   2   1
07   06   05   04   03   02   01   00   99   98

Printed in Great Britain by
Creative Print & Design (Wales), Ebbw Vale

Contents

1 Development of the Marketing Concept   **1**
1.1   An Early Historical Perspective   1
1.2   The Modern Era   3
1.3   Different Types of Business Orientation   10
1.4   Summary   11

2 Marketing and the Macro-environment   **13**
2.1   The Micro-environment   13
2.2   The Proximate Macro-environment   19
2.3   The Wider Macro-environment   21
2.4   Other Macro-environmental Factors   24
2.5   Summary   25

3 Customers and Marketing   **27**
3.1   Segmentation Defined   27
3.2   Targeted Marketing Efforts   28
3.3   Effective Segmentation   29
3.4   Segmentation Bases in Consumer Product Markets   30
3.5   Segmentation Bases in Industrial Product Markets   37
3.6   Effective Segmentation   39
3.7   Product Positioning   40
3.8   Summary   41

4 Buyer Behaviour   **42**
4.1   Importance of Understanding Customer Motives   42
4.2   Social and Cultural Influences   42
4.3   Specific Social Influences   44
4.4   Models of Consumer Behaviour   54
4.5   Organisational Buying Behaviour   60
4.6   Summary   68

5   Marketing Information Systems and Forecasting   **70**
   5.1   Introduction   70
   5.2   Marketing Information Systems   71
   5.3   Component Parts of the System   73
   5.4   Designing, Implementing and Controlling an MkIS   83
   5.5   Cost–Benefit Aspects of MkIS   84
   5.6   Forecasting   86
   5.7   Forecasting Methods I – Subjective Methods   91
   5.8   Forecasting Methods II – Objective Methods   92
   5.9   Summary   99

6   Marketing Research   **101**
   6.1   Introduction   101
   6.2   Definition of Marketing Research   102
   6.3   Marketing Research and Marketing Information Systems   102
   6.4   Types of Marketing Research   104
   6.5   Stages in the Research Process   107
   6.6   Tools of Marketing Research   108
   6.7   Main Research Areas   113
   6.8   Summary   116

7   Products and Services   **118**
   7.1   Defining the Product   118
   7.2   Categories of Products   119
   7.3   Product Management   122
   7.4   New Products   123
   7.5   Product Mix and Product Line   127
   7.6   Product Life-cycle   128
   7.7   Product Diffusion and Adoption   134
   7.8   Portfolio Models   136
   7.9   Packaging   146
   7.10 Summary   147

8   Prices   **149**
   8.1   The Importance of Pricing   149
   8.2   Pricing Perspectives   150
   8.3   Pricing Decisions   150
   8.4   Concepts of Pricing   152
   8.5   Tactical Pricing Issues   165
   8.6   Summary   166

9   Channels of Distribution   **168**
   9.1   Introduction   168
   9.2   Channels of Distribution and the Marketing Concept   169
   9.3   Indirect versus Direct Systems   170

9.4	The Nature of Distribution	173
9.5	Strategic Elements of Channel Choice	175
9.6	Changes in the Structure of Retailing	183
9.7	Summary	189

10 Logistics Management — **191**

10.1	Scope of Logistics Management	191
10.2	History and Development of Logistics Management	194
10.3	Definitions	197
10.4	The Distribution Process	197
10.5	A Systems Approach to PDM	200
10.6	Monitoring and Control of PDM	202
10.7	Summary	206

11 Managing Selling — **209**

11.1	Importance of Personal Selling to the Organisation	209
11.2	Benefits of Personal Selling	211
11.3	The Broader Task of Selling	211
11.4	Different Types of Selling Task	213
11.5	Selling Skills and Qualities	215
11.6	The Selling Routine	216
11.7	Sales Management	226
11.8	Summary	233

12 Above and Below-the-line Promotion — **235**

12.1	Introduction	235
12.2	Real and Implied Product Attributes	236
12.3	Needs and Wants	238
12.4	The Marketing Communications Mix	240
12.5	The Marketing Communications Process	243
12.6	Above-the-line Promotion	249
12.7	Advertising Models	250
12.8	Below-the-line Promotion	255
12.9	The Main Elements of Sales Promotion	256
12.10	Summary	263

13 Public Relations — **266**

13.1	Intoduction	266
13.2	The Role and Nature of Public Relations	269
13.3	What PR is Not	273
13.4	The Need for Public Relations	276
13.5	Publics	276
13.6	Media Used in Public Relations	284
13.7	Internal and Relationship Marketing	287
13.8	Summary	288

viii   *Contents*

14   International Marketing   **290**
   14.1   International Marketing Definitions   290
   14.2   The Significance of International Marketing   290
   14.3   A Macro-overview of International Trade   293
   14.4   The Four Ps of the International Marketing Mix 295
   14.5   Sales Channels   300
   14.6   Cultural and Environmental Factors   303
   14.7   Summary   304

15   Marketing Planning   **307**
   15.1   Marketing Planning in the Context of Corporate
        Planning   307
   15.2   An Overview of Marketing Planning   309
   15.3   Summary   316

References   318
Index   320

1 Development of the Marketing Concept

The concept of marketing is not a particularly complicated or even original idea. Sayings such as 'the customer comes first' or 'the customer is always right' have been used by forward-thinking merchants and entrepreneurs throughout the ages. Based on that age-old principle, marketing is really a more formalised business orientation that has developed into a management discipline over the years.

1.1 An Early Historical Perspective

Marketing is principally concerned with exchange or trade. Trade in its most basic form has existed ever since mankind has been capable of producing a surplus. Historically, this surplus was usually agricultural produce which was often traded for manufactured goods such as textiles or earthenware. Exchange brought into existence places that facilitated trade, such as village fairs and local markets. The emergence of trade allowed people to specialise in producing particular goods and services which could be exchanged in markets for other goods they needed.

The period 1760–1830 saw the United Kingdom's economy transformed during the so-called Industrial Revolution, losing its dependence on agriculture with a dramatic increase in industrial production. Before the Industrial Revolution, the production and distribution of goods tended to be on a small scale. Industrialisation resulted in dramatic gains in productivity, mainly due to the development of machines. Production became more geographically concentrated and was carried out in purpose-built mills or factories. Enterprises became larger, production-runs longer and products more standardised. Firms produced in volume, not only for a local market, but for a national and even an international market. The growth of the 'factory system' caused the migration of the population from the countryside to the new and rapidly expanding industrial towns.

Because of developments during the period of the Industrial Revolution, firms could produce more in terms of volume than the local economy could absorb. Consumption therefore became dispersed over greater geographical distances and producers no longer had immediate contact with their markets. To get over this problem, many forward-thinking entrepreneurs of the time started to plan their business operations in a 'marketing orientated' manner, although the terms 'marketing' or 'marketing orientation' were not formally used to describe this process until well into the twentieth century as we explain later.

In order for producers to be able to manufacture goods and services that would appeal and sell in widely dispersed markets, it became necessary for them to carefully analyse and interpret the needs and wants of customers and to manufacture products which would 'fit in' with those needs and wants.

The process of matching the resources of a firm to the needs and wants of the marketplace is called **entrepreneurship**. Men such as Josiah Wedgwood (1730–95) came to epitomise the traditional entrepreneur with their ability to 'sense' what the market wanted in terms of design, quality and price, then organise production and distribution to satisfy effective demand at a profit. The early entrepreneurs were practising an early, albeit simplistic, form of marketing activity, although it was not called marketing as such.

A craftsman, such as a blacksmith or potter, develops a high degree of skill in a particular activity. Industrialisation took the processes of specialisation and division of labour a stage further, resulting in greater productivity which, in turn, reduced costs and hence the selling price of products. However, the rise in job specialisation also increased the need for exchange. Larger-scale production meant that marketing channels had to be created to facilitate the distribution of goods to enable the effective demand from the much larger market to be met. This development laid the foundations of the modern industrial economy, which is still based on the fundamental concept of trade or exchange.

During the first half of the nineteenth century Britain was the dominant force in the world economy, and the main factor underlying its industrial growth was the development in international trade. Britain was first and foremost a trading nation which had secured supplies of raw materials and held a virtual monopoly in the supply of manufactured goods to the relatively underdeveloped countries which collectively made up the British Empire.

Activity

Suppose that the United Kingdom had not been at the forefront of the Industrial Revolution. Do you feel that we would be better off or worse off as a nation nowadays?

The immediate answer is probably: 'We would be worse off'. However, the thought processes that such a question would invoke are:

- Sometimes it is better to follow than to lead, so we might have been better off;
- Living on past glories tends to make a nation complacent;
- When you are in the lead there is less for which to compete.

The question is of course hypothetical, so there can be no right or wrong answer. It is, however, a fruitful question as a source of debate.

1.2 The Modern Era

The first half of the twentieth century saw the emergence of Germany and the United States as competing industrial powers. Although the United Kingdom faced fierce competition from the economically emerging nations in the areas of textiles, coal and steel, the British economy continued along a path of industrial expansion in the period up to the First World War. The incomes generated in other countries resulted in a worldwide increase in total effective demand for goods and services. The total value of UK trade increased even though its share of international trade started to decline.

In order to better understand the notion of marketing orientation, which puts customers first, we must trace back its historical development as it took place in the United Kingdom. We must also examine the different philosophical views that pertained in relation to business at different periods of time.

Adam Smith

Perhaps the most enduring of quotations that emphasises marketing orientation comes from Adam Smith at the time of the Industrial Revolution when he wrote in his now classic *Wealth of Nations*:

'Consumption is the sole end and purpose of all production and the interests of the producer ought to be attended to only as far as it may be necessary for promoting that of the consumer.'

However, he went on in this same quotation to point out that producers do not take this obvious logic seriously:

'The maxim is so perfectly self evident that it would be absurd to attempt to prove it. But in the mercantile system, the interest of the consumer is almost constantly sacrificed to that of producers who seem to consider production, and not consumption, as the ultimate end and object of all industry and commerce.'

This was long-sighted vision on the part of Adam Smith and it was said at the time of the Industrial Revolution. It is also true that the notion of marketing orientation and putting customers first has only been taken up relatively recently as we shortly explain.

Activity

Why do you feel it took until the twentieth century to formally recognise marketing orientation, even though it was first informally recognised and practiced by some entrepreneurs at the time of the Industrial Revolution?

This, perhaps, is a rather difficult question and it is probably more useful as a topic for debate. The answer lies in the fact that theory in marketing, and indeed most other business disciplines, is established by observing the phenomenon (as a kind of case study or series of case studies) and then establishing that a trend exists. Once this becomes an established tendency (through statistical or behavioural observation) then it becomes a theory. By its very vagueness, you will see later that such theory comes in for much criticism. In the case of the recognition of marketing orientation it was not until the twentieth century, as we shall see, that the trends referred to here became known as marketing orientation. In the physical sciences is perhaps easier to establish theories, because most of the experiments are laboratory-based, and observation and statistical testing prove or disprove a theory. In the behavioural sciences (such as marketing) theory rests upon observing the phenomenon as it happens and then recording what happened. Only when sufficient happenings have taken place and trends established can it be called a theory, and even then such theories are often not based upon hard evidence. This is why many physical scientists tend to eschew the behavioural sciences, because of their imprecision, and indeed the behavioural sciences are sometimes collectively referred to as: 'soft sciences'.

Before we examine the notion of marketing orientation in more detail, it is worthwhile reflecting for a moment on the three principal types of production:

- **Job production** – which is essentially 'one-off' production where every aspect of production and manufacture is done as a separate task from the design stage to the completion stage. Here, skilled personnel are needed in design and manufacturing processes as 'no two jobs are alike'. As such, it tends to be a relatively expensive process.
- **Batch production** – is similar in terms of its philosophy to job production, but the numbers produced are more than one. Sometimes a batch is produced, followed by another similar batch later, and the times between batches are a reflection of when products are needed by customers.

These are the two types of production that pertained in world manufacture until 1913. This is the date that Henry Ford set up the first-ever continuous flow line production assembly plant in Detroit, USA to manufacture the model 'T' Ford motor car. The first model 'T' Ford was produced in 1908 using batch production methods, and this car was developed out of the original model 'A' Ford which dated back to 1903. This, then, was the start of mass or flow production.

- **Flow production** – is where all aspects of manufacture are broken down into their simplest components of labour. It uses a continuous production line and, as such, unskilled (and less individually expensive) labour can be used. More to the point, it is a quicker and more efficient method of production and the savings in production costs should mean that these can be passed onto customers in terms of reduced prices.

Activity

List three types of products that are typically manufactured under each of the headings:

- Job production;
- Batch production;
- Flow production.

Under job production 'one-off' products like shipbuilding, power stations and hospitals should be cited. Under batch production, typical products are, 'designer' clothes, mining machinery and machine tools, although the latter two can be job production when they are 'one-off' products. Flow production is appropriate for motor cars, televisions and mass produced clothing.

Henry Ford was not secretive about this outstanding development in manufacturing technique. In fact he opened up his Detroit plant for inspection as a model for world manufacturing and before long other motor manufacturers in the USA emulated this system. In a very short space of time the cost of purchasing cars was reduced to approximately one-third of what it was during the days of batch production. Consequently, in the USA, motoring became available to many classes of consumer who would have never hitherto considered purchasing a motor car because of its capital cost. By 1923 over two million model 'T' Fords had been produced and sold.

Despite the apparent advantage of flow production technology, the system did not gain widespread approval and adoption in the United Kingdom where manufacturers preferred to stick with job and batch production. This was not due to chauvinism on the part of British people, but it was owing to the fact that society in the UK was very unequal with the majority of the country's wealth being concentrated in very few hands and the vast majority within society being very poor with relatively few people falling between these two extremes. In the USA society was more equal with wealth being more equally spread between the extremes of the wealthy and the poor. Consequently, in the USA it was easier to market these much cheaper cars to middle-income layers. In the UK, there were very few people in middle-income brackets to which to market them. Most people fell in the lowest layer, and here it was a situation of subsistence living so even if cars had been given away people would not have been able to afford to run them. The rich on the other hand would not have been interested in such things as mass produced cars, preferring to order 'bespoke' automobiles from British manufacturers which more befitted their status within society.

Second World War

The Second World War, which started on 3 September 1939, was the flashpoint in the UK for the widespread adoption of flow production technology. Men either volunteered or were conscripted to the armed forces, unless they were in protected professions where their contribution to the war effort was deemed to be better fulfilled in a non-combative role. Factories switched from making civilian goods to making goods and materials to assist the war effort. The result was that the factories had to be staffed largely by women, most of whom had never worked before in a productive capacity, as the UK was then a very male-dominated society. All of this had to be done quickly, and it was realised that training would take many years. The answer was to adopt flow production technology, so advice was taken from the Americans who helped to switch over factories and production systems to the manufacture of munitions and related war goods by an essentially female workforce using flow production techniques. The 'experiment' worked remarkably well, and it is now widely recognised that without this adaptable and industrious female workforce the outcome of the war could have been significantly different.

The war officially ended on 7 May 1945, but rationing ended more than nine years later on 3 July 1954. Consequently, war shortages still pertained until well after the war, and it made sense to continue using flow production line techniques in a civilian goods manufacturing context, as such manufacturing techniques were seen to be more efficient in terms of attempting to overcome these shortages. Needless to say, there was much disquiet on the part of men returning after the war to find that their skilled jobs were at risk, and in many cases their original jobs no longer existed as a result of these new manufacturing techniques.

The government during the war was a coalition government led by Winston Churchill, and party politics did not officially feature because the top priority was to try to win the war. Although Churchill, who led the Conservative party, was much admired as a war leader, this popularity did not carry over to the general election in July 1945 when he was ousted by Clement Atlee who, as leader of the new Labour government, embarked on a programme of nationalisation and wide-ranging social reforms. Churchill was widely held to be responsible for the prewar depression, so the popular vote went to Atlee whose proposed reforms were to bring about a radical redistribution of wealth through common ownership and better wages and working conditions for the less well off. The first industry to be nationalised was the coal industry on 1 January 1947, followed by rail on 1 January 1948 and electricity on 1 April of that year, and these were followed by a number of other major industries.

High personal taxation

During this period from the end of the Second World War until the late 1960s, taxes rose with the top rate of personal taxation being 98 per cent on investment income. Strangely nowadays perhaps, investment income, being deemed to be 'not worked for' income, attracted extra taxation of 15 per cent on top of 83 per cent which was the top rate insofar as earned income was concerned. The idea was to tax inherited income, into which most income of this nature fell, but it was certainly a disincentive to savers who also happened to be high earners. These high rates of taxation lasted well into the 1970s, and in the tax year 1974/5 the rates, after tax free personal allowances had been taken off, were as shown in Table 1.1.

Death duties (now termed 'Capital Transfer Tax') were set at punitive levels and the rich were debarred from taking their assets abroad. In fact foreign holidays were discouraged and at one time the maximum amount of currency that individuals were allowed to take abroad as 'spending money' was £20. Many stately home property which are now owned by the

Table 1.1 **Basic and higher rates of tax for 1974/5**

Slice of income	Rate	Total income (after deduction of allowances)	Total tax
£4500 (£0–£4500)	33%	£4500	£1485
£500 (£4500–£5000)	38%	£5000	£1675
£1000 (£5000–£6000)	43%	£6000	£2105
£1000 (£6000–£7000)	48%	£7000	£2585
£1000 (£7000–£8000)	53%	£8000	£3115
£2000 (£8000–£10000)	58%	£10000	£4275
£2000 (£10000–£12000)	63%	£12000	£5535
£3000 (£12000–£15000)	68%	£15000	£7575
£5000 (£15000–£20000)	73%	£20000	£11225
Remainder	83%		

An additional rate of 15% is charged on all investment income apart from normally the first £2000. The top investment income rate is thus 83% + 15% = 98%

Source: HM Inspector of Taxes 1974/75 Tax Tables, p. 22.

National Trust are the results of agreements with the tax authorities upon the death of benefactors whereby inherited property was given to the state in lieu of death duties.

During the 1950s and 1960s we also witnessed the emergence of the so-called 'welfare state' with increased social benefits for absence from work through illness (although the actual start of the welfare state is more truly attributed to Lloyd George, the Liberal Prime Minister on 4 May 1911 when he introduced the National Health Insurance Bill). Increased child allowances and numerous other forms of assistance were established to help the less better off. Wages rose at far more than the rate of inflation and we witnessed the ascent of a more powerful trade union movement which successfully fought for better conditions and wages for their members.

Redistribution of wealth

The net effect of all of this was to redistribute wealth such that the rich became less rich and the poorer became much better off. The polarisation within society that existed before the Second World War disappeared as Britain moved towards a more egalitarian society. In terms of the net effect of all this upon marketing, it meant that goods which had hitherto been classed as luxury products had become utility products which were needed as part of everyday living. A good example of this is the telephone which was a luxury service well into the 1960s, but which is nowadays very much a utility item and required as a virtual necessity for those wishing to pursue a 'modern' lifestyle. This has meant that people tend to need more 'belongings' in terms of gadgets and accessories, so although the population might have expanded numerically it has also expanded in terms of greater individual purchasing power. People also need more in terms of clothes and personal belongings. For instance, during the postwar rationing period it was commonplace to only have two pairs of shoes – one pair as 'best' and the other pair for everyday use – a far cry from the multifarious sets of footwear that most people now possess as part of their general wardrobe.

Silent revolution

This switch in the personal incomes pyramid and its effect on purchasing patterns is what sociologists call 'the silent revolution'. We shall go on to explain its implications as far as marketing is concerned.

In terms of our time perspective, we have now explained what happened up to around the late 1950s when demand usually exceeded supply and production was the starting point for business planning. However, this was a time when war shortages almost imperceptibly began to be fulfilled, together with increased spending power and a generally satisfied feeling of 'well-being' being experienced by the population as a whole as a result of the silent revolution. Shortages began to be a thing of the past. This was the era when the then Conservative Prime Minister, Harold Macmillan said of the population: 'You have never had it so good!' However, management did not react to a slowing down of company sales by investigating their customers with a view to ascertaining their true needs and then manufacturing products to suit these needs. This would have been the logical thing to do. Instead, they employed functional aids to selling in order to persuade customers that they needed more or tried to convince them that what they had was in premature need of replacement. There was still an attitude that production should be at the start of business planning, so a whole raft of tactical approaches were imported from the USA in terms of sales techniques, sales promotional methods and advertising. Some of these tactics made good business sense and are still in use today, but a number were nothing less than confidence tricks and many people suffered as a result. The 1960s thus became the era of the 'hard sell', and to a certain extent the poor image that often surrounds marketing nowadays is a result of these techniques that came to the UK during the 1960s.

To compound the problem there was very little around in terms of consumer protection that was enshrined in the legal system, as the era of consumerism and its attendant laws to assist consumers belonged very much to the 1970s. This was a time during which the unscrupulous benefitted at the expense of many consumers.

Activity

How would you respond if somebody asked you to defend marketing on the basis that it was no more than a fancy word for selling?

This should be relatively easy to do in terms of explaining sales orientation and marketing orientation. Although it comes later in the text when we look at marketing in more detail, it could also be answered on the basis that selling is really part of marketing. Marketing includes selling, together with a consideration of advertising, pricing, the product or service, distribution channels and logistics, a study of customers and the segments into which they fall, marketing research to discover customers' needs, and more besides.

Today, we have a situation where a large number of producers compete for a share of a finite market, not only in the domestic, but in the world arena. It is no longer enough to produce a good product, as it was in time of shortages or rationing when producers enjoyed a 'sellers' market'. Today, for producers to achieve a sufficient level of effective demand, they must produce goods and services that the market perceives as valuable and, of more importance, that the customers will actually buy in sufficient volume. The final customer's needs and wants not only have to be taken into account, but the identification and satisfaction of these needs and wants has become the most important factor in the long-term survival of a firm. This, then, is the cornerstone of marketing orientation.

1.3 **Different Types of Business Orientation**

Marketing maturity tends to be a gradual developmental process, and by evolving through lower stages of development enlightened firms begin to appreciate that the satisfaction of consumers' needs and wants is the rationale for everything the company does. Such companies have progressed to a marketing orientation. Of all the stakeholders in a business enterprise the customer is by far the most important, for it is by the satisfaction of customers' needs and the profits that should result from doing so that all other stakeholders'needs are satisfied.

To summarise what has been said and to give an idea of what is now universally recognised within business, it can be said that, generally speaking , there are three basic types of business orientation:

- Production orientation;
- Sales orientation; and
- Marketing orientation.

Each of these is now briefly explained.

Production orientation

In the nineteenth and early twentieth centuries, the primary purpose of all business and industrial activity was thought to be production. Manufacturers were in a 'supplier's market' and were faced with a virtually insatiable demand for anything that could be produced. Henry Ford made a famous statement when he produced his first production line model 'T' Ford:

'You can have any colour you like, as long as it is black.'

This was certainly a production-orientated statement, and during this period firms concentrated on improving production efficiency in an attempt to bring down costs. In America in the economic recession of the 1920s and 1930s, to simply produce was no longer good enough and firms had to begin to focus their attention on the changing needs of the marketplace. This ultimately led to the idea of marketing orientation and it was in America in the 1930s that the origin of this commonsense philosophy can be formed.

Sales orientation

Gradually business people began to appreciate that in a highly competitive environment it was simply not enough to produce goods as efficiently as possible. The sales department was thought to hold the key to the firm's prosperity and survival, and sales volume became the success criterion. In a sales-orientated firm, selling is a major management function and is often given status equal with that of production and finance. Here the emphasis is on 'pushing' a company's products or services to sometimes unwilling customers.

Marketing orientation

Under the marketing concept it is the customer who becomes the centre of business attention. Firms no longer see production or sales as the key to prosperity, growth and survival, but the identification and satisfaction of customers' needs and wants. In a marketing-orientated organisation, the whole firm appreciates the central importance of the customer and realises that without satisfied customers there will be no business.

The Chartered Institute of Marketing sums up what marketing is in its formal definition of the subject:

'Marketing is the management process responsible for identifying, anticipating and satisfying customer requirements profitably.'

An alternative definition is put forward by the American Marketing Association:

'Marketing is the process of planning and executing the conception, pricing, promotion and distribution of ideas, goods and services to create exchanges that satisfy individual and organisational objectives.'

The Chartered Institute of Marketing's definition perhaps more succinctly sums up the overall aim of marketing, but it is felt that the American Marketing Association's definition is more precise as it identifies the tools with which marketing realises its objectives. These tools are collectively known as the 'marketing mix' – a term introduced by Neil Borden which essentially means manipulating the 'four P's' (a term coined by E. Jerome McCarthy which embraces price, product, place and promotion) in their most effective way. This theme is expanded in later chapters.

1.4 **Summary**

In this chapter we have described how marketing has come to occupy the important place it holds in business today. It is really only since the end of the Second World War that marketing has developed in the United Kingdom as a formalised business concept with a codified philosophy and a set of techniques. It has also been demonstrated that marketing is now central to planning in businesses that operate in a competitive environment. The marketing-orientated firm achieves its business objectives by identifying and anticipating the changing needs and wants of specifically defined target markets. The subject of **targeting** is addressed in Chapter 3. The techniques actually used for identifying customer requirements, under the heading of **marketing research,** are discussed in Chapter 6. Business planning, therefore, starts with customers, and it is the responsibility of market-ing to marshall these requirements through the marketing plan into the corporate business plan. As a consequence, it is from customers' needs, and subsequent marketing planning to meet these needs, that other functions in a business operation take their respective leads.

Chapter Review Questions

In terms of long-term business planning, do you feel that the initial driving force behind such planning is

- production,
- finance,
- sales, or
- marketing;

when a company is

1 Production-orientated,
2 Sales-orientated, or
3 Marketing-orientated?

The obvious answer might be: production, sales and marketing in that order. In the case of production orientation this is clearly the case, because production pro-duces what it wants to produce and demand for products tends to outstrip their supply. In the case of sales orientation it is not sales that is the driving force, because sales tactics are merely the tools that are used to move products that have not been automatically taken up by the marketplace. Thus, production is still the driving force in a sales-orientated organisation. In the case of a marketing-orientated company, customers' needs are the starting point for business plan-ning, and these are discovered through marketing research and other means. It is thus marketing that ultimately interprets these requirements into physical prod-ucts and appropriate messages that are designed to appeal to customers' needs.

2 Marketing and the Organisation's Micro- and Macro-environments

2.1 The Micro-environment

The term micro-environment denotes those elements over which the marketing firm has control or which it can use in order to gain information that will better help it in its marketing operations. In other words, these are elements which can be manipulated, or used to glean information, in order to provide fuller satisfaction to the company's customers. The objective of marketing philosophy as discussed in Chapter 1 is to make profits through satisfying customers. This is accomplished through the manipulation of the variables over which a company has control in such a way as to optimise this objective. The variables are what Borden has termed 'the marketing mix', which is a combination of all the 'ingredients' in a 'recipe' that is designed to prove most attractive to customers. In this case the ingredients are individual elements that marketing can manipulate into the most appropriate mix. McCarthy further dubbed the variables which the company can control in order to reach its target market the 'four Ps'. Each of these is discussed in detail in later chapters, but a brief discussion now follows upon each of these elements of the marketing mix together with an explanation of how they fit into the overall notion of marketing.

The 'four Ps' and the marketing mix

The 'four Ps' stands for:

1 Product,
2 Price,
3 Place, and
4 Promotion.

Product and price are obvious, but perhaps place and promotion need more explanation.

Place, it is felt, might better be termed 'placement' because it comprises two distinct elements. The first is channels of distribution – that is the outlets and methods through which a company's goods or services are sold. Thus a channel could be certain types of retail outlet or it could be salespeople selling a company's industrial products through, say, a channel which comprises buyers in the chemical industry. The other element of place refers to logistics which relates to the physical warehousing and transportation of goods from the manufacturer to the end customer. Thus, placement might be a better descriptor as it refers to the placing of goods or services from the supplier to the customer. In fact, place has its own individual 'mix' which is termed the 'distribution mix'.

Promotion also has its individual 'mix' which is called the 'promotional mix'. This promotional mix comprises advertising, selling and sales promotion. In fact promotion is a bit of a misnomer because in advertising agency circles the mention of promotion almost inevitable means 'sales promotion'. Some writers are now separating selling away from promotion and calling it 'people', because it is too important an element of marketing to be lumped in with promotion, although in reality it is still promotion through word of mouth. This fifth P (people) are those who contact customers on a regular basis with the objective of ultimately gaining orders, and these people comprise the sales-force. We can thus see that selling is a component part of overall marketing. There are two more Ps for service marketing, but these are dealt with in a later chapter.

Activity

Consider the distinction between the idea of the marketing mix and McCarthy's four Ps. Are they the same, or do you feel that there is a distinction.

In marketing literature the terms are quite often used interchangeably, but the reality is that McCarthy's four Ps are very specific as the tools that can be used by marketing people to target customers (see Figure 2.2 for a fuller explanation). The marketing mix on the other hand is wider than this and includes customers and their individual and group buying behaviour, and the market segments into which they fall. It also includes appropriate strategies for targeting these groups of customers. Again, this is explained more fully in the next section.

Models of marketing

Figure 2.1 attempts to sum up what is meant by marketing at a very simple level. In fact it is one of the earliest models ever attempted to explain what was meant by marketing. The figure shows information coming from customers to the supplying company. This information is noted and goods or services are supplied to customers in line with their needs. The information flow represents an exchange of ideas whilst the operation flow represents an exchange of meanings.

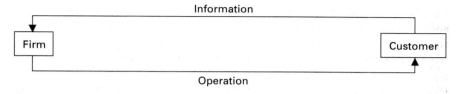

Fig 2.1   Simple diagrammatic representation of marketing

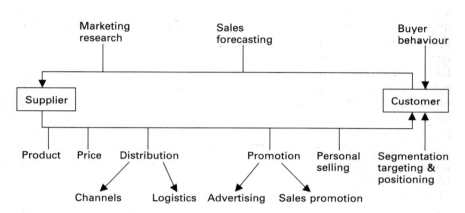

Fig 2.2   Model of the process of marketing

Figure 2.2 is, perhaps, a more precise diagram of what is meant by marketing and one which we can begin to understand from what has already been said. This more complex model better explains what we are now beginning to understand about marketing. The bottom line represents the elements of the marketing mix over which a company has control. These elements are manipulated in such a way as to best suit customers' needs and tastes and this represents an operational flow where things have to be done in order to arrive at the optimum marketing mix. Remember too that there are sub-mixes within the individual elements of the marketing mix. This bottom line also equates to the earlier notion of the four Ps, or rather the five Ps as personal selling has been separated from promotion and becomes 'people'.

The top line represents an information flow from the market to the firm. Data is collected through discussions and interviews with customers on an informal and formal basis. A whole range of techniques are available for this process which is collectively termed marketing research. A more advanced strategic model which incorporates marketing research is embodied in a marketing information system (MkIS) and this is dealt with in a later chapter. In addition, data is collected from customers in relation to their likely future purchases and this is known as sales forecasting. Another raft of techniques is available for the subject of sales forecasting which lies at the very heart of marketing and business planning and this is covered in a later chapter.

Thus we begin to see how marketing orientation works. Customers are the starting point and sales forecasting and marketing research determine their likely requirements and tastes. This information is processed internally within the organisation and products and promotional messages are devised to suit customers' needs, to allay their purchasing fears and to reinforce their expectations. Goods and services are supplied as and when required in the quantities needed and when they are requested – not later and not earlier. This latter point is reinforced because modern marketing dictates that customers demand their goods on a timely basis and this lies at the base of the latest notion of 'just-in-time' manufacturing and the supply of raw materials and components. This is covered later in the text and has tremendous implications for modern marketing.

Customers are also segmented (or divided) according to their various needs and requirements in order that different messages can be relayed and product modifications made to suit the specific desires of smaller groups of customers. The subject of segmentation, together with the strategic implications of targeting and positioning form the basis of the next chapter. Finally, customers behave in a certain way towards purchasing products and services. Such behaviour is influenced by family, by people from work, from societies and clubs to which individual buyers belong, plus a whole host of other competing influences. This is termed 'buyer behaviour' and again this is supported by a whole array of techniques and theories under the headings of consumer buying behaviour and organisational buying behaviour, all of which is dealt with in Chapter 4.

Activity

A quotation often cited by non-marketing people is: 'Marketing is simply an elegant term for selling'. Refute this allegation.

This should be relatively easy. You should simply explain that selling is but one element in the marketing mix, whereas marketing is much broader than this. As you proceed through the text you will discover that marketing pervades a modern organisation, as customer satisfaction should be the driving force for all businesses.

The place of marketing alongside other elements of business

Marketing is but one function within business. Arguably it is the most critical function because it interprets customers' needs and requirements into products and services and repeat business without which a business cannot continue. In fact a modern view of marketing puts customers in the centre with marketing as the interpretative function surrounding the customer, with other major functions of business around this as shown in Figure 2.3. The idea is that all functions of business should be geared towards the satisfactions of customers' requirements and this has led to the new notion of customer care which is dealt with in a later chapter.

At a more traditional level, marketing is often found alongside other major functions within business, and Figure 2.4 illustrates this relationship. This organisation chart does not, of course, refer to all business organisations and to a large extent it is the 'ideal' theoretical structure. Companies tend to evolve and develop in a non-textbook manner, and in practice many different organisation charts can be found as a result of all kinds of illogicalities that defy modern management thinking. Such illogical functions might well exist because of the forceful personality of a head of department whose department has assumed a position of power within an organisation through his or her own personal disposition when there is no managerial justification for putting it in such a position of power in line management. An example could be the material control department which might report direct to the managing director rather than being a subfunction within the purchasing department. Another example, quite commonly found, is a situation where a sales director can be found in the line alongside a marketing director. In such a situation, it might be a forceful sales director in a sales-driven organisation who will not assume the responsibility for marketing, but who is too powerful to put into a subordinate

Fig 2.3   The place of marketing in the modern organisation

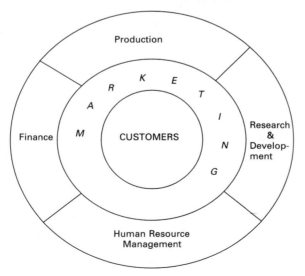

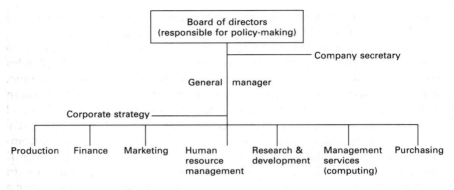

Fig 2.4   A traditional organisation chart

position under marketing. With this background in mind, a 'textbook' organisation chart might be as shown in Figure 2.4. In this organisation chart we can see the place of marketing alongside other major functions of line management.

At the top there is the board of directors who are responsible for giving the organisation its strategic direction. Members of the board are not necessarily full-time employees of the company. Indeed, in many larger companies they tend to be from outside the organisation and the expertise they lend to the board can be on a variety of criteria. Such people could, for instance, be strategy experts, financial experts, people who lend distinction to an organisation (for example somebody with a title), and people who are there because they are on the board of directors of other companies and can bring a cross fertilisation of ideas, financial linkages and potential inter-firm dealings.

The general manager is the person who translates policy into tactics and is responsible for the day-to-day operations of the company. In most companies the general manager is a member of the board of directors and in such cases his or her title would then be managing director.

The company secretary is responsible for legal and administrative matters in addition to serving as the secretary to the board of directors. This person also ensures that board meetings take place at intervals stipulated in the company's articles of association, and that policies that are decided are implemented. For this reason, the role of company secretary is a lateral relationship and is not in the line of command. This also applies to the relatively new function of corporate strategy, whose function may be carried out by general management but is often a separate, relatively small, function whose role it is to ensure that all subdivisions in the organisation have a plan (for example a marketing plan) and that each of these plans fits into the overall corporate plan without there being any mismatches (for example marketing might plan to market more than the firm can produce). The subject of marketing planning is dealt with later in the text.

The major line functions are responsible for translating strategy into tactics in terms of the organisation's everyday operations and this includes such matters as manufacturing, training and recruitment, design and selling. As was discussed in the first chapter, marketing is a relatively modern function and it encompasses the function of selling (although as discussed earlier, in many organisations the two functions are sometimes separated). In many organisations, heads of these line functions are sometimes members of the board of directors in which case they would then have 'director' behind their title (for example marketing director, financial director). In such cases their responsibilities would cover both strategic matters (being a member of the board of directors) and tactical matters (being a functional head of department).

Activity

In the organisation chart shown in Figure 2.4, apart from the general manager, which do you feel is the most important function in a business concern?

This should have opened up a useful debate to which there is no precise answer as it all depends upon the individual circumstances of the company. However, it can be said that in retailing organisations the role of the purchasing department is of paramount importance, because it is mark-up on goods purchased and then sold that determines the prosperity of the company. In fast-moving consumer goods manufacture, branding of products is often very important and here marketing might be the most important function. In engineered products when delivery and quality is important the prime function might be production. In a financial services company it might be finance. There is thus no correct or incorrect answer as it is all a matter of emphasis.

2.2 The Proximate Macro-environment

The term macro-environment denotes all forces and agencies external to the marketing firm itself. Some of these will be closer to the operation of the firm than others; for example a firm's suppliers, agents, distributors and other distributive intermediaries and competing firms. These 'closer' external constituents are often collectively referred to as the firm's **proximate macro-environment** to distinguish them from the wider external forces found, for example, in the legal, cultural, economic and technological sub-environments.

This area consists of people, organisations and forces within the firm's immediate external environment. Of particular importance to marketing firms are the sub-environments of suppliers, competitors and distributors (intermediaries). These sub-environments can each have a significant effect upon the marketing firm.

The supplier environment

This consists of other business firms or individuals who provide the marketing firm with raw materials, product constituents, services or, in the case of retailing firms, possibly the finished goods themselves. Firms, whether they be retailers or manufacturers, will often depend on numerous suppliers. The buyer/supplier relationship is one of mutual economic interdependence, both parties relying on the other for their commercial well-being. Although both parties are seeking stability and security from their relationship, factors in the supplier environment are subject to change, such as industrial disputes which will affect delivery of materials to the buying company, or a sudden increase in raw material prices which forces suppliers to raise their prices. Whatever the product or service being purchased by the marketing firm, unexpected developments in the supplier environment can have an immediate and potentially serious effect on the firm's commercial operations. Because of this, marketing management, by means of the marketing intelligence component of its marketing information system, should continually monitor changes and potential changes in the supplier environment and have contingency plans ready to deal with potentially adverse developments. The marketing information system is covered in a later chapter.

The distributive environment

Much reliance is placed on marketing intermediaries such as wholesalers, factors, agents and distributors to ensure that their products reach the final consumer. To a casual observer, it may seem that the conventional method of distribution in any particular industry is relatively static. This is because changes in the distributive environment occur relatively slowly, and there is therefore a danger of marketing firms failing to appreciate the commercial significance of cumulative change. Existing channels may be declining in popularity over time, while new channels may be developing unnoticed by the marketing firm. Nowhere has this 'creeping' change been more apparent over recent years than in the retailing of fast-moving consumer goods (FMCG). In the 1960s well over half of all FMCG retail trade was accounted for in the independent sector, plus a further large proportion to the Co-operative Societies. Nowadays, the sector represented by the larger food multiples has grown well in excess of this proportion. This theme is expanded in Chapter 9.

The competitive environment

Management must be alert to the potential threat of other companies marketing similar and substitute products whether they be of domestic or foreign origin. In some industries there may be many hundreds of manufacturers worldwide posing a potential competitive threat. In other industries, there may only be a few. Whatever the type, size and composition of the industry in question, it is essential that marketing management has a full understanding of competitive forces. Companies need to establish exactly who their competitors are and the benefits they are offering to the market. Armed with this knowledge, the company will have a greater opportunity to compete effectively.

Activity

For an organisation of your choice, cite three examples of individual firms or organisations that fall under each of the sub-divisions of the proximate marketing environment.

This should be a matter of thinking around local, national or international organisations, about whom you have read, or with which you are familiar. In reality the list can be endless.

2.3 The Wider Macro-environment

Changes in the wider macro-environment may not be as close to the marketing firm's day-to-day operations, but they are just as important. The main factors making up these wider macro-environmental forces fall into four groups:

1 Political and legal factors;
2 Economic factors;
3 Social and cultural factors; and
4 Technological factors.

(Often referred to as the 'PEST' factors in the marketing analytical context, a useful *aide-mémoire*, although in some texts it is sometimes referred to as 'STEP'.)

To the above is sometimes added 'competitive factors', although in a 'PEST' analysis relating to a specific organisation, 'competitive factors' tend to be subsumed under 'economic factors'. Such a PEST analysis means listing all possible points that may affect the organisation under review, under each of the PEST headings.

The political and legal environment

To many companies, domestic political considerations are likely to be of prime concern. However, firms involved in international operations are faced with the additional dimension of international political developments. Many firms export and may have joint ventures or subsidiary companies abroad. In many countries, particularly those in the so-called 'Third World' or more latterly termed 'developing nations', the domestic political and economic situation is usually less stable than in the UK. Marketing firms operating in such volatile conditions clearly have to monitor the local political situation very carefully.

Many of the legal, economic and social developments, in our own society and in others, are the direct result of political decisions put into practice; for example the privatisation of state industries or the control of inflation.

In summary, whatever industry the marketing firm is involved in, changes in the political and legal environments at both the domestic and international levels can affect the company and therefore need to be fully understood.

The economic environment

Economic factors are of concern to marketing firms because they are likely to influence, among other things, demand, costs, prices and profits. These economic factors are largely outside the control of the individual firm, but their effects on individual enterprises can be profound. Political and economic forces are often strongly related. A much quoted example in this context is the 'oil crisis' caused by the Middle East war in 1973 which produced economic shock waves throughout the western world, resulting in dramatically increased crude oil prices. This in turn increased energy costs as well as the cost of many oil-based raw materials such as plastics and synthetic fibres, and contributed significantly to a world economic recession, demonstrating how dramatic economic change can upset the traditional structures and balances in the world business environment.

As can be seen, changes in world economic forces are potentially highly significant to marketing firms, particularly those engaged in international marketing. However, an understanding of economic changes and forces in the domestic economy is also of vital importance as, clearly, it is these forces which have the most immediate impact.

One such factor is a high level of unemployment, which decreases the effective demand for many luxury consumer goods, adversely affecting the demand for the industrial machinery required to produce such goods. Other domestic economic variables are the rate of inflation and the level of domestic interest rates, which affect the potential return from new investments and can inhibit the adoption and diffusion of new technologies. In addition to these more indirect factors, competitive firms can also pose a threat to the marketing company so their activities should be closely monitored.

It is therefore vital that marketing firms continually monitor the economic environment at both domestic and world levels. Economic changes pose a set of opportunities and threats, and by understanding and carefully monitoring the economic environment, firms should be in a position to guard against potential threats and to capitalise on opportunities.

The socio-cultural environment

This is perhaps the most difficult element of the macro-environment to evaluate, manifesting itself in changing tastes, purchasing behaviour and changing priorities. The types of goods and services demanded by consumers are a function of their social conditioning and their consequent attitudes and beliefs.

Core cultural values are those firmly established within a society and are therefore difficult to change. They are perpetuated through family, the church, education and the institutions of society and act as relatively fixed parameters within which marketing firms are forced to operate. Secondary cultural values, however, tend to be less strong and therefore more likely to undergo change. Generally, social change is preceded by changes over time in a society's secondary cultural values, for example the change in social attitude towards credit. As recently as the 1960s, personal credit, or hire purchase as it is sometimes known, was generally frowned upon and people having such arrangements tended not to discuss them in public. Today, offering instant credit has become an integral part of marketing, with many of us regularly using credit cards and store accounts. Indeed, for many people it is often the availability and terms of credit offered that are major factors in deciding to purchase a particular product.

Marketing firms have also had to respond to changes in attitude towards health; for example, in the food industry people are now questioning the desirability of including artificial preservatives, colourings and other chemicals in the food they eat. The decline in the popularity of smoking is a classic example of how changes in social attitudes have posed a significant threat to an industry, forcing tobacco manufacturers to diversify out of tobacco products and into new areas of growth.

Changes in attitudes towards working women have led to an increase in demand for convenience foods, 'one-stop' shopping and the widespread adoption of such time-saving devices as microwave cookers. Marketing firms have had to react to these changes. In addition. changes in moral attitudes from the individualism of the 'permissive society' of the 1960s and early 1970s to the present emphasis on health, economic security and more stable relationships, are all contributory factors to a dynamically changing socio-cultural environment which must be considered by companies when planning for the future.

The technological environment

Technology is a major macro-environmental variable which has influenced the development of many of the products we take for granted today; for example, television, calculators, video recorders and desk-top computers. Marketing firms themselves play a part in technological progress, many having their own research department or sponsoring research through universities and other institutions, thus playing a part in innovating new developments and new applications.

One example of how technological change has affected marketing activities is in the development of electronic point of sale (EPOS) data capture at the retail level. The 'laser checkout' reads a bar code on the product being purchased and stores information which is used to analyse sales and re-order stock, as well as giving customers a printed readout of what they have purchased and the price charged. Manufacturers of fast-moving consumer goods, particularly packaged grocery products, have been forced to respond to these technological innovations by incorporating bar codes on their product labels or packaging. In this way, a change in the technological environment has affected the products and services that firms produce and the way in which firms carry out their business operations.

Activity

For an organisation of your choice conduct a PEST analysis.

The answer to this depends, of course, upon the organisation you have chosen. As an approximate guide, you should have been able to cite around 10 or more separate factors under each of the four headings.

2.4 Other Macro-environmental Factors

The macro-environmental factors discussed so far are not intended to form an exhaustive list, but merely to demonstrate the principal areas of environmental change. Other sub-environments may be important to marketing management, for example in some countries the religious environment may pose an important source of opportunities and threats for firms. In the UK, demographic changes are considered important by a number of firms.

In general, the UK population has been stable at approximately 56 million for a number of years, but the birth rate is falling, while people are living longer. Firms which produce goods and services suitable for babies and small children (for example Mothercare) have seen their traditional markets remain static or decline slightly. Such companies have tended to diversify, offering products targeted at older age groups. A larger older sector of the population offers opportunities for firms to produce goods and services to satisfy their particular needs. The over-55 age group are the modern marketer's current major opportunity. In all advanced economies such as the UK and USA it is this age group that has the largest disposable income, and special products and services such as holidays and pension-related financial services are being marketed to this sector.

2.5 **Summary**

In this chapter we have examined the company's micro-environment and investigated variables over which it has control in terms of the marketing mix. This led to a description of marketing and its various subdivisions including information from the marketplace in terms of forecasting and marketing research. Marketing was then looked at alongside other business functions, and its place in line management was noted.

The company's proximate macro-environment was then examined under supplier, distributive and competitive environments, and finally the wider macro-environment was examined under the headings of political and legal, economic, socio-cultural and technological environments.

The chapter can be summed up by looking what has been covered in terms of a number of layers in the environment from customers, to marketing and resources of the company, to the organisation's proximate macro-environment and finally to its wider macro-environment. This is illustrated in Figure 2.5. The outer layer consists of the wider macro-environmental PEST factors.

The next layer concerns the proximate macro-environment factors cited under 2.2, but also includes the organisation's 'publics' which is a public relations term dealt with in detail in a later chapter, but which essentially means any group of individuals who are affected by or are in touch with the company in any context (for those who supply finance or those who live near the company's manufacturing plant).

The next layer is the organisation's strategic marketing planning and control system and the details of this are dealt with in a later chapter. The tactics that deliver the strategy are the four Ps and these are in the next layer. The final inner circle is the most important as it is customers from which all planning must start. The phrase of being a 'customer led' organisation is at the very heart of marketing orientation.

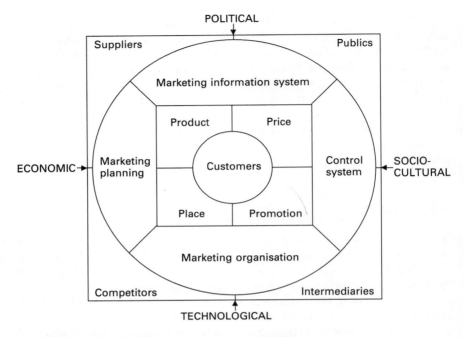

Fig 2.5   An organisation's various environments

Chapter Review Question

Distinguish between the proximate macro-environment and the wider macro-environment.

This should have been easy. The former falls under the headings of

- the supplier environment,
- the distributive environment, and
- the competitive environment;

while the latter encompasses

- political,
- economic,
- socio-cultural, and
- technological factors.

3 Customers and Marketing

3.1 Segmentation Defined

The essence of the marketing concept is the idea of placing customer needs at the centre of the organisation's decision-making. As seen in the previous chapter, the need to adopt this approach stems from a number of factors, including increased competition, better-informed and educated customers and, perhaps most importantly, changing patterns of demand. Primarily it is the change in patterns of demand that has given rise to the need to segment markets. This change stems from the fact that higher standards of living and a trend towards individualism has meant that consumers are now more able to exercise their choice in the marketplace.

Market segmentation can be defined as the process of breaking down the total market for a product or service into distinct sub-groups or segments where each segment may conceivably represent a separate target market to be reached with a distinctive marketing mix. Segmentation and the subsequent strategies of targeting and positioning start by recognising that increasingly within the total demand/market for a product, specific tastes, needs and demand may differ. It breaks down the total market for a product or service into individual clusters of customers, or segments. Here, customers who share similar demand preferences are grouped together within each segment.

Effective segmentation is achieved when customers sharing similar patterns of demand are grouped together and where each group or segment differs in the pattern of demand from other segments in the market. In most markets, be they for consumer or industrial products, some kind of segmentation can be accomplished on this basis.

Activity

In order that you can more fully appreciate the idea of segmentation, think of the following products and decide if segmentation is possible:

- dishwasher detergent;
- washing powder;
- chocolates; and
- motor cars.

For dishwasher detergent, if we are considering this only for household use, the answer is 'no' in that separate groups of purchasers are not identified. However, if one is considering dishwasher detergent both for households and for industrial use, then the answer must be yes because for canteen or restaurant use it will be packed in larger sizes and probably in more utilitarian packaging.

Washing powder is generally a product that has not been segmentable, but more recently different formulations of washing powder have been introduced – for severe stains, for coloured clothes, for white clothes, for woollens, and so on. However, the best-selling and highly promoted brands tend not to segment and are keen to promote a uniform image to sustain their market-share.

Chocolates are definitely segmentable in terms of groups of people to whom they are meant to appeal, and attempts are made to give a 'personality' to specific brands.

Motor cars are obviously segmentable into, for example, sports cars, estate cars, saloon cars, together with different versions under each of these categories in terms of engine size and tuning. In fact, manufacturers now tend to make a virtue of the fact that of the many vehicles produced only a few need be the same.

3.2 Targeted Marketing Efforts

Most companies now realise that they cannot effectively serve all the segments in a market, and must instead target their marketing efforts. For example, in developing a new car, the manufacturing firm will have to make a decision on many issues, such as should it be a two, four, or five-seater model, with a 1000, 2000 or 3000 cc engine? Should it have leather, fabric or plastic seats? The overriding factor when deciding these issues is customer demand. Some customers (segments) may want a five-seater 2000 cc model with leather upholstery, while others may prefer a four-seater with a 1000 cc engine and fabric seats. One solution would be to compromise and produce a four-seater 1500 cc model with leather seats and fabric trim. Clearly, such a model would go some way to meeting the requirements of both groups of buyers, but there is a danger that because the needs of neither market segment are precisely met, most of the potential customers will purchase from other suppliers who do cater for their specific requirements. Ironically, one of the biggest postwar car failures was the much heralded and much hyped American Ford Edsel car. This is a car that was said to be produced following extensive marketing research, the results of which were aggregated, and the end product was a car that satisfied the true needs of very few buyers making it the most spectacular flop in modern motoring history. Ironically, it is now very much sought after as a collectors' car.

Target marketing is thus defined as the identification of those market segments that are the most likely purchasers of a company's products.

Specifically, the advantages of target marketing are:

1 Marketing opportunities and unfilled 'gaps' in a market may be more accurately appraised and identified. Such gaps can be real (for example sweet, strong, harsh or mild) or they can be illusionary in terms of the way people want to view the product (for example happy, aloof, silly or moody). In the case of the former, product attributes can fulfil these criteria whereas for the latter these attributes might well have to be implanted in the minds of customers through an appropriate advertising message.
2 Market and product appeals through manipulation of the marketing mix can be more delicately tuned to the needs of the potential customer.
3 Marketing effort can be concentrated on the market segment(s) which offer the greatest potential for the company to achieve its goals – be they goals to maximise profit potential or to secure the best long-term position for the product or any other appropriate goal.

Activity

In terms of the tactics involved in targeting, what must a company do in order to target its marketing efforts towards a specific goup of customers?

A company should devise a different marketing mix for different segments of the market. This essentially means manipulating the marketing mix, which was considered in the last chapter, to suit individually chosen market segments and the process of this manipulation is called market targeting.

3.3 Effective Segmentation

Theoretically, the base(s) used for segmentation should lead to segments that are:

1 **Measurable/identifiable**   Here, the base(s) used should preferably lead to ease of identification in terms of who is in each segment. It should also be capable of measurement in terms of the potential customers in each segment.
2 **Accessible**   Here, the base(s) used should ideally lead to the company being able to reach selected market targets with their individual marketing efforts.
3 **Meaningful**   The base(s) used must lead to segments which have different preferences or needs and show clear variations in market behaviour and response to individually designed marketing mixes.

4 Substantial   The base(s) used should lead to segments which are suffi-
ciently large to be economically and practically worthwhile serving as
discrete market targets with a distinctive marketing mix.

The third criterion is particularly important for effective segmentation, as it
is an essential prerequisite when attempting to identify and select market
targets.

In segmentation, targeting and positioning, a company must identify
distinct subsets of customers in the total market for a product where any
subset might eventually be selected as a market target, and for which a
distinctive marketing mix will be developed. The following represents the
sequential steps in conducting a segmentation, targeting and positioning
exercise for any given product market:

1 Select base(s) for segmentation and identify appropriate market
segments.
2 Evaluate and appraise the market segments resulting from the first step.
3 Select an overall market targeting strategy.
4 Select specific target segments.
5 Develop a product positioning strategy for each target segment.
6 Develop an appropriate marketing mix for each chosen target segment in
order to support the product positioning strategy.

3.4 **Segmentation Bases in Consumer Product Markets**

Geographic segmentation

This consists of dividing a country into regions that normally represent an
individual sales person's territory. In bigger companies, these larger regions
are then broken down into areas with individual regionalal manager controlling salespeople in distinct areas. In international marketing, different
countries may be deemed to constitute different market segments.

Demographic segmentation

This consists of a wide variety of bases for subdividing markets, and each of
these is now discussed:

- **Age** is a good segmentational variable for such items as clothes where the
  fashion-conscious young are more susceptible to regular changes in style,
  and older segments are perhaps more concerned with such factors as
  quality and comfort.
- **Sex** is a strong segment in terms of goods which are specifically targeted
  towards males or females and again an obvious example is clothing.
  Here, fashion is a powerful element when purchasing, and a whole industry surrounds this criterion.

- **Income** as a segmentation base is perhaps less popular in the United Kingdom than it is in the USA. This is probably due to our conservative nature and matters like income tend to be regarded in a very private manner. It would indeed be difficult and embarrasing asking this question as part of a marketing research survey. In the UK we tend to use the next segmentation variable, 'social class', and from this a person's income is deduced.
- **Social class** is probably the single most used variable for research purposes, and the National Readership Survey divides everybody in the UK into the categories shown in Table 3.1.

Activity

Consider the so-called 'silent revolution' referred to in Chapter 1 and consider the situation pre-World War Two when wealth was polarised into a minority who possessed most of the wealth and the majority who possessed very little. Now look at the percentage distribution of the population amongst the social grades in Table 3.1. It can be seen that these percentages relate more to a normal distribution curve than was the situation between the wars. In terms of marketing, what is the implication of this observation?

The implication is that this more even distribution amongst the social classes, and thus of wealth, has meant that consumers are able to afford more in terms of personal possessions. Articles classed as luxury goods between the wars are now classed as utility goods and are needed in order to partake in a 'modern' lifestyle. Thus individuals need a larger and more complicated and larger bundle of possessions. A good example of a service that was a luxury possession between the wars is a telephone. Now it is a utility product that is essential for domestic and social purposes for the majority of the population. In addition, goods are now

Table 3.1 **Social class and grade structure (United Kingdom)**

A	Upper middle class (higher managerial, administrative or professional) which comprises about 3 per cent of the population
B	Middle class (intermediate managerial, administrative or professional) which comprises approximately 10 per cent of the population
C1	Lower middle class (supervisory, clerical, junior administrative or professional) containing around 25 per cent of the population
C2	Skilled working class (skilled manual workers) who comprise around 30 per cent of the population
D	Working class (semi- and unskilled manual workers) or around 27 per cent of the population
E	Lowest levels of subsistence (state pensioners with no other income, widows, casual and lowest grade earners) who form the remaining 5 per cent, or thereabouts, of the population.

expected to last for a shorter period of time with a good example being clothes where fashion rather than functionality is more important. On the aspect of clothes, people also have more comprehensive wardrobes to suit different social and work occasions.

Continuing the list of demographic bases:

- **Education** is often related to social class, because, as a generalisation, the better educated tend to get the better jobs. It is generally acknowledged that a person's media habits are related to education. Accordingly, news-papers design to aim their news and content towards the upper or lower ends of the social spectrum, and encourage advertisers to target their advertising appropriately depending upon whether the product has an up-market or down-market appeal. In fact they publicise their readership profile of the percentage of ABC1, etc. groups that actually read their newspapers or magazines and this information is ascertained through independent auditors. This is done principally to alert advertising agen-cies who will place their clients' advertising according to the social classes towards whom their products are targeted.
- **Nationality** or ethnic background now constitutes a growing and distinc-tive segment for potential target marketing. Food products, clothing and hair-care products are obvious examples of products that fit into this segmenttion variable.
- **Political** is perhaps a less obvious segmentation base. An individual's political leanings might well influence the way he or she behaves in terms of purchases made. Such purchases are of course reflected in the types of newspaper and other media that are read, and this in turn contains advertising which is aimed at people who read such media, so political leanings might be more significant than at first sight.
- **Family size** will have an effect on the amount or size of purchases, so this is certainly a meaningful segmentation variable.
- **Family life cycle** is a logical follow on to the above and this will tend to determine the purchase of many consumer durable products. This is based on the notion that consumers pass through a series of quite distinct phases in their lives, each phase giving rise to different purchasing patterns and needs. For example, an unmarried person living at home will probably have very different purchasing patterns from someone of the same age who has left home and is recently married. Wells and Gubar have put forward what is now an internationally recognised clas-sification system in relation to life-cycle, and these stages are shown in Table 3.2.
- **SAGACITY** is a refinement of the family life-cycle grouping system. This is a system which believes that people have different behavioural patterns and aspirations as they proceed through life, and identifies four main stages of the life-cycle as:

Table 3.2   **Family life-cycle segmentation base**

Bachelor stage	young single people not living with parents (which gave rise to the category of 'Yuppies' or 'young, upwardly-mobile persons')
Newly marrieds – no children	(sometimes referred to as 'Dinkies' meaning 'double income – no kids')
Full nest I	with the youngest child being under six years of age
Full nest II	where the youngest child is six or over
Full nest III	is an older married couple with dependent children living at home
Empty nest I	with no children living at home, but the family head is in work (sometimes referred to as 'Woopies' meaning 'well off older persons')
Empty nest II	where the family head is retired
Solitary survivor in work	
Solitary survivor retired	

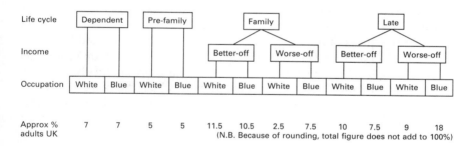

Approx %   7   7   5   5   11.5   10.5   2.5   7.5   10   7.5   9   18
adults UK   (N.B. Because of rounding, total figure does not add to 100%)

Source: Research Services Limited.

Fig 3.1   Sagacity life-cycle groupings

– *Dependent* (mainly under 24 living at home)
– *Pre-family* (under-35 s who have established their own household, but without children)
– *Family* (couples under 65 with one or more children in the household)
– *Late* (adults whose children have left home or who are over 35 and childless)

Income groups are then defined as being in categories: 'better off' and 'worse off'. Occupation groups are defined as white (collar) – or the A, B and C1 social groups and blue (collar) – or the C2, D and E social groups. The system works as shown in Figure 3.1.

- **Type of neighbourhood and dwelling (ACORN)** is a relatively new segmentation base and it uses as its underlying philosophy the fact that the type of dwelling and area a person lives in is a good predictor of likely purchasing behaviour including the types of products and brands which might be purchased. This classification analyses homes, rather than individuals, as a basis for segmentation. It is termed the ACORN system (A Classification of Residential Neighbourhoods). The source of this is the 10-yearly population census which is undertaken during every year ending with one – the next being due in 2001. The system was developed by Richard Webber for Consolidated Analysis Centres Incorporated (CACI). It breaks down the census of population into various categories of homes as shown in Table 3.3.

These ACORN classifications are further subdivided into yet smaller groupings. For instance, group C which refers to 'older housing of intermediate status', is broken down into:

  C8   Mixed owner-occupied and council estates
  C9   Small town centres and flats above shops
  C10   Villages with non-farm employment
  C11   Older private shousing skilled workers

- **Mosaic system** This system is an extension of the ACORN system except that this is based upon individual postal codes (or zip code as it is referred to in some parts of the world). Each postal code in the United Kingdom consists of up to seven letters and figures. An individual code represents approximately ten dwellings and each of these groups of dwellings is given an individual Mosaic categorisation, of which there are 58 categories. The idea of 'mosaic' comes from the notion that if a different colour was ascribed to each category and superimposed on a map of the United

Table 3.3 **ACORN classification system**

Acorn group	Type of dwelling	Approx % UK population
A	Agricultural areas	3
B	Modern family housing, higher incomes	18
C	Older housing of intermediate status	17
D	Poor quality older terraced housing	4
E	Better-off council estates	13
F	Less well-off council estates	9
G	Poorest council estates	7
H	Multi-racial areas	4
I	High status non-family areas	4
J	Affluent suburban housing	16
K	Better-off retirement areas	4
U	Unclassified	1

Source: CACI.

Kingdom then the resulting pattern would resemble a mosaic. The full Mosaic listing is not reproduced here, but by way of illustration some are described below:

M1	High status retirement areas with many single pensioners	1.0% of population
M15	Lower income older terraced housing	1.5% "
M25	Smart inner-city flats, company lets, very few children	1.5% "
M33	Council estates, often Scottish flats, with worst overcrowding	1.3% "
M46	Post-1981 housing in areas of highest income and status	0.2% "
M50	Newly built private estates, factory workers, young families	3.3% "
M57	Hamlets and scattered farms	0.7% "

Taken together, the demographic bases described above probably constitute the most popular bases for segmentation in consumer product markets, since they are often associated with differences in consumer demand and as such they are meaningful to advertisers. For instance, occupation and social class are linked because of the way that occupation is used to define social class. It is, therefore, relatively easy to reach the different social classes through their different media and shopping habits, although boundaries between the purchasing power of different classes become blurred when, for example, skilled manual workers are able to earn higher incomes than their counterparts in lower or even intermediate management.

Direct or behavioural segmentation

This appeals to marketing people on the basis that it takes customer purchasing behaviour as the starting point for segmentation. Such bases include:

- **Usage status** when a distinction might be made between say 'light', 'medium' and 'heavy' users of a particular product.
- **Brand loyalty status** where customers can be divided into a number of groups according to their loyalty, or their propensity to repurchase the brand again. Status categories are:

  Hard core loyals who purchase the same brand every time;
  Soft core loyals who have divided loyalties between two or more brands and purchase any of these on a random basis;
  Shifting loyals who are sometimes called 'brand switchers' in that they buy one brand, and stay with it for a certain period, and then purchase another brand and stay with it for a certain period. They may then return to the original brand;

Switchers who show no particular preference or loyalty to one particular brand, so their purchasing pattern cannot be clearly determined.

- **Benefits sought** is a segmentation base that determines the principal expectation(s) that a purchaser is seeking from the product. For instance, in the case of a motor oil purchasers might be looking for cheapness, a well-known brand, its viscosity or its engine protection reputation.
- **Occasions for purchase** also falls under this category. The best example of this probably relates to the purchase of holidays.

Lifestyle or psychographic segmentation

This is based on the idea that individuals have characteristic patterns of living which may be reflected in the products and brands which they purchase. The advertising agency Young and Rubican has come up with a classification system called 'Four Cs' where 'C' stands for consumers. These categories are:

- *Mainstreamers* or the largest group who do not want to 'stand out from the crowd'. They are the biggest segment (over 40 per cent of the population) and tend to purchase branded products over supermarket brands.
- *Reformers* are people who tend to be creative and caring, many doing charitable work. They are largely responsible for the purchase of supermarket brands.
- *Aspirers* are usually younger people who are ambitious and keen to 'get on' at all costs. Their purchases tend to reflect the latest models and designs.
- *Succeeders* are those who have 'made it' and do not see the need for status symbols that aspirers seek. They like to be in control of what they are doing and this includes their purchases where they generally have very clear and firm ideas of what they see as a good product and what they see as being a less useful product.

Activity

Consider the following products and services. Suggest some of the more obvious segmentation bases in respect of each of these.

- Insurance services
- Holidays
- Coffee
- Frozen foods

Insurance services are segmented in numerous ways and insurance products are then tailor-made to suit these specific segments. Examples are car insurance, health insurance, property insurance, pension plans and domestic appliance extended warranty insurance.

Holidays can, for example, be segmented on the basis of activity holidays, sightseeing holidays, exotic destination holidays, beach holidays and historic venue holidays.

Coffee can be segmented on the basis of taste, ease of preparation (ground coffee or instant coffee) or occasions for use (for example some are more appropriate for evening drinking whilst others might be more suitable for breakfast drinking).

Frozen foods can be, for instance, ready meals for convenience eating, exotic foods, standard frozen vegetables, chips, ice cream or frozen desserts. All of these products are designed to suit different eating occasions like 'a quick and easy meal', 'special occasions', and so forth.

3.5 Segmentation Bases in Industrial Product Markets

Segmenting an industrial product market introduces a number of additional bases, uses similar bases and also precludes some of the ones more frequently used for consumer product markets. The most frequently encountered bases in this context are:

- **Type of application/end use** For example adhesives for home, office and industrial use.
- **Geographical** For example Scotland, Wales, North West, North East, South East, East Anglia. Or by country/region as in the USA, Pacific Rim, Middle East and so on.
- **Benefits sought** Closely related to the above, but more in terms of what the product actually does for the purchasing company; for example detergents for general cleaning or detergents that are actually used in the production process.
- **Type of customer** For example banks or insurance companies or people who purchase for public authority undertakings.
- **Product/technology** For example fibres for the carpet industry or the clothing industry.
- **Customer size** For example larger customers, might receive different 'treatment' to smaller customers, and this segmentation variable is called 'key account selling' whereby the sales manager deals directly with major accounts.
- **Usage rate** For example light users or heavy users; regular or sporadic users.
- **Loyalty of customer** For example regular purchasers of the company's products (be they for large or small purchases) and sporadic purchasers. Here again, the treatment given to loyal customers might differ to that accorded to occasional customers.
- **Purchasing procedures** For example centralised versus decentralised purchasing (which can affect the buyer/seller relationship); the extent to which purchasing is carried out by tightly defined, or more flexible,

specifications which allows the seller more latitude in terms of making suggestions; the extent to which purchasing is by tender (that is by some kind of closed bidding system) or by open negotiation.

- **Situational factors**   These consider the tactical role of the purchasing circumstances. In some purchasing situations it requires a more detailed knowledge of the customer, whereas in others the buyer/seller relationship is kept strictly to commercial matters.
- **Personal characteristics**   These relate to the people who make purchasing decisions.

As with consumer markets, industrial market segmentation may be on an indirect (associative) or a direct (behavioural) basis. A variety of bases may be also be used in conjunction with each other in order to obtain successively smaller sub-segments of the market. The essential criteria given earlier for bases of consumer market segmentation – being identifiable, accessible, substantial and, most important, meaningful – are equally applicable to bases for industrial market segmentation.

A 'nested' approach to segmetation was suggested by Shapiro and Bonoma in 1984 on the basis of a hierarchy ranging from the broad to the specific as shown in Figure 3.2. At the centre we have people who actually make buying decisions and their personalities must be considered. Then comes situational factors which concern the tactical role of the purchasing situation and which demand customer knowledge. Purchasing approaches examine customer purchasing practices (for example who actually makes buying decisions – which is considered in more detail in the next chapter

---

Fig 3.2   A nested approach to segmentation in industrial markets

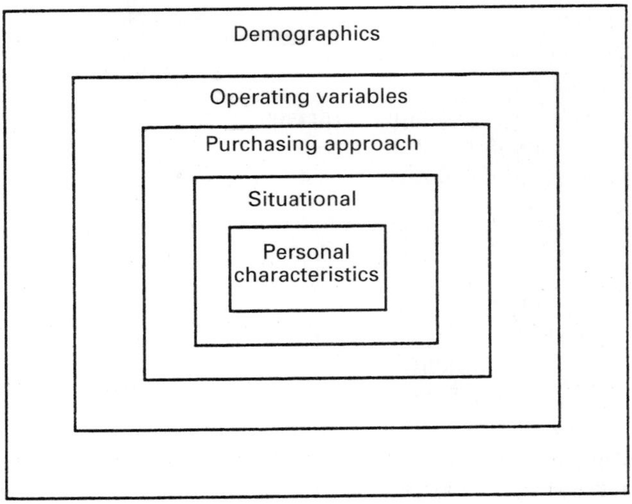

under the decision-making unit). Operating variables allow a more exact pinpointing of potential and existing customers within the final category, which is demographic variables, or the broad description of the segments related to customer needs and patterns of usage.

Activity

Consider the following industrial products or services and suggest likely segmentation bases:

- valves
- banking services
- artificial fibres
- adhesives
- paints

In the case of valves the most obvious base is by end-use – for the water industry, for the oil industry, for the gas industry.

Banking services can be based upon the requirement that is needed – an overdraft for working capital, a bank loan for a more permanent requirement, a source of investment.

Artificial fibres are another example of end-use segmentation – fibres for spinning into carpet yarn or, say, clothing yarn.

Adhesives might be for use in an office, or for heavier industrial applications.

Paints can be for exterior or interior use, with different types of finishes required, and, of course, with different types of colours.

3.6 Effective Segmentation

Once market segments have been identified, the marketer's task is to assess these various segments. This appraisal should be in relation to sales and profit potential, or, in the case of non-profit organisations, their ability to add to organisational aims. This means that each segment should be viewed in terms of its overall size, projected rate of growth, actual and potential competition, nature of competitive strategies and customer needs. Companies that decide to follow a concentrated or a differentiated targeting strategy must then decide which of the segments in the market it wishes to serve. Such a decision to select specific target markets must be based on some of the factors outlined earlier, including company resources, competition, segment potential and company objectives.

There are four characteristics which will make a market segment particularly attractive:

1 It has sufficient current profit and sales potential to meet the organisation's aims and objectives.

2 Competition in the segment is not too intense.
3 There is good potential for future growth.
4 The segment has some previously unidentified requirements that the company has recognised and is now in a position to serve especially well.

3.7 **Product Positioning**

A company has to develop a product positioning strategy for each segment it chooses to serve. This relates to the task of ensuring that its products occupy a planned-for place in chosen target markets, pertinent to opposing competition in the marketplace. The notion of product/brand positioning is applicable to both industrial and consumer markets, and the key aspects of this approach are based upon the following suppositions.

1 All products and brands have both objective attributes (for example sweet/sour, dark/light, fast/slow) and subjective attributes (for example modern/unfashionable, happy/sad, youthful/elderly).
2 Potential purchasers might think about one or more of these attributes when deliberating which product and/or brand to purchase.
3 Potential customers have their own thoughts about how the various competing products or brands rate for each of these particular attributes. In other words, the positioning of the brand along the parameters of these attributes (for example 'entertaining' on the one hand, to 'mundane' at the other extreme) takes place in the mind of the customer.

Once this is done it is then possible to establish important attributes in choosing between different brands or products, together with the customer's perception of the position of competitors' products in relation to these characteristics, and then to establish the most advantageous position for the company within this particular segment of the market.

The final step in the appraisal of segmentation, targeting and positioning is developing appropriate marketing mixes. This involves the design of marketing programmes which will support the chosen positional strategy in the selected target markets. The company must therefore determine the 'four Ps' of its marketing mix – that is what price, product, distribution (place) and promotional strategies will be necessary to achieve the desired position in the market.

There are four acknowledged strategic options for target marketing:

1 Undifferentiated marketing where there is one single marketing mix for every potential customer in the market.
2 Differentiated marketing where there are many marketing mixes for different segments of the market.

3 Concentrated marketing which has a single marketing mix for a segment of the total market.

4 Custom marketing which attempts to satisfy each individual customer's requirements with a separate marketing mix.

3.8 Summary

We can now appreciate how marketing begins to work. Having defined the purpose of segmentation we have looked at the obvious and the less obvious bases for segmentation in both consumer and industrial markets. We have also ascertained that, used well, the techniques and concepts described in this chapter can contribute significantly to overall company marketing success. Market segmentation, targeting and positioning decisions are thus more strategic than they are tactical.

Segmentation variables should be examined in detail, especially new segments. These should then be authenticated in terms of viability and potential profit. Targeting investigates specific segments in terms of how they should be approached. Positioning relates to how the product is perceived in the minds of consumers, and a suitable marketing mix should then be designed.

Chapter Review Question

For the following product categories, determine which of the four strategic options quoted best fit each of the categories listed:

- a meal out
- mining machinery
- washing powder
- chocolates

A meal out – custom marketing; Mining machinery – concentrated marketing; Washing powder – undifferentiated marketing; Chocolates – differentiated marketing.

4 Buyer Behaviour

4.1 Importance of Understanding Customer Motives

The task of marketing is to identify consumers' needs and wants accurately, then to develop products and services that will satisfy them. For marketing to be successful, it is not sufficient to merely discover what customers require, but to find out why it is required. Only by gaining a deep and comprehensive understanding of buyer behaviour can marketing's goals be realised. Such an understanding of buyer behaviour works to the mutual advantage of the consumer and marketer, allowing the marketer to become better equipped to satisfy the consumer's needs efficiently and establish a loyal group of customers with positive attitudes towards the company's products.

Consumer behaviour can be formally defined as: the acts of individuals directly involved in obtaining and using economic goods and services, including the decision processes that precede and determine these acts. The underlying concepts of this chapter form a system in which the individual consumer is the core, surrounded by an immediate and a wider environment that influences his or her goals. These goals are ultimately satisfied by passing through a number of problem-solving stages leading to purchase decisions. The study and practice of marketing draws on a great many sources that contribute theory, information, inspiration and advice. In the past, the main input to the theory of consumer behaviour has come from psychology. More recently, the interdisciplinary importance of consumer behaviour has increased such that sociology, anthropology, economics and mathematics also contribute to the science relating to this subject.

4.2 Social and Cultural Influences

Culture is 'learned' behaviour that has been passed down over time, reinforced in our daily lives through the family unit and through educational and religious institutions. Cultural influences, therefore, are powerful ones and if a company does not understand the culture in which a particular market operates, it cannot hope to develop products and market them successfully in that market.

It is important to recognise that culture, although immensely powerful, is not fixed forever. Changes in culture tend to be slow and are not fully assimilated until a generation or more has passed. An example of this is the custom of marriage, which has been openly challenged in the UK over the past 20 years. When couples first began to set up home together and raise families outside marriage, society, for the most part, adopted an attitude of condemnation, whereas today there is a much more relaxed attitude to those who choose to ignore the convention.

The twentieth century has witnessed significant cultural changes, for example, changing attitudes towards work and pleasure. It is no longer accepted that work should be difficult or injurious to mind or body, and many employers make great efforts to ensure that the workplace is as pleasant an environment as possible, realising that this probably increases productivity. Employees now more frequently regard work as a means to earn the money to spend on goods or services that give them pleasure, and not just to pay for the necessities of life. The shortened working week, paid holidays and labour-saving devices in the home have all led to increased leisure time that influences how, when and what the consumer buys. Another major cultural change in this century is the changing role of women in society. Increased independence and economic power have not only changed the lives of women, but have also influenced society's and women's own perception of their socio-economic role.

In most western societies today, when considering culture, we must also consider subcultures. Immigrant communities have become large enough in many countries to form a significant proportion of the population of that country, and marketers must consider them because of their interactive influence on society and because, in some cases, they constitute individual market segments for certain product areas. Subcultures can also exist within the same racial groups sharing common nationality. Their bases may be geographical, religious or linguistic differences, and marketers must recognise these differences and should regard them as providing opportunities rather than posing problems.

Activity

Why do you feel modern marketing practise increasingly needs to take buyer behaviour motives into consideration when devising new or modified products and services?

It would be easy to repeat what has already been said so far in this chapter and this would be an acceptable answer. However, the question asks for **modern** marketing practice and herein is the clue. The world is becoming increasingly cosmopolitan with movements of groups of people from one country to another and an assimilation of their sub-culture into that of the new country. There has also been a move towards more gregarious tastes through travel and foreign holidays. We have already looked at segmentation bases in the previous chapter and from this you will have seen that many sophisticated sub-segments are now possible. More precise targeting of marketing efforts is necessary to reach these sub-segments and this has led to the growth of more direct methods of marketing. It is, therefore, essential that marketers understand the buying motives of such sub-groups when manipulating their marketing mixes through promotional appeals, new product designs and other strategies in order to more precisely target such sub-groups.

4.3 **Specific Social Influences**

Social class

This is the most prominent social influence. Traditionally, one of the chief determinants of social class was income, but since pay structures have altered a great deal in terms of the lower C2, D and E categories moving more towards levels previously enjoyed by the higher A, B and C1 categories over the past 30 years or so, classification of consumers on the basis of 'lifestyle' is becoming more meaningful today. Income aside, social class is an indicator of lifestyle and its existence exerts a strong influence on individual consumers and their behaviour. There is evidence to suggest that whatever income level a consumer reaches during his or her lifetime, basic attitudes and preferences do not change radically. As consumers, we usually identify with a particular class or group, but often it is not the actual social class that is revealing, but that which the consumer aspires to. Income and/or education allows young people to 'cross' social class barriers and adopt lifestyles which are different from those of their parents. They will tend to absorb the influences of the group to which they aspire and gradually reject the lifestyles of their parents and relations. It can thus be seen that occupation is a strong determinant towards an individual's behavioural patterns, which include buyer behaviour.

When studying social class, the marketer should make decisions on the basis of information revealed by objectively-designed research, without any preconceptions or associations with inferiority or superiority in 'lower' or 'higher' social groupings. This is the only way that changes in behaviour can be identified.

Activity

What are the implications of the last statement that encourages marketers to make decisions based on information revealed by research rather than upon preconceptions related to individuals belonging to higher and lower social groups.

In the past people were less mobile in the physical sense and there was every likelihood that individuals would stay in the locality in which they were born, and they would probably take up similar occupations to those of their parents. The family unit was relatively stable and divorce was a rare occurrence. Thus, one could in those days make generalisations about social class being relatively 'permanent' from one generation to the next.

However, there is now even an expectation that young better-educated people will move to different parts of the country or even to different parts of the world. Higher education is now much more widely available to the broader spectrum of social groups, and young people are now able to attain qualifications and expertise that their parents could only dream about. As they become better qualified, so the positions they are able to attain are different to those of their parents. Such positions usually entail greater mobility. The bonding of the family group becomes eroded and family meetings between children and parents take place only at holiday periods because of the distances involved in travelling. The probability is that children have taken on different social attitudes from those of the parents with whom they were brought up. Indeed, many such parent/offspring meetings are sometimes seen as being stressful, because parents cannot appreciate that their children have 'changed so much'.

Reference groups

This can be described as group of people whose standards of conduct mould an individual's dispositions, beliefs and values. This group can be small or large. Reference groups can range from the immediate family to the place of work. They can also be found in a person's social life. An individual is unlikely to deviate too far from the behavioural norms laid down by the members of a club or hobby group. Reference group theory does not state that individualism cannot exist within a group, but it does suggest that even rigid independent thinkers will at least be aware of what is considered 'normal' within a group.

In a small group like the family the advice and opinions of those who are regarded as knowledgeable will be highly regarded. Such people are termed 'opinion leaders'. Other influences extraneous to groups might also be at work in opinion forming, and here there are opinion leaders outside of the immediate group. Their opinions are taken up by 'opinion followers'. In the case of a number of products a deliberate direct appeal is made to the so called 'snob appeal' by using a marketing strategy of making a company's products acceptable to opinion leaders, or famous personalities (who are paid for their endorsement) in the hope that other sectors of the population will follow them.

The family is perhaps the strongest reference group for most people because of its intimacy and relative permanence. Strong associations mean that individuals within this group will influence each other. The family life-cycle traditionally contains six stages, although more recently different divisions have been quoted. These divisions are:

1 **Unmarried** Here, financial commitments and family responsibilities tend to be low, with disposable income being high. These younger unmarried consumers tend to be more leisure-orientated and more fashion conscious. This segment thus comprises a very important market for many new and innovative products.

2 **Young newly-married couples – no children** This group focuses its expenditure on those items considered necessary for setting up home.

3 **Young married couples with children** Outlay here is children-orientated, and there is little surplus cash for luxury items. Although they are receptive to new product ideas, this group sees economy as being the overriding factor when making purchases.

4 **Older married couples still with children at home** Disposable income will probably have increased, often with both parents working and children being relatively independent. In some cases children may be working and the parents are able to engage increasingly in leisure activities often in the form of more than the 'standard' annual holiday. Consumer durables, including major items of furniture, are often replaced at this stage. Such purchases are often made with different motivations to the original motivations of strict functionality and economy that was necessary at an earlier life-cycle stage.

5 **Older married couples with no children living in the home** Here, disposable income can be quite high. However, tastes are likely to be firmly rooted reflected in unchanging purchasing patterns. Thus marketers will have difficulty when attempting to change predispositions, so the best policy will be through attempts to refine and add value rather than to introduce new concepts and ideas.

6 **Older retired couples and single people** At this stage, most consumer durables have been purchased although occasional replacements will be required. Purchasing is low and patterns of purchasing are conservative and predictable. This group of consumers is increasing rapidly. Such people tend to be less reliant solely on the state pension, many having subscribed to occupational pensions from former employers, which boosts the state pension. This allows this group to lead more active lives and the tourist industry now actively targets this particular market segment.

In the past the tendency was for clearer demarcations of purchasing responsibility in terms of which partner was responsible for which purchases. Nowadays, this distinction is far less clear-cut as family roles have tended to merge in terms of women taking on traditionally-viewed male roles and vice versa. Marketers should, therefore, engage in research before determining whom to target for their marketing efforts.

Activity

Do you feel that social class or family life-cycle is the best base for segmentation?

The two are interlinked, because one can belong to a particular social class, yet be in any of the family life-cycle stages that have been mentioned. This means that marketing appeals can be made to particular classes within each of the stages that have been cited.

Individual buyer behaviour

As well as being influenced by the outside environment, people also have their own individual beliefs. It is important that we should know what these are in order that we can better understand how individuals respond to marketing efforts. Individuals are different in terms of how they look, their education, their feelings and their responses to marketing efforts. Some will behave predictably and others less predictably according to an individual's personality. The individual consumer absorbs information and develops attitudes and perceptions, and in marketing terms this will affect an individual's needs as well as determining how to satisfy them. The task of marketing is to identify patterns of behaviour which are predictable under given conditions and which will increase the marketer's ability to satisfy customer needs, and this process is at the very base of marketing. In order to more fully understand this we shall concentrate on five psychological concepts which are recognised as being very important when attempting to understand buyer behaviour:

1 **Personality and self-concept** This concerns how we think other people see us and how we see ourselves. As individuals we might wish to create a picture of ourselves that is acceptable to our reference group, and this is communicated to the outside world by our individual behaviour. Marketers are interested in this behaviour as it relates to our purchase and consumption of goods. The sum of this behaviour is an individual self-statement and is a non-verbal form of communication. This self-image is expressed in a way which relates to our inner selves and this promotes acceptance within a group. Direct advertising appeals to the self-image are now being made through behavioural segmentation bases that were discussed in the previous chapter.

   'Self' is influenced by social interaction and people make purchases that are consistent with their self-concept in order to protect and enhance it. The constant process of re-evaluating and modifying the self-concept results from a changing environment and changing personal situations.

   Personality is the principal component of the self-concept, and it has a strong effect upon buyer behaviour. Many purchase decisions are likely to reflect personality, and marketers must consider personality when making marketing appeals. Psychological theory suggests that we are born with instinctive desires which cannot be satisfied in a socially acceptable manner and which are thus repressed. The task of marketing in this context is to appeal to inner needs, whilst, at the same time, providing products which enable them to be satisfied in a socially acceptable way.

2 **Motivation**   An early thinker insofar as motivation is concerned was the psychologist Sigmund Freud (1856–1939). His theories have been criticised but are of fundamental value. He was responsible for identifying three levels of consciousness:

- The conscious which includes all sensations and experiences of which we are aware;
- The pre-conscious which includes the memories and thoughts which we have stored from our experiences and which we can bring to mind when we wish;
- The unconscious which is the major driving force behind our behaviour, and this includes our wishes and desires of which we are not always aware.

Within these levels of consciousness there are mental forces at work attempting to reconcile our instincts with the social world in which we live, and since these are not always in accord we experience emotional difficulties. The Freudian terms for these are:

- The *Id* which is the reservoir for all our physiological and sensual instincts. It is selfish and seeks instant gratification regardless of social consequences;
- The *superego* which develops as we grow and learn from family, friends, teachers and other influences. It functions as our internal representation of the values and morals of the society in which we have grown up. It is a potent force and comes into conflict with the demands made by our *id* for the gratification of what might be antisocial desires;
- The *ego* which attempts to resolve the conflict between the *id* and the *superego* and tries to redirect our *id* impulses into socially and morally acceptable modes of expression.

Marketers are interested in motivation when it relates to purchasing behaviour. This behaviour relates to the motive for wishing to possess the goods or services in question, and it has been termed 'goal-related behaviour'. For a motive to exist, there must be a corresponding need. Motives like hunger, thirst, warmth and shelter are physiological. Others, like approval, success and prestige are psychological. Motives like staying alive are instinctive whilst motives like cleanliness, tidiness and proficiency are learned during life. We can also discern between rational and emotional motives. Most purchasing decisions are a composite of these, and quite often a deciding factor might be price which is of course more of an economic restriction than a motive. It can, therefore, be seen that a number of motives might be at play when making a purchasing decision – some stronger than others – and the final decision might be a compromise solution.

In 1954 the psychologist Abraham Maslow put forward his classic 'hierarchy of needs' which is shown in Figure 4.1. This hierarchy is now central to much thinking in buyer behaviour. Physiological needs are concerned with self-preservation and these are the basic needs of life involving those elements required to sustain and advance the human race. Safety needs relate to protection against danger and deprivation. Once the more basic needs have been satisfied behaviour is influenced by the need for belonging, association and acceptance by others. In many texts the next two needs are put together, but here we have separated respect and self-esteem in terms of confidence, competence and knowledge and have then placed achievement in terms of qualifications and recognition above this. The final need is what Maslow termed 'self-actualisation' which means self-fulfilment in terms of becoming all that one is capable of being at the pinnacle of personal potential.

It is argued that when more basic needs like hunger ant thirst have been satisfied, then individuals will move towards satisfying higher-order needs towards the apex of the pyramid and look increasingly for

Fig 4.1 Hierarchy of needs

Source: After Maslow (1954).

satisfactions which will increase status and social acceptability. When the apex has been reached and other satisfactions have been achieved, the prime motivation is then one of acquiring products and accomplishing activities which allow self-expression. This can be in the form of hobbies, particularly collecting, which may have been desired for a long time, but have been neglected until those lower-order needs have been satisfied. It is of course not possible to formulate marketing strategies on the hierarchy theory on its own. Its real value is that it suggests that marketers should understand and direct their efforts at the specific needs of their customers, wherever the goods one is attempting to promote is in the hierarchy.

Activity

Think of one product or service that falls into each of the six sections of the pyramid in Figure 4.1.

The answer to this will differ between different individuals according to their particular circumstances and backgrounds. The lower-order needs are easiest, but higher-order needs will differ according to their backgrounds and aspirations. It is also more probable that higher-order needs will tend to be fulfilled as individuals become older towards the retirement period of life; at this time attainments, although perhaps not perfect in terms of original aspirations, are recognised as having been achieved as far as possible. It is then that people start looking for self-actualisation in terms of hobbies and recreations that had not been possible previously owing to the pressures of working life.

Maslow was not the only theorist to focus upon human needs as the motivating force behind human behaviour. McGregor argued that two sets of theories (theories X and Y) motivate people, particularly within the workplace, and since the workplace is where attitudes and opinions are accumulated his works has indirect relevance to marketing. Under theory X certain assumptions are made:

- people have an inherent dislike for work and will avoid it if possible;
- because of this, they must be coerced, controlled, directed and threatened with punishment in order to complete their work satisfactorily;
- people like to be directed and don't crave responsibility. They have little ambition and want security.

Under theory Y he makes an alternative set of assumptions:

- people are not naturally passive or resistant to organisational needs. They have become so as the result of experience in organisations;
- motivation and the capacity to develop and assume responsibility are

all present and it is management's responsibility to develop these characteristics;
- it is management's responsibility to organise production towards economic ends, but it is also their task to arrange conditions and methods of operation so that people can achieve their own goals best by directing their own efforts towards organisational objectives;
- if the right conditions prevail, individuals will not only accept responsibility, they will actively seek it;
- most of the population is capable of imagination, ingenuity and creativity in problem-solving within an organisation;
- industrialisation has meant that such capabilities are underutilised.

There are thus two ways in which human behaviour can be interpreted, depending upon whether the observer assumes theory X or theory Y. What McGregor argued was that management by control (theory X) was based on an inaccurate set of negative assumptions, and that organisations would work more effectively if 'management by objectives' (MBO), or theory Y, was applied.

Frederick Herzberg (1966) also contributed to motivation theory through his *Motivation-hygiene* theory. He believed that performance is at its pinnacle when people are satisfied with their jobs as long as the necessary resources are provided to carry out this work effectively. Satisfaction with work and personal happiness do not necessarily work in harmony, but when they do and the person is stretched to the limits of his or her ability then there may be a feeling of 'self-actualisation' (see Figure 4.1). Whilst this feeling might be more evident in recreational or home situations, it is less common in the workplace because of the conditions and deadlines imposed in an occupational situation. According to Herzberg, self-actualisation depends on what he terms *'motivators'*, which he distinguishes from *'hygiene factors'*. Motivators can positively contribute to satisfaction at work, whereas hygiene factors cannot promote satisfaction, but they can prevent dissatisfaction. He uses the medical analogy to describe hygiene factors and cited the case of unhygienic conditions as being a source of infection which may make a person unhealthy. In an organisation, hygiene factors are:

- financial reward;
- supervision;
- working conditions;
- company policy;
- status and relationships with colleagues.

Similarly, in an organisation, motivators are:

- recognition for achievement;
- opportunities for advancement;

- responsibility;
- the job itself.

It can be seen that motivating factors are those which are part of the job whereas hygiene factors are more concerned with the job environment.

Activity

Under this section headed **motivation** we have discussed theories put forward by Freud, Maslow, McGregor and Herzberg. What do you feel is the practical value of these theories to marketers?

At this stage, those of a cynical inclination might be tempted to say: 'Very little'. Those who are a little kinder might see some relevance in Maslow's hierarchy of needs, but might view the rest as being irrelevant. Others might see some indirect bearing in the theories of the others in terms of discussing 'motivation' in a less direct sense in the knowledge that how we are motivated might reflect the way we purchase. However, the real point is that in order for marketing to develop as a science it must have theories. Theories are a way in which thinkers can communicate with each other in concise terms, and these theories have central relevance to the subject of motivation. As marketers, we are interested in motivation from a purchasing behaviour point of view so their relevance is justified because as marketers our knowledge would be incomplete without an understanding of the basic building blocks behind motivation.

3 **Perception**   Unlike motivation, which requires a reaction to a stimulus, perception relates to the meaning that is assigned to that stimulus. As marketers we are interested in how buyers perceive and react to products in relation to such matters as quality, aesthetics, price and image, since products not only exist in practical terms but are also perceived by consumers in relation to need-satisfaction. This perception by the buyer is affected by the nature of the product itself, by the circumstances of the individual buyer, and by the buyer's innate situation in terms of how ready they are to make the purchase (whether they need it at a particular point in time). It is, or course, necessary that the product or service (that is, the stimulus) receives the attention of the potential buyer. Buyers have numerous stimuli competing for their attention so marketers must make their stimuli as interesting and attractive as possible, since potential buyers only act on information that is retained; this is the foundation of how the product or service is communicated together with the choice of media. There is of course no certainty that perception of a product or service will be as the marketer expected, even though the marketer has successfully alerted the consumer to a particular offering through successful manipulation of the marketing mix. Consumers might be influ-

enced by all kinds of illogical motives as well as the practical ones presented to them by the marketer. These might be favourable or unfavourable preconceptions from personal experience, from peer group or family advice, or from other psychological motives, all combining to alter and shape the final perception and indeed the ultimate buying decision.

4 **Attitudes**   Our strongest basic attitudes are implanted in our formative years and come largely from the influence of our close family group and other social interactions. More refined attitudes develop later. In marketing terms, the sum total of our attitudes can be regarded as a set of cognitions which a potential buyer has in relation to a potential purchase or a purchasing environment. This is why certain stores or companies go out of their way to engender favourable attitudes, and it is why manufacturers seek to induce loyalty towards their particular brand or product. Once this attitude has been established in the mind of the consumer, it might be difficult to alter. Even a minor dissatisfaction can cause a fundamental shift in disposition. This process can work for and against a manufacturer or retail establishment, and a method of attempting to change attitudes is through promotional appeals and through a programme of public relations. These subjects are dealt with more fully in later chapters.

5 **Learning**   Experience precedes learning and this can alter perceptions and attitudes. It also intensifies a shift in behaviour, so when a buyer perceives that certain products are more favourable than others within his or her reference group, repeat purchases are made to promote this acceptability. Every time a satisfactory purchase is made, the consumer becomes less likely to depart from this purchasing behaviour. The result is *brand loyalty*, and the ultimate success of marketing is in terms of customers making repeat purchases or becoming brand-loyal.

In the context of marketing, learning is a result of information received through advertising or other publicity, or through some reference group or other. In order to have an effect on motives or attitudes, marketing effort should associate the product with positive drives and reinforcing messages.

A fundamental aim of marketers is to bring about satisfaction for their customers, and this is cardinal to the concept of marketing. Having looked at some of the issues which make up consumer behaviour, we can now look at the consumer's central goal. Because they are continually occupied in the quest for satisfaction, competitive offerings will always have potential appeal, so that firms must seek continuous improvement to the products or services and the levels of support they provide. This is a matter of balancing costs and potential profit with customer demands, as 'total satisfaction', except in a minority of cases, is an unrealistically expensive goal.

4.4 **Models of Consumer Behaviour**

Now that we have examined the psychological factors that influence consumer buyer behaviour we are now in a position to examine some consumer behaviour models. The aim is to bring together our present understanding by presenting a series of models that endeavour to explain the purchase decision process in relation to pertinent variables.

The buyer decision process

Different buying tasks present different levels of complexity to the purchaser. The 'AIDA' model which is presented in Figure 4.2 considers the steps leading to a purchase in the form of a sequential problem-solving process. This classical model was first proposed by E. K. Strong (1925) and it is still useful today because it is easy to apply and describes the activities involved in the buyer decision process. Products and services vary in the complexity of decision-making involved in their acquisition. The purchase of a new shower unit, for instance, is more complicated than the purchase of a tube of shower gel.

Robinson, Faris and Wind (1967) put forward a model that viewed purchasing as a problem. This is shown in Figure 4.3 and describes the activities involved in the purchasing process. An individual needs a particular product. Information will be sought from a variety of sources including family and friends ('word of mouth'), from advertising, catalogues, visits to retail establishments, and from many other sources. The more complex the product, the greater will tend to be this information search. The task

Fig 4.2   AIDA model of buying behaviour

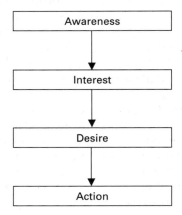

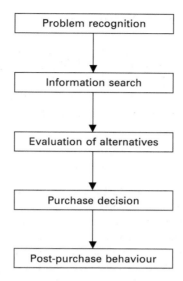

Fig 4.3   The buyer decision model

of marketing is to ensure that the company's products receive high exposure during this *information search* period, and that the best points of the
product are emphasised during the *evaluation of alternatives* phase. This
will put the company's product in the best light prior to the *purchase
decision*, because even then the consumer is still susceptible to further
influences in making the correct choice. Marketers must also be aware
of *post-purchase behaviour* because this can affect repeat business, and
forward-looking companies attach as much importance to after-sales service as they do to making the initial sale. This reduces the degree of dissatisfaction (or dissonance) in the case of genuine complaints. One method
that is now practised for sales of major items like new motor cars is where
companies follow up a sale by some form of communication by letter or
telephone with their customers. This builds confidence in the mind of the
customer in having made the 'correct' purchasing decision. The terminol-
ogy that has been attached to this kind of after-sales follow-up is 'customer
care'.

A knowledge of how the buyer decision process works is critical to the
success of marketing strategy. For simple products, the task of marketing is
to direct the purchasing routine in favour of the company's products, perhaps through an effective mass-advertising campaign. For more complicated purchases it is more important that customers are helped in their
problem-solving process and that reassure once is provided to show that
their choice has been a wise one.

Activity

Of the two models that have been put forward in relation to the buyer decision process which do you feel is most useful as a tool of marketing?

The AIDA model is perhaps more of a tool for marketers in that they must ensure that their products or services display the characteristics of creating attention, generating interest, forming a desire to possess, and bringing about action through purchasing. The other model is perhaps less useful in that it merely describes the consumer decision-making process from problem recognition (that the product or service is needed), to post-purchase behaviour (how they feel after the purchase has been made).

The adoption process

The buyer decision model (Figure 4.3) was not specifically designed for new products, and its substance was concerned with search and problem-solving. The model shown in Figure 4.4 was devised by Everett Rogers (1962) pp.

Fig 4.4   The adoption process

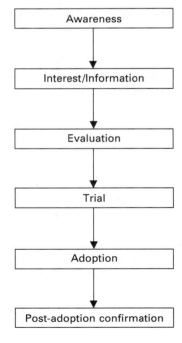

79–86, and relates to new products. It begins with awareness. Marketers must first create awareness and then assist customers through subsequent stages of the process. Consumers cannot begin to consider a new product or service as a solution to need-related problems without this awareness. Successful innovative products should attempt to be problem-solving as far as the customer is concerned.

Awareness can come about as a result of the marketing effort of the company or simply by 'word of mouth' communication. If the product has potential *interest* and appeal, then potential purchasers will seek further *information*. Consumers then *evaluate* the new product against existing products, and then make an initial adoption by obtaining a *trial* sample, which might be a free sample or a *trial* purchase. The *adoption* stage is when a decision is made whether to use the product (in the case of a fast-moving consumer good on a repeat purchase basis). *Post-adoption confirmation* is when the product has been adopted and the consumer is seeking reassurance about the wisdom of the purchase. After a major purchase, dissonance (usually termed cognitive dissonance) is present in the sign of unease that what was thought to be value for money at the time of purchase may not, after all, turn out to be true value. Such dissonance should be countered by the provision of some kind of follow-up – either written or through the telephone.

A more detailed model is suggested in Figure 4.5 which develops the adoption process. A series of inputs feed into the knowledge base. The 'self' input includes the psychological notions of perception, attitudes, motivation and learning. Similar to other inputs, they set the scene for knowledge to be interpreted into a favourable situation of awareness. Figure 4.5 also shows that persuasion governs the rate of adoption which is affected by relative advantage, compatibility, complexity, trial opportunity and observability. The model also allows for review after the decision stage, and here consumers can be sensitive to the influence of external information sources from promotional appeals and from such influences as reference groups.

It can be seen that various inputs contribute to *knowledge*, ranging from personal factors to company marketing activity. *Persuasion* is an important phase and here a number of factors which are functions of the product itself can lead to the *decision* whether or not to purchase the new product or service in question. The decision means adoption or rejection. If it is adoption, then good experience can lead to its continued adoption, but if the experience of the product or service is bad then it will be discontinued. Conversely, rejection might be the decision and this can be followed by continued rejection, or later adoption, perhaps in the latter case through hearing good experience of reference group members who have purchased. Continued adoption and later adoption need *confirmation* in order to continue the repeat-purchase pattern.

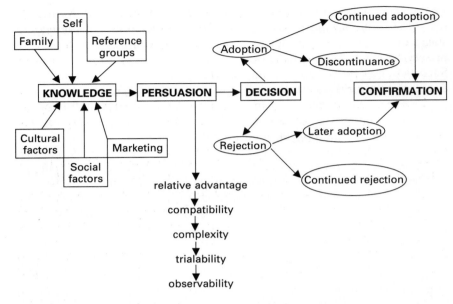

Fig 4.5   New product purchasing decision process

Activity

What do you feel is meant by each of the terms that are cited under *Persuasion* in Figure 4.5?

- 'Relative advantage' means how much better the service or product is over other offerings in the marketplace.
- 'Compatibility' is the degree to which the product or service conforms to the buyer's purchasing needs.
- 'Complexity' is a function of the product or service in that, for instance, a new brand of toothpaste is less complex than an innovatory type of food processor.
- 'Trialability' is again a function of the product or service and it simply relates to how easy it is to try it out at as small a cost as possible. For instance, a new brand of toothpaste might be given away free as a trial sample or at most the price would be the cost of a single purchase. A video recorder might be supplied as a demonstration model for a short period on loan. A new car, on the other hand, can be demonstrated on a test drive, but it is quite often some time after the purchase has been made that real opinions about the newly purchased car are formed.
- 'Observability' is also a function of products in particular, because like motor cars they can be observed in use. However, a service like an insurance policy is a more abstract concept, so it is rates low on this factor as it relies more upon description and other evidence for its sale.

The diffusion of innovations is a process that is examined in detail in Chapter 7 under 'product' considerations. It is, however, important that we look at innovator categories insofar as purchasing behaviour is concerned, because consumers as individuals can be more or less receptive to new product or service ideas.

The process of the diffusion of innovations proposes that certain groups of consumers will take on new ideas more quickly than other groups, and they tend to influence later consumer groups. These group have particular common features:

1 **Innovators** are the first small segment to take on new product ideas, and they are likely to be younger people from well-educated, relatively affluent backgrounds having a high social status. They are more probably unprejudiced, discerning people whose understanding of the new product has been more objectively ascertained than through salespeople or company promotional material.
2 **Early adopters** possess some of the characteristics of innovators, but they are more part of 'local' systems, acting as opinion leaders within their specific group.
3 **Early majority** adopters tend to be above average in terms of social class, and rely upon company promotional efforts for data. Opinion leaders of the early adopter category will tend to be their biggest inspiration.
4 **Late majority** adopters tend to adopt the product or service because it has become generally accepted by earlier groups.
5 **Laggards** make up the final group. They tend to be more careful and older and of a lower socio-economic standing.

Clearly, adopter categories will tend to differ depending upon the new product or service being marketed.

Hierarchy of effects

Lavidge and Steiner (1961) produced a 'hierarchy of effects' model of purchasing behaviour. Their model starts at the *awareness* stage, but it could be argued that there is a stage prior to this when the potential purchaser is completely unaware of the product or service offering, and it is through marketing communication that such awareness is made known. The model is described in Figure 4.6.

Activity

Consider the models of purchasing behaviour that have been discussed. Now consider three phases of purchasing as being: the pre-transaction phase, the transaction phase and the post-transaction phase. Which component parts of each model fall under each of these purchasing phases?

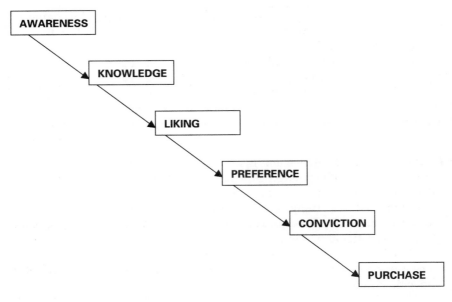

Fig 4.6   The innovation/adoption model

	pre-transaction	transaction	post-transaction
Fig 4.2	awareness, interest, desire	action	
Fig 4.3	problem-recognition, information-search	evaluation of alternatives, purchase decision,	post-purchase behaviour
Fig 4.4	awareness, interest, information	evaluation, adoption	post-adoption confirmation
Fig 4.5	knowledge	persuasion, decision	confirmation
Fig 4.6	awareness, knowledge	liking, preference, conviction, purchase	

4.5 Organisational Buying Behaviour

The term 'organisational buying' reflects purchasing in three different buying situations as shown in Figure 4.7. Industrial buying and organisation buying tend to be used interchangeably in the literature, but as we can see industrial buying is really a subset of organisational buying. The process of organisational buying behaviour differs from consumer buying in that the psychological and emotional considerations attached to the latter should not apply here. However, organisational buyers are human, so clearly some 'emotion' might be involved, but generally it can be said that commercial

Fig 4.7   Elements of organisational buying

considerations are of prime significance when arriving at purchasing decisions.

Activity

Think of three purchasing situations involved in each of the three sub-headings of organisational buying:

- Industrial buying: purchasing man-made fibres for a spinning plant; purchasing a new lathe for the actory's machine shop; purchasing silicon chips for incorporation in the motherboard of a computer.
- Buying for resale: purchasing fruit and vegetables for a supermarket chain; purchasing fashion clothing for the next selling season; a wholesaler purchasing fancy glassware from an overseas factory for stockholding with a view to promoting it for onward sale to domestic retail outlets.
- Institutional buying: purchasing uniforms for the fire service; purchasing medical equipment for a hospital; purchasing stationery materials for a local government department.

The principal similarity between consumer and organisational purchasing is that they both represent a need-satisfying process. This need reflects itself in buying behaviour, and this is why it is important that marketers understand purchasing motives in order to effectively target their marketing efforts in a way that satisfies these needs.

Activity

In each of the sub-divisions that comprise organisational buying, what do you feel will be the principal criterion when making purchasing decisions?

This is a difficult one, but it should make you think about the constraints under which purchasing in each of the three situations described operates. It depends, of course, upon individual buying situations in terms of the importance that is attached to each, and it also depends upon the type of purchase being made, so what follows is really a generalisation.

In industrial buying the principal criterion will be to keep production satisfied in terms of raw materials and components in order that they can complete work for the company's customers.

In buying for resale the principal criterion will be to purchase at a 'keen' price in order to apply a reasonable mark-up and keep the company profitable.

In institutional buying the main criterion will be in terms of budget constraints. Typically, institutional buying activity is indirectly funded by the public through revenue that is raised through various taxes and levies. Spending should, therefore, be kept within the predetermined spending limits that have been agreed as part of the funding process.

It can be seen that organisational purchasers have to work with more stringent purchasing constraints because they have the commercial and budgetary interests of their respective organisations to serve. They also have logistical factors like delivery schedules to maintain. There is little opportunity for 'impulse' purchasing in which everyday consumers can indulge. As purchasing professionals they should have a great deal of technical and commercial knowledge about their prospective purchases.

Models of organisational buying

In Figure 4.8 we propose a model of the organisational purchasing decision process. It is, perhaps, more precise in its application than the models that were suggested for consumer buying behaviour, as items for purchase require a more business-like description through a formal specification at the *need description* and *product specification* stages. Likely suppliers tend to be more rigorously vetted prior to a first order being placed, and it is not uncommon for purchasing and other executives to visit the supplying company beforehand, in order to ascertain whether or not the supplying company measures up to quality, financial and other reliability criteria. The purchase routine specification will instruct the supplying company in relation to quantities to be delivered at specific dates through a delivery schedule if the entire order is not all needed at once.

Having said that organisational purchasing is more 'scientific' than consumer goods purchasing, individual organisational purchasers are of course subjected to the marketing actions and efforts of their current and potential suppliers. Reference groups also exist within organisational situations and there can be influences from outside of the purchasing department, and these factors are dealt with later in this chapter. It should also be recognised that individual buyers have discrete psychological attributes which can also influence decision-making.

Figure 4.9 shows a more refined model that was developed by Wind (1978). He contended that it is critical for marketers to locate powerful buyers, because they tend to have a more direct say in purchasing decisions at the negotiation stage. This does not ultimately mean those who are most

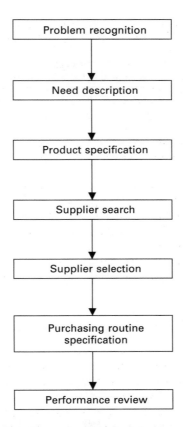

Fig 4.8   The organisational purchasing decision process

important within the organisation at which the marketing approach is being directed. Buyers of relatively low status may be able to impede a purchase for a variety of reasons, and five power bases have been identified in this respect:

1 **Reward**   The ability to provide monetary, social, political, or psychological rewards to others for compliance.
2 **Coercive**   The ability to withhold monetary payments or other punishments for non-compliance.
3 **Attraction**   The ability to elicit compliance from others because they like you.
4 **Expert**   The ability to elicit compliance because of actual or reputed technical expertise.
5 **Status**   Compliance from the ability derived from a legitimate position of power in a company.

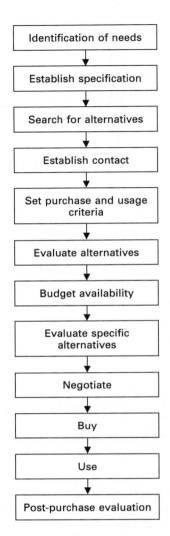

Fig 4.9   Wind's organisational purchasing model

Organisational and consumer purchasing compared

Activity

How do purchasers in organisational buying situations differ from consumer buyers in their purchasing decision-making processes?

- Rationality of purchasing motives;
- Derived demand, especially in industrial buying situations, where demand is dependent upon purchases further down the supply chain and this creates demand further up the chain;
- Small numbers of individual buyers;
- Large number of influences on individual buyers;
- Often multi-person purchasing decision-making unit;
- Suppliers are sometimes in active competition with each other;
- Industrial customers may have more power;
- Many products are pre-specified by the buyer's organisation;
- Commercial relationships between buyers and sellers are often long-term;
- Unequal purchasing power of customers;
- Distribution is more direct;
- Higher value of purchases;
- There is sometimes a geographical concentration of purchasers;
- Company policies, for instance in relation to suppliers being 'listed' for a particular quality standard, may act as a constraint on the buyer;
- Possible 'reciprocal' purchasing arrangements, in that certain markets may be closed off because of a mutual trading agreement;
- A sale is often preceded by lengthy negotiation;
- Relationships between buyers and sellers tend to be more long-term, rather than depending on a single commercial transaction.

The structured nature of organisational purchasing

Each time a consumer makes a purchase from a retailer, a derived demand is created for a series of materials and components which make up the final product. Added to this is an elaborate chain of supply from companies who buy and sell ancillary products like packaging materials, machinery and maintenance equipment. In order that companies can control this steady flow of goods and services, they must organise their purchasing activities so that they have:

1 a constant supply of goods and services of the requisite quality as and when required;
2 a system which monitors supplier performance in terms of the above; and
3 a system of review of existing and potential suppliers.

The larger the organisation, the more structured the methods of buying should be, and there should be an established procedure for each of the steps outlined in Figure 4.8. Purchasing will tend to be more critical in flow production situations than in a jobbing works. Even a minor delivery or quality problem could cause substantial losses in terms of lost production and loss of customer goodwill. Organisational purchasers tend to be far more demanding than consumer purchasers because of the implications just outlined, so the notion of 'customer care', which is dealt with in more detail later in the text, has profound significance in modern marketing.

Organisational buying situations

Three major types of organisational buying situation have been identified, together with the problems surrounding each, as shown in Figure 4.10. From the viewpoint of suppliers' marketing departments, each of these purchasing situations suggests a different marketing mix. This is in order to

Fig 4.10   Organisational buying situations

(a) STRAIGHT REBUY
- continuing or recurrent item or commodity
- involves little purchasing effort
- routinely dealt with within current purchasing arrangements
- suppliers are already known
- represents much of purchasing activity in many companies
- past experience has established a reliable supply pattern
- difficult for new suppliers to enter the market

(b) MODIFIED REBUY
- continuing need but at an expanded (or decreased) level
- minor changes to product specification needing additional information
- change of regular supplier for some reason
- possibly due to some outside event (e.g. shortage of material)
- companies who are not already supplying sometimes attempt to convert straight rebuy into modified rebuy
- internal circumstances (e.g. new buyer) might want to look for cost reductions or better service or better quality
- sometimes develops from new buy or new task

(c) NEW TASK
- unfamiliar or new product or new specification
- extensive need description
- supplier search
- challenging purchasing task as no past experience to draw upon
- infrequent occurrence
- sets the pattern for more routine straight rebuy and modified rebuy situations later
- creative marketers will anticipate this event and will make appropriate marketing appeals

fit the particular circumstances, depending upon whether the company is an 'in' supplier currently supplying, or an 'out' supplier seeking to become an 'in' supplier.

Activity

What do you feel are the principal characteristics of organisational demand?

- Demand is derived from the demand for other products further down the distribution chain;
- Price tends to be relatively stable;
- Demand tends to fluctuate because it is often linked to external economic circumstances and there is sometimes evidence of stocking up on the part of purchasers.

The decision-making unit (DMU)

The scope and roles of organisational buyers vary widely according to the type of service or commodity being purchased and whether purchasing is a centralised or decentralised function. Large retail chains now tend to centralise their purchasing in order to employ specialist buyers who can negotiate keen terms and conditions. Some companies employ buyers who have only superficial knowledge of the products offered and handle only the commercial aspects of the sale. Whatever the buying structure, organisational salespersons know that the buyer is not always the final decision-maker.

Fig 4.11 The decision-making unit (DMU) or buying centre

Gatekeepers	control the flow of information to and from the people who buy (e.g. the buyer's secretary or an assistant buyer)
Users	are individuals who work with, or use the product. Depending upon how purchasing decisions are made, they are sometimes involved in product specification
Deciders	are people who make the buying decision. In many cases this is the buyer, but on some occasions it can be the specifier or in a tightly budgeted situation the accountant
Buyers	have authority to sign orders and make the purchase. They may also help to shape the specification, but their principal role is in supplier negotiation and selection
Influencers	can affect the buying decision in different ways (e.g. technical people may have helped in a major or minor way to develop the product specification)

The predominant difference between consumer and organisational buying is that organisational buying often involves group decision-making. Webster and Wind (1972) proposed that there were distinct roles in the purchasing process, sometimes taken up by different individuals, and sometimes the same individuals combining some of these roles as shown in Figure 4.11. They termed this idea the notion of the 'buying centre' or the decision-making unit (DMU).

Activity

Apart from using sales representatives, what means do organisational marketers have for targeting the DMU?

- Direct mail
- Press advertising
- Sales literature
- Editorial publicity
- Exhibitions
- Seminars and demonstrations
- Public relations
- Sponsored films
- House magazines
- Posters
- Radio and TV (although these might be relatively expensive)

Future developments in organisational purchasing

Nowadays manufacturing companies (especially those operating flow line production) are moving towards holding less stocks of components and raw materials. In some manufacturing situations, stockholding is theoretically non-existent. This is termed *just-in-time* management, or *lean manufacturing*. It requires delivery of goods exactly when required with zero defects. Should defects occur, the company's production will soon be stopped so reliability of supply is of prime importance. In such situations relationships tend to be long-term, and it is just as common for buyers to visit sellers as it is for sellers to visit buyers (the traditional pattern). The idea of buyers sourcing sellers is termed *reverse marketing* (as opposed to *traditional marketing* when the seller meets buyers). The term used to describe these longer-term relationships is *relationship marketing*.

It is important to recognise that just as consumer goods buyers are responsive to the actions of sellers, industrial buyers are individuals who possess personalities. The personal impression that the buyer or a member of the DMU has of a company's image, as well as the personal accord that the salesperson can achieve, can profoundly influence the purchasing decision. This human factor also extends to individual relationships which the buyer might have with colleagues within the selling organisation. As we move towards longer-term relationships, so this trend will increase and the notion of customer care will become increasingly important. Companies have 'personalities' which is an amalgam of attitudes and policies reflected in the way outside people view the organisation.

4.6 Summary

Although we have identified factors that are common to consumer and organisational buying behaviour, it is emphasised that the two markets should be approached differently. The requirements of consumers are established and the marketing response is communicated mainly through the mass media and direct-response marketing methods like 'individualised personal mailings' from a mailing list. In organisational markets, buyers and sellers also communicate through the mass media, but to a lesser extent as they also rely upon personal interaction. Organisational buyers tend to work to obtain satisfaction in relation to the company's commercial needs. Much consumer behaviour has a psychological foundation, and although organisational purchasers have an explicit rationale for their actions this does not imply that they are inflexible to receiving psychological influences. Marketers should not overlook the psychological factors that drive industrial customers. Nowhere is this more important than in a market where the products or services on offer are broadly similar; it is here that organisational marketers must attempt to modify their marketing advances to serve specific idiosyncratic needs and requirements.

5 Marketing Information Systems and Forecasting

5.1 **Introduction**

Information is the life-blood of successful marketing. With the possible exception of the accounting function of the firm, marketing, as a functional area of management, depends on and makes use of information more than any other management discipline. Information can be of great strategic value to the professional marketer, as well as contributing to tactical and more routine operational decision-making. Knowing what kind of information to obtain and how to make effective use of it once you have got it, are the key skills of strategic marketing management. The possession and use of information gives the firm a chance of gaining a competitive advantage over the competition. Armies often win wars, not because they have superior military power, but because they have more effective intelligence-gathering procedures. Likewise commercial firms are waging a sort of commercial war in a free-market competitive economy. They too will have a better chance of 'winning' if they have superior intelligence to their competitors.

In a purposeful, proactive marketing organisation the acquisition and management of information cannot be left to chance, it is far too important a commodity for that. All aspects of information including its collection, storage, processing, retrieval and use must be managed. The marketing-oriented firm needs some form of process to carry out this important activity; what is needed is some form of system devoted to the management of the entire information-needs of the organisation. Such a system is the subject of the first part of this chapter and is referred to as a marketing information system (MkIS). As we shall see, marketing research is part of an integrated marketing information system. Marketing research is covered in this chapter, although a more comprehensive treatment of the subject is given in the next chapter.

Marketing is the management process that anticipates and delivers customer value more effectively and efficiently than the competition and, in a profit-making organisation, does so at an acceptable level of profit. Note the word anticipate. Many markets are dynamic rather than static, and the only thing really certain about the future is that it will be different from today. Marketing management needs to anticipate and stay ahead of these changes. Much marketing decision-making at the strategic level requires some form of prediction or forecast of likely future conditions across a wide variety of areas. Marketing information systems can be used to provide information for use in a wide range of decision areas. Not all of these involve forecasting by any means. However it would be true to say of any information system or decision-support system, that the end product is usually a decision about the future made in the present often based largely on information about the past. This process by its very nature involves forecasting. Hence the second part of this chapter is devoted to this very important marketing area, forecasting. Because of the limitation of space the authors have based many of their examples in this part of the chapter on sales forecasting. However, the reader should note that the techniques discussed can be used to forecast a wide range of different things. For example in logistics the forecasting of production materials or component parts is likely to be very important, while in production error-processes can be predicted and monitored. In fact forecasting is used in many areas of business decision-making.

5.2 **Marketing Information Systems**

As we mentioned in the introduction, a marketing information system (MkIS) is really a systematic process for the management of marketing information. The term 'system' often conjures up thoughts of computers in the minds of many people, especially those managing or working in smaller enterprises. They feel it must be too sophisticated for their business and must require a great deal of technical skill to design and implement. In fact nothing could be further from the truth. Every firm must organise the collection, storage and distribution of information to its managers if it is going to function effectively. As we shall see, such a system can be purely manual. Hence companies of all sizes are carrying out information audits in an attempt to design systems that will meet their information needs and give them a competitive edge. One of the best definitions of a marketing information system is given by Professor Philip Kotler of Nothwestern University in the United States:

'A Marketing Information System (MkIS) consists of people, equipment and procedures to gather, sort, analyse, evaluate and distribute needed, timely and accurate information to marketing decision makers.' (Kotler, 1997)

A formal MkIS can be of great benefit to any organisation no matter what its size or the level of managerial sophistication. As for the term 'system' conjuring up visions of complex computer networks, again this view is entirely false. It is true today that in many companies an MkIS is operated as part of a computer system, and even in smaller companies there is often a personal computer in the office. If no computing capability is available the design and implementation of an MkIS is still possible. There is no reason why an MkIS can not be based entirely on a manual system of reference cards and files. Such a system will lack the ease of storage and retrieval of a computer system, but some form of manual system is far better than having no system at all and merely leaving the management of information to chance. To manage a business well is to manage its future, and to manage its future is to manage information. Information is a valuable resource and must be as carefully managed as any other valuable resource – for example human resources, financial resources and so on. It cannot be left to chance, and management needs some form of system to try to ensure that information from a diverse set of sources is collected, stored, analysed and distributed effectively at the right time and to the people who require it to make certain marketing decisions. This, in essence, is what the concept of an integrated marketing information system is all about.

Activity

'To manage a business well is to manage its future, and to manage its future is to manage information.'

To what extent do you think the above statement is true and why? Use examples where possible to illustrate the points made.

The first thing here is to discuss what you think management is all about and there are a number of ways of looking at the role of management within the organisation. Getting things done using other people to do it is a view of management often expressed. Making decisions about the future in the present using information obtained from the past and the present is another interesting 'definition'. The next thing is to examine the concept of strategy. Strategy is long-term in nature and is concerned with the broad general direction of the organisation in the future often over a five to ten-year time horizon or even longer.

Of course day-to-day operational activities and operations need to be managed effectively. This process is usually carried out by 'middle' managers, while more senior managers concern themselves almost exclusively with matters that will affect the future direction and performance of the organisation. Long-term strategic decisions and not made on a whim; far from it, they are made on the basis of information. A good example to use here is the US software giant Microsoft. Microsoft is coming to an arrangement with the University of Cambridge to set up a software development campus along the same lines as the Microsoft complex near Seattle in the north-western United States. The objective of the firm is not to simply develop 'Windows 98' or whatever, but to develop a computing concept for the next century that most people would not even be able to understand at present. Microsoft are thinking strategically far ahead into the next millennium and have based their investment decision, due to cost the firm billions of US dollars, on the best information available.

Marketing information systems are not simply the province of larger, more sophisticated and technically-competent organisations. In fact the smaller, entrepreneurial type of firm has potentially the most to gain from the adoption of such a system, no matter how sophisticated the system might be or whether it is a manual or computerised system. Evidence from Day and Reynolds (1996), and other researchers working at the 'marketing entrepreneurship interface', suggest that generally smaller, newer firms make less-effective use of information than larger firms. Many small firms could dramatically increase their marketing capability, literally overnight, if they were to make full use of the information at their disposal. Such a system need not cost a lot of money or indeed any money at all. As we shall discuss later much valuable information is generated every day simply in the course of the firm carrying out its business activities. Much more information can be collected externally with very little cost and little effort and without the necessity of employing conventional marketing research procedures. Even formal marketing research can be carried out by small firms on a limited budget with a little thought and imagination. So few small firms make effective use of marketing information that those that do, all other things being equal, are likely to gain a significant competitive advantage.

5.3 Component Parts of the System

Perhaps the most straightforward design of a marketing information system is that suggested by Kotler (1997). Kotler suggests such a system should be made up of four separate but interrelated component parts. Three of these component parts or sub-systems collect and produce information. The fourth sub-system takes the information provided from the other three parts and processes it, models it and carries out other procedures on the data that enhances its value to marketing decision-makers. When most people think of marketing information they tend to immediately think of marketing research. Of course formally-produced marketing research information is very valuable to all firms, however formal marketing research is not the only form or source of marketing information. The modern firm needs to gather information from whatever sources it can and needs to make effective use of this information. The MkIS is a system that ideally will carry out all of these information functions in a systematic and planned manner. The concept of an integrated marketing information system is shown in Figure 5.1.

Internal accounting system

All firms generate data as part of the general process of carrying out their business. The generation, recording, storage and retrieval of such data is

MARKETING INFORMATION SYSTEM

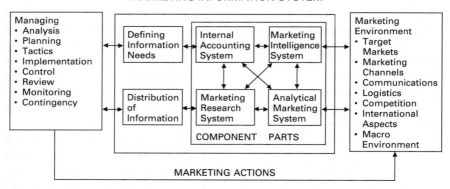

Fig 5.1   A marketing information system

referred to by Kotler as the 'internal accounting system of the firm'. The term tends to evoke thoughts of financial and cost-accounting information, but actually it refers to all information received and generated by the firm. Perhaps a better name for this system would be the 'internal documentary system of the firm' as it is more accurately descriptive. Firms tend to use standard commercial forms and documents that are universally recognised and understood by people in other businesses. Such standard business forms and documents can be purchased from any business stationers, and the individual firm then has it's name and logo printed on the top of the form. Such internally generated forms and documents are usually in the form of multiple copies, often in triplicate. One copy is sent to the customer and others are stored in various places within the documentary system of the firm – for example the accounts department or the sales office. In public limited companies the accounts have to be audited by a qualified accountant under the Companies Act. Management is required to keep copies of all incoming and internally generated commercial forms and documents for a period of six years.

Internally generated data and data inwardly received comes in many forms. For example purchase orders are received by the marketing firm from customers, and delivery notes are generated by the firm to be signed by the customer on delivery. The time between the dates on the two documents gives the total order processing time. This can be monitored to make sure pre-determined service delivery levels are being adhered to. When defective goods are returned to the marketing firm for whatever reason, a goods return slip is usually generated. Again this document can be used to monitor quality performance of either internally manufactured goods or goods bought in from other suppliers. Total number of goods returned or total number of complaints about goods as a percentage of goods sold provide measurable standards of performance. Sales-force expenses as a percentage of sales, number of telephone enquiries converted into sales, orders for particular products which might indicate seasonal or cyclical demand are also useful. This list is almost endless, as are the uses to which internally generated and internally received data can be put for marketing planning, monitoring and control purposes. The list given here is merely indicative and by no means claims to be exhaustive. Further examples are given in the next section when we discuss collecting data internally for sales forecasting purposes.

An important point to bear in mind in the management of marketing firms is that such information is available and can be retrieved from within the internal documentary system or 'internal accounting' system of the firm with a little effort and at little cost. The management of many firms have a wide variety of valuable marketing information quite literally 'right under their feet' so to speak. It is not enough to simply know that such a wealth of data exists, although this is a necessary condition. To be of any practical value as a planning, monitoring and control resource management need to know how to use it effectively. The fact is that the value of virtually any data set can be significantly enhanced by applying certain analytical techniques and procedures to it. This will be discussed further in the section covering the fourth component part of the system, the Analytical Marketing system.

The marketing intelligence system

We saw in the previous section that firms produce a wealth of information internally through the very process of managing and administering their business. Apart from the official purpose for which such information was generated – for example sending out invoices, auditing and so on – it often remains a neglected marketing resource. There are other information sources that are often underutilised by marketing management, if collected and used at all. The type of information we are talking about here is not formally-collected marketing research information, that will be discussed under the next heading, but information collected as and when it present itself, often in an *ad hoc* fashion. The system that attempts to collect, collate and manage this source of 'loosely' collected information is often referred to as the 'marketing intelligence system'. Kotler, who has pioneered work in this area, defines this system in the following manner:

'A Marketing Intelligence System is a set of procedures and sources used by managers to obtain their everyday information about pertinent developments in the marketing environment.' (Kotler, 1997)

In the course of carrying out there business for the firm, various members of staff may come across potentially valuable and interesting information. In many firms such information is thought to be of little or no consequence. Often the people who might have access to such information may be of a lower working status within the firm, and they do not think that what they have to say would be of interest to management. Unfortunately it is often management themselves that and to blame through a condescending attitude to staff lower down the 'pecking order' than themselves. For example, the attitude that 'he is only the van driver' or 'she is only a telephonist' and therefore could not possibly have anything of any value to say, still prevails in many organisations even today.

Members of the sales force are out working in the marketplace every day. They make it their business to keep themselves informed of what is going on in terms of developments in the market, competitors' products, prices and concessions, in terms of customers and future customers and their future purchasing plans. Salespeople attend conferences and conventions, attend courses to further their careers such as those leading to the qualifications of the Institute of Management or the Chartered Institute of Marketing, and so on. They man the stands at trade shows and exhibitions, attend sponsored events and assist with hospitality. They make it their business to network effectively with other sales people within the industry, and strive to keep abreast of changes and capitalise on opportunities as they present themselves. Sales people are usually very intelligent, they have to be to stay in such a job. However, they are often underestimated. The possess a wealth of marketing intelligence gathered during the course of their job, but how many firms make full use of this potentially valuable and important source of commercial intelligence. The use of sales personnel to collect and supply marketing intelligence is but one example of the type of information that can make up a firm's marketing intelligence system. Lorry drivers, van delivery drivers, receptionists, maintenance engineers and others all come in contact with suppliers and/or customers during the course of their work, and all have the potential to contribute to the marketing intelligence gathering arm of the firms MkIS.

A diagrammatic representation of a firm's marketing intelligence system is shown in Figure 5.2.

The marketing research system

Marketing research is discussed separately and in more depth in Chapter 6 and me give only a summary of the subject here. This is the final input to the marketing information system, the other component part, as we shall see in the following section, produces output. The marketing research system makes use of both secondary data (data already in existence) and primary data (that collected for a specific piece of research for the first time).

Secondary data
Secondary data can come from many sources; for example, every college and university library is full of secondary data. Some of these sources, such

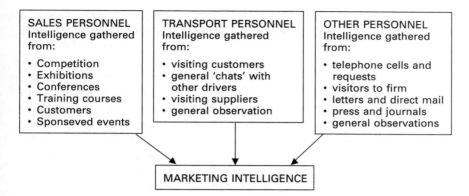

Fig 5.2 The marketing intelligence system as a sub-system of the overall MkIS

as the libraries collection of past MBA dissertations, for example, used to be someone's primary data at the time the data were originally collected. Secondary data include a whole range of official government sources usually collected under the direction of the Central Statistical Office in London. This data is collected on a regular basis, much of it but by no means all on an annual basis, to assist various government departments and agencies make better and more effective decisions on matters concerning social and economic policy. They have not collected such data to help marketing researchers directly. Some of the surveys commissioned by the Central Statistical Office cost literally millions of pounds to carry out. The Census of Population surveys every household in the country every ten years with intercensal samples in between the main census. The Census of Production surveys every firm over a certain size throughout the whole country on an annual basis. These two surveys alone would cost many millions of pounds to carry out and they are but examples of a wide range of similar work carried out for the government. A market researcher can purchase all of these government reports from Her Majesty's Stationary Office (HMSO) for a few pounds. If you do not want to spend even that amount they are usually available in the larger public libraries – for example Manchester public library has an excellent commercial section – or from the better University business schools or similar institutions – for example the London Business School, the London School of Economics, UMIST, Warwick and so on. Secondary data also comes in the form of 'multi-user reports' such as 'Keynote' or 'Mintel' publications. These publications usually cover one industry in the case of Keynote, or four or five product areas as in the case of Mintel. Mintel also do in-depth special reports on particular industries. These reports are available from the publishers themselves, or again many university business school libraries hold a range of them.

Other secondary sources include, as mentioned earlier, dissertations and theses which are available from individual university libraries or on order through the British Library. Academic books and journal articles are another important source of secondary material. Most of the major newspapers are now kept by libraries on either microfiche or compact disc, and these publications have good sections on markets and general business and economic topics. Company reports and abstracted company data are kept on Extel and McCarthy systems, again these days usually on compact disc for use with a computerised retrieval system, although some of the smaller libraries still use a manual card type of system. The list of secondary sources given here is not intended to be exhaustive, but at least gives a good illustration of the type and form of secondary data available to marketing information consultants or researchers.

Primary data

Primary data collection basically takes four forms:

1 **Interviews** – these are usually qualitative and exploratory in nature. Depth interviews, where respondents are interviewed individually, and group discussions, where a group of 8 to 12 people are interviewed in a group setting are the most common form of this type of data collection. Depth interviews and group discussions can be totally exploratory and unstructured, semi-structured in as much as the interviewer (or moderator in the case of group discussions) has at least some idea of the question areas to be covered in the interview session, or very structured. Structured interviews are not meant to be a formal 'question and answer session' and they still retain the degree of pragmatism and flexibility common to all qualitative research approaches. However, they are conducted be means of an interview schedule, and more formal techniques such as the presentation of attitudinal rating cards or the use of projective techniques such as sentence completion tests are administered during the interview session. Depth interviews and group discussions are usually, but not exclusively, used at the start of the research process, hence the term 'exploratory' research. The results are not intended to be conclusive, indeed depth interviews and group discussions are usually conducted with a relatively small sample of respondents and hence the qualitative results are from too small a sample to have any theoretical statistical validity.

Interviews such as these are more often used to try to get a feel for the research situation at hand. Unless the researcher is already experienced in conducting marketing research in a particular field or industry, and many researchers are experts in a particular field, then the researcher will need to educate himself/herself in the fundamentals of the research topic. This is really the role of exploratory, qualitative research based on the depth interview and group discussion techniques. These techniques are fairly versatile and can also be used during or even after the main body of the research has been conducted, usually to go back and qualify or clarify certain points. These techniques will be discussed further in the next chapter.

2 **Observation** – this type of primary data collection can include human observation and the use of electrical or mechanical devises such as cameras, tape recorders and so forth. Some marketing research firms specialise in 'audit'-type services, and these are also a form of observational technique. The retail audit, as the name suggests, is a research process which monitors the sale and other related information such as price, of a wide range of products within stores. The manufacturers of such products can pay the auditing company to 'track' the product sales of their own products and collect information on competitors' products. The consumer panel is similar in many ways to the retail audit except that brand purchase is monitored or 'audited' in peoples' homes. For both the retail audit and the consumer panel, use is made of modern information technology in the form of bar-code readers and computer modems, to both record and transmit the information to the research company.

Observation might involve use of a video camera to observe traffic passing a potential retail site, or an electrode on the road counting the traffic in order to calculate a poster-site's rental rates. It can involve 'things' observing people, again cameras and tape recorders or even turnstyles monitoring or counting people as they move around a store. It can involve people observing things such as a quality control inspector observing a production process. And finally it can involve people observing people. A good example of the latter would be an undercover store detective, but the same principle is used in marketing research in the form of 'mystery shoppers' who visit stores in the guise of ordinary shoppers to check out their prices, service and other matters. Observation is a particularly important marketing research technique and is often used in conjunction with other methods. It is particularly valuable in research situations in which it is difficult to ask respondents questions, for example when researching the behaviour of very small children or small animals such as cats and dogs, in order to develop a new baby food or pet food.

3 **Surveys** – usually involve the use of a questionnaire to collect the information from respondents. Questionnaires come in many different forms and can be administered in many different ways. Many are sent by post for self-completion, and sometimes interviewers call on households or hold interviews in the street or shopping mall. Questionnaires are sent by post, by fax and even these days on the internet. Questionnaires are usually used by researchers to collect more quantitative information than say the information obtained from depth interviews or observational techniques. This data is coded and fed in to a computer file and processed using a standard data-analysis package. A variety of statistical procedures

are available to the researcher in such data-processing packages as well as the capability to produce graphs, charts and other forms of graphical information to aid presentation of the findings. Surveys are used extensively all over the world, for all sorts of reasons and by all sorts of organisations, not just commercial firms. However, whatever the purpose of the research survey and whatever the nature of the organisation, be it University, government department or political polling organisation, the basic principles of survey and questionnaire design are the same. We will investigate the use of surveys in a little more depth in the next chapter.

4 **Experimentation** – can be used in a 'laboratory setting' or a field setting. In a laboratory setting, experiments are easier for the researcher to control. For example under artificial controlled conditions the researcher can take into account any outside influences that might be affecting the experimental results. A 'blind' paired comparison test into the texture or taste of competing food products such as tinned ham is a good example. Factors that might influence a consumer's preference, such as knowing the brand name or knowing the price or seeing advertising, can be either eliminated from the experiment altogether or at least statistically accounted for in the test results. When we say laboratory, we do not necessarily mean laboratory in the same way that chemists or physicists use the term, although some marketing experiments involving recall or the measurement of certain physical parameters such as blood pressure or heart rate may well be conducted in such a place. So-called 'lab' experiments in marketing are often carried out in Town Halls or other venues in the centre of towns and cities, and are often referred to as 'hall tests'.

The problem with laboratory-type experiments is that although they are easier to design, set up and conduct than field experiments, results from such tests may not have much validity in the wider 'real' world. Laboratory experiments, by their nature, are often undertaken in a heavily controlled artificial environment. What a person remembers about an advertisement they have been shown under controlled conditions may not necessarily be the same as what they are able to recall in a busy High Street on the way to work. Because of this, laboratory experiments are said to have a high level of 'internal validity' but a relatively low level of 'external validity'. This point will be covered further in the next chapter.

Field experiments as the name suggests are undertaken out in the real world, rather than in a heavily controlled artificial laboratory environment. They are not necessarily carried out in a field, however, as one of our students seemed to think. The best example of a field experiment is what has become known as a 'test market', whose basic principle is as follows. A certain area of the country is chosen for the test, and this has to be representative of the wider market for it to have any validity, or at least any differences must be taken into account statistically by the researcher. Television areas are often chosen because there is a great deal of demographic and other secondary data already available to the researcher by TV region. A control area is also chosen as a 'bench mark' so that the researcher can see what is happening in the market anyway, and which has nothing to do with the actual test variables. New products, new pack, promotions, advertising and other marketing 'tools' are usually tested in a limited 'test market' environment so that all of the problems can be identified and put right prior to going national with a product launch, advertising campaign or whatever. Because test market operations usually take place in a 'real world' setting they are difficult to control for external influences. The dynamic and often chaotic nature of the real world often makes it difficult to measure the test results and separate them from effects that are happening anyway, although proper use of a control group reduces this problem. Because of these problems field-type experiments are said to generally have a high degree of external validity, but a relatively low level of internal validity. You will notice that this is the exact opposite to what was claimed for a laboratory-type experiment.

The analytical marketing system

This sub-system of the overall MkIS does not produce any new data as such. Rather it takes the data from the other three component parts of the system in the form of input data and enhances its value. Users of the system are able to do this by applying what might be termed 'management science' techniques to the data thereby transforming it into a form that makes it more easily understood and more valuable to the marketing decision-maker. The techniques applied to the data by the marketing management scientist are usually statistical in nature and many computer packages are commercially available that can carry out quite sophisticated analyses. Such packages are reasonably priced and within the budget of even the smallest firm, and can usually be run on a personal computer.

It is beyond the remit of an introductory text such as this to cover the subject of management science or operational research, but the following examples should give the reader at least a general 'feel' for this subject area:

- **Simulation** – marketers often want to know what likely problems may occur in a given situation without having to actually experience the situation in 'real life'. It is possible to simulate many marketing situations using statistical or mathematical techniques. For example 'queuing theory' can be used to predict the effects of bottlenecks in the flow of customers within a hypermarket. Markov chains, sometimes referred to as 'brand switching matrices' can be used to simulate the competitive response to a price cut or promotion and the affect on relative brand shares using probability to predict brand-switching behaviour.

- **Optimisation** – linear programming can be used to calculate optimum levels of output, marketing mix elements and so on. Marginal analysis making use of differential and integral calculus can assist management in making similar decisions, particular the optimisation of the overall marketing mix.
- **Forecasting** – this subject is covered in more depth later on in this chapter and so only a mention of the actual techniques is given here. Information collected from formal marketing research and marketing intelligence gathering of internally generated information can be used as input data in a wide variety of forecasting models. Data collected over a period of time can be extrapolated into the future by the use of time-series techniques. The use of such techniques also allows the manager to model seasonality and cyclical effects. Trend-fitting, using the mathematical functions of known curves, can also be used to forecast sales and model likely future product life-cycles. Linear and multiple regression are more sophisticated forecasting techniques which make use of 'econometric' procedures.
- **Hypothesis testing** – in many marketing situations, particularly in marketing experiments, managers have certain hypotheses or strong ideas that they want to test scientifically. Methods such as Chi Square and analysis of variance allows the scientific testing of the relative differences in the effectiveness of marketing variables.

The above techniques are by no means the only techniques available to marketing scientists to enable them to enhance the value of marketing information, in fact the list is not intended to be exhaustive. However, they do convey the general principles of what goes on within an analytical marketing system. A diagrammatic representation of such a system is shown in Figure 5.3.

Fig 5.3 Analytical markety system

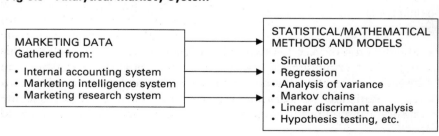

MARKETING DATA
Gathered from:

- Internal accounting system
- Marketing intelligence system
- Marketing research system

STATISTICAL/MATHEMATICAL
METHODS AND MODELS

- Simulation
- Regression
- Analysis of variance
- Markov chains
- Linear discrimant analysis
- Hypothesis testing, etc.

Activity

Can sales people provide management with useful marketing intelligence?

Sales people are basically working for the firm in order to sell. Their primary skill is selling. Often the remuneration package offered to the sales force by management is heavily loaded towards earned commission. If they do not sell they do not earn any commission. Sales people on such terms tend to be concerned only with selling, they have little time for anything else. If they 'don't sell they don't eat', so to speak and this tends to concentrate their minds.

Hence it is not that sales people are incapable of providing useful marketing intelligence, but rather a question of whether they have the time to do so. If they are expected to adopt this expanded role and provide management with such intelligence reports then they must be given the time to do so. The pressure to sell, sell, sell must, to a certain extent, be lessened. Providing such intelligence must be built in to their remuneration package.

Sales people are 'in the front line'. They come in contact with customers and sales people from other competing firms. They are actually 'out there' performing in the marketplace. They have the opportunity to collect much highly valuable marketing intelligence but they must be given the encouragement, time and financial incentive to do so.

5.4 Designing, Implementing and Controlling an MkIS

Design

Marketing information systems are intended to aid marketing decision-making. If they do not do that then they are more of a hindrance than a help. In order to make sure such a system meets the needs of the users within the marketing firm, great attention must be paid to the design of the system. Every organisation is different and therefore different information requirements and different ways of doing things. The MkIS must be designed to fit in with the way marketing personnel go about their daily business. Access and use of the system must be as easy and as natural to potential users as the use of a telephone or word processor for it to be used naturally and effectively.

The first step in the design process is to carry out an analysis of how people do their job – how they pass on the results of their work in the form of information, and how they communicate with other members of the marketing team. This process might be called a 'systems analysis'. After this a form of 'information audit' is required to find out what information each member of the marketing team requires in order to carry out their particular job effectively. When these exercises have been carried out and the results carefully analysed, management will be in a much better position to design an effective system.

Implementation

New ideas, new procedures and even new managers are often met with a certain amount of suspicion and scepticism. Before any new system is implemented all staff should have the nature and the purpose of the new system fully explained to them. Emphasis should be placed on how the system will improve job efficiency, increase staff productivity and make working life more pleasant for all staff. Some people will have fears about the impact of the new system on their job security. It should be fully explained to all staff that the system is there for the benefit of all and is in no way intended to replace anyone. Full staff training should take place before the system comes into use. It is no use introducing the system and then let staff simply 'get on with it'. Obviously some staff will cope but the majority will not and this will probably breed distrust and resistance towards the new system. Any new system should have the full support of top management otherwise it will be simply regarded as the latest management 'fad' and will not be taken seriously. Any new system takes time to get used to and those personnel responsible for its implementation should have patience if it develops slower than expected or if there are a few initial problems.

Control

As we mentioned earlier, there is a tendency amongst marketing staff to regard any new system with a certain amount of suspicion. They may regard it as yet another demand on their time, as more bureaucracy, form filling and time wasting. Many think that if they just let the new system die a natural death people will get fed up with it and things will revert back to normal. For the new system to survive someone must be given authority and responsibility for its upkeep and management. An MkIS manager could be appointed who would make sure that proper procedures were followed, that the correct information was produced and sent to the correct people and, if necessary, returned. The manager should be stationed at an 'information centre' which could act as the hub for the whole system. This might be an office or even simply a desk within an office. The important thing is that the management and upkeep of the system is not simply left to chance but that there is someone with responsibility and authority to keep the system working.

5.5 Cost–Benefit Aspects of MkIS

Ideally a MkIS will have been carefully designed to produce information which is relevant, pertinent and useful to the users of the system in terms of assisting them in improving their marketing decision-making. In fact the entire rationale for a firm adopting a formally designed MkIS is that the system helps members of the marketing team make better decisions or

enables them to make decisions faster. Management do not want to go to
the time, expense and trouble involved in designing and implementing an
MkIS just for the sake of it, or to make the firm look as if it is up to date
in adopting the latest marketing ideas. They only want such a system if it
directly or indirectly generates a financial return.

Information, just like any other 'product', has a marginal cost and a
marginal value. Theoretically the marketing firm should continue to collect
and store information up to the point where the marginal cost of information equals the marginal value. We say theoretically, because in reality it
would probably be rather difficult to actually calculate the cost and revenue
functions of marketing information and certainly difficult to work out the
marginal value of an additional piece of information. Working out the
marginal cost of collecting, processing and storing an additional piece of
information would perhaps be less difficult. The principle of applying
marginal analysis to marketing information is shown in Figure 5.4.

Looking at Figure 5.4(a) we see that the firm is collecting $X1$ amount of
information and the marginal cost $C1$ of collecting this amount of information is greater than the marginal value $V1$. Hence the firm is experiencing
negative net value at the margin. The value of an additional piece of
information is less than the cost of providing it. In Figure 5.4(b) we see the

Fig. 5.4   Applying marginal analysis to marketing information

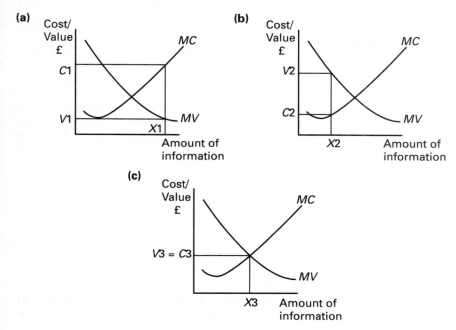

opposite situation. The firm is collecting $X2$ amount of information. At this level the marginal cost $C2$ well below the marginal value $V2$ so it would pay the firm to go on collecting information as the are experiencing positive returns from its collection, albeit at a diminishing rate. In the final diagram Figure 5.4(c), we can see that at the information level $X3$ the marginal cost $C3$ is just equal to the marginal value $V3$. At this point the value of collecting marketing information is maximised and hence this is the optimal level of data from a cost/value point of view.

Activity

Explain the terms 'information audit' and 'systems analysis' in the context of planning an MkIS.

An MkIS is not intended to produce information just for the sake of it. It is not simply information that marketing staff want, but it is pertinent information. In designing the system attention should be paid to establishing the type and the amount of information users of the system require in order to carry out their particular marketing functions as efficiently as possible. A questionnaire survey could be carried out with questionnaires being sent to each staff member asking them questions about their information needs. These could then be followed up by individual interviews or group sessions. This process audits what information is being used at the present time and identifies how information acquisition, storage and dissemination amongst staff could be improved. This is what is meant by the term 'information audit'.

   The administrative systems of marketing departments will vary among different organisations. There will be some similarities, but generally the way a marketing department arranges and carries out their various tasks is likely to differ from firm to firm and will be influenced by a number of factors. These factors will include the type of industry the firm is in, the size of firm, whether it markets products or services or both, whether it is involved internationally, whether it is involved in the marketing of consumer goods and/or services, or whether it is involved in industrial or business-to-business marketing activities. Because the process of marketing differs to some extent between organisations it stands to reason that the kind of marketing information system required by firms will also differ. In order for management to have any chance at all in designing an effective MkIS for a company it will have to be designed on an individual basis; there are general principles that may be followed, but no universal 'laws'. To do this management will have to have a thorough understanding of the marketing processes and procedures used by staff within the firm. The MkIS can then be designed to reflect the way marketing operations and procedures are actually undertaken within the firm. It is this process that is often referred to as 'systems analysis'.

5.6 Forecasting

Managerial decision-making involves forecasting future conditions and such decisions tend to be long-term and strategic in nature rather than operational. Forecasting information helps management in making the operational decisions that take up a lot of time day to day. It is frequently said that forecasting is the key to success, and that poor forecasting can lead to high inventories and associated costs which eat into working capital, or to under-production and unrealised market potential. A major research exercise carried out by Ledbetter WN and Cox JE (1977) showed that forecasting techniques were used by 88 per cent of the 500 largest industrial companies in the USA, and that forecasting was more widely used than any other planning technique.

Forecasting is important in almost all areas of the firm, but the forecasting of sales is particularly important since they are the base upon which all company plans are built. There are several methods available to the forecaster: subjective or objective methods or a combination of the two (for example Bayesian statistical forecasting).

Activity

Do you agree with the position that the production of accurate sales forecasts are essential to any foreward-looking marketing organisation. Fully support your views.

Marketing management requires sales forecasting information in order to plan and generally make informed and effective decisions about the future. Much of a manager's time is concerned about making decisions to do with the future, in the present, with little to guide him or her except what has happened in the past. Hence in most of our decision-making we are forced to 'take a position' on likely future events. We use forecasts every day; whether we actually call them forecasts is another matter.

The marketing or sales managers, out of practical necessity, will also have to predict future conditions especially, in their particular case, the position regarding future sales. They will need accurate sales forecasts to make a wide variety of decisions for different points in time. For example, in marketing short-term sales forecasts are required for products in order to plan the total promotional effort and sales strategies. Such forecasts define the primary targets that the selling operation must achieve and provide the generating force behind the managerial process of setting objectives, planning, organising and coordinating. The sales budget and individual sales peoples' quotas are derived from the short-term forecast which serves as an immediate planning tool in the setting of short-term objectives and in the scheduling of resources within the marketing department. Short-term sales forecasting has been used here by way of illustration. Management also requires forecasting information to make medium and long-term decisions.

Forecasting terminology

In many texts the term **forecast** refers to objective, quantitative techniques, and **predict** denotes subjective estimates. In this chapter the terms **subjective** and **objective forecast** will be used.

The development of a forecasting system requires a considerable amount of data to be collected and analysed for usefulness and validity. The company's ability to acquire relevant data influences which of the wide choice of forecasting techniques should be used, and a forecast will only be as good as the data used in its compilation.

Data collection

Following the decision about how much time, energy and money is to be spent on the data collection stage of the forecasting process, it has to be decided where to obtain the necessary data. There are two main categories of existing data:

1 **Internal data** generated within the company itself; for example previous company plans, sales statistics and other internal records.
2 **Secondary data** from external sources; for example government and trade statistics and published marketing research surveys.

Most forecasting situations use both sources. Data can also be generated expressly for the forecasting task using marketing research, for example through a sample survey. This is an expensive way of collecting data and existing data should be looked at first as, in some situations, it may be sufficient.

Internal data sources

Internal documentation and records are a valuable source of potentially useful information, especially in the case of immediate and short-term forecasting. There are questions that can only be answered by a close look at the company's own data, which should be collected, recorded and stored as routine.

The most useful and most economic source of internal data is **desk research**, which should form the starting point for data collection in any forecasting exercise. The accuracy of such data can easily be validated by the departmental manager concerned, but on the other hand it may be difficult for the forecaster to obtain the information due to inflexibility of the system or lack of cooperation from some departments. To succeed in obtaining appropriate internal data the forecaster must know the firm and its staff well and must have authority from top management to encourage full cooperation.

Firstly, the forecaster should take a **systems analysis** approach, looking carefully at what records are kept and how data are obtained, altered, processed and circulated throughout the firm, recording every document as well as noting its type, the function it serves, its origin and destination. Most company systems start with an inquiry from a customer and end with a customer's invoice. A picture must be built up of the overall system, from individual members of staff to the total departmental system and ultimately the company as a whole. 'Unofficial' records kept by members of staff for their own use are often very useful to the forecaster, but they may only come to light after a careful search.

Data from the sales department

The sales department is where the company and its customers interact and therefore it should provide a great deal of information, including:

1 **Sales volume by product and by product group.** These combine to give total sales volume, but also show each product or product group in the overall mix in terms of its contribution to total volume.
2 **Sales volume by area.** Areas include either salespersons' territories, standard media areas as used by the Joint Industry Committee for Television Advertising Research (JICTAR), or other geographical areas.
3 **Sales volumes by market segment.** Segmentation may be regional or, in industrial markets, by type of industry. It will show which segments are likely to remain static, which are declining and which show growth possibilities. Where the company deals with a small number of large companies, segmentation may be by customer, and any change in demand from any of these may be highly important when forecasting sales and material requirements.
4 **Sales volume by type of channel of distribution.** In a firm that has a multi-channel distribution policy, the effectiveness and profitability of each channel can be calculated. It also allows for trends in the pattern of distribution to be identified and used when forecasting future channel requirements. Channel information by geographical area may show a difference in the profitability between various types of channel in different parts of the country, allowing for profitable geographical channel differentiation. A more realistic forecast can be developed from information gathered by type of retail outlet, agents, wholesalers, distributors and factors, revealing promising channel opportunities and resulting in more effective channel management.
5 **Sales volume over time.** This reveals actual sales and units sold and allows for seasonal variations, inflation and price adjustments to be taken into consideration.
6 **Pricing information.** The effects of price increases and decreases can be established through historical information, giving an opportunity to forecast the effects of future changes.
7 **Communication-mix information.** The effects of previous advertising campaigns, sponsorship, direct-mail programmes or exhibitions can be evaluated, as can the effects of various levels of expenditure in marketing communications, giving a guide to future effectiveness.

8 Sales promotional data. This allows assessment of past promotional campaigns in terms of their individual effects on sales.
9 Sales representatives' records and reports. The customer-file kept by professional sales representatives contains detailed information on live customers such as company information, likely future requirements and so on, and the reports that they make to the sales office contain much information that is useful to the forecaster.
10 Enquiries received and quotations sent. Written and verbal enquiries from customers leading to a detailed quotation being submitted provide information that is useful to the forecaster, especially if patterns can be established in the percentage of enquiries that are followed by orders and the time that elapses between quotation and order. The number of quotations converted into orders indicates the firm's market-share.

Data from other departments

Accounts department
Accurate cost data is available from the management accountant, and previous management reports are also a useful source of information on such matters as:

- Number of new customers in a given period;
- Number of withdrawals;
- Number of items sold by product in volume and monetary terms;
- Total sales by salesperson, area, division, and so on.

Production capacity can be forecast using the information on staff which is given in management accounting reports, including absenteeism. Historical information can be obtained from past budgets with variance analysis showing budgeted figures against actual figures. Information such as orders received, dispatched and on hand will be most accessible in the accounts department.

Purchasing department
Useful information to be gathered here includes old purchase orders, material lists, requisitions, material status schedule reports, information on suppliers and stock control data relating to re-order levels, buffer and safety stock levels, economic order quantities and stockturn by inventory item.

Dispatch department
Here the forecaster will find chronological information on what goods were dispatched and how, including copies of advice notes and other delivery documents.

Production department
Works orders, material lists, design information, order completion dates and much other useful information can be easily obtained from this source.

Departmental plans

Activity and changes in company policy or methods of operation already planned could have significant bearing on a forecast. For example, plans to expand the sales department or increase promotional activity will affect a sales forecast.

In addition to the above sources of information, other departments such as personnel and research and development also provide useful information, and the choice of sources will depend on the type of forecast required.

5.7 Forecasting Methods I – Subjective Methods

These are **qualitative** techniques relying on human judgement rather than on numerical calculating. They are sometimes known as **intuitive techniques** using experience and judgement. There are a number of subjective techniques as follows.

Executive opinion (or jury) method

The sales or marketing manager makes an informed subjective forecast which he then discusses with other executives from production, finance and other departments, who deliver a 'verdict' on the forecast. Thus the forecast is based on the collective experience of the group.

Advantages

- The sales forecast is put together by people with many years' experience in a particular industry.
- The final forecast is based on the collective experience of a group, rather than on the opinion of a single executive.
- Because the final forecast is based on a consensus of opinion, variations in individual subjective estimates are eliminated.
- Because of the status of the contributing panel, the figures are seen as having a high level of source credibility by the people who use the information.

Disadvantages

- Production of a pessimistic forecast by a sales person whose sales quotas or targets are linked to payments of bonus or commission in order to boost earnings.
- Forecasts based on guesswork because of salespeople not having enough time to devote to producing them. The salesperson's expanded role leaves little time for forecasting activity, especially when a large number of product forecasts are required on a regular basis.

Customer-use projections

Survey techniques such as market research surveys or simply conversations between the sales representative and existing and potential customers can a make clear the purchase intentions of customers and/or users. Test marketing, in a small representative area, is also used to produce forecasts and in many ways is similar to surveys.

Advantages

- Prospective purchasers provide information on what and how much they are likely to buy in the future.
- Information is elicited with the use of proven marketing research methodology such as sample surveys, projective techniques and questionnaires.
- Production of sales forecasts can be subcontracted to professional market research agencies, particularly useful when time is short.

Disadvantages

- Sample surveys are expensive and very time-consuming, and not suited to producing forecasts on a regular basis.
- There may be variance between what respondents say they are going to purchase and their actual purchases.
- There is a limit to how often the same people (that is, a company's purchasing manager) can be approached.

It does appear from evidence that the jury of executive opinion and salesforce composite methods have greater application than customer-use projections, particularly in industrial markets where a close relationship exists between supplier and customer.

5.8 Forecasting Methods II – Objective Methods

Objective methods of forecasting are **statistical** or **mathematical** in nature. Historical data are analysed to identify a pattern or relationship between variables and this pattern is then extended or extrapolated into the future to make a forecast. Objective methods of forecasting can be classified by considering the underlying models involved. They fall into two categories: **time series models** and **causal models**.

Time series models

Time series analysis uses the historical series of only one variable to develop a model for predicting future values. The forecasting situation is treated rather like a 'black box', with no attempt made to discover the other factors which might affect its behaviour.

Because time series models treat the variable to be forecast as a function of time only, they are most useful when other conditions are expected to remain relatively constant, most likely true of the **short-term** rather than the long-term future. Hence such methods are particularly suited to short-term, operational, routine forecasting – usually up to six months or one year ahead of current time.

Time series methods are not very useful when there is no discernible pattern of demand. Their whole purpose is to identify patterns in historical data, model these, and extrapolate them into the future. Such methods are unlikely to be successful in forecasting future demand when the historical time series is very erratic. In addition, because it is assumed that future demand is a function of time only, causal factors cannot be taken into consideration. For example, such models would not be able to incorporate the impact of changes in management policy.

Causal models

Causal models exploit the relationship between the time series of the variable being examined and one or more other time series. If other variables are found to correlate with the variable of interest, a causal model can be constructed incorporating coefficients that give the relative strengths of the various causal factors. For example, the sales of a product may be related to the price of the product, advertising expenditure and the price of competitors' products. If the forecaster can estimate the relationship between sales and the independent variables, then the forecast values of the independent variables can be used to predict future values of the dependent variable (in this case, sales).

Such techniques are epitomised by two of the simpler models, **moving averages** and **exponential smoothing** which will be looked at here. Other, more sophisticated, time series models include **decomposition models** and **auto-regressive moving averages** (Box–Jenkins) techniques.

Example of objective methods (moving averages)

A coverage of the more sophisticated quantitative techniques are beyond the scope of this text; detailed coverage of the technical aspects of exponential smoothing and causal techniques are covered in more advanced, specialist texts on forecasting. What we have provide here is an example of one of the more simple objective techniques, moving averages. This method is merely to illustrate what we mean by 'objective methods of forecasting' and allows the reader to compare and contrast objective methods with the coverage of subjective methods given earlier.

Simple moving average

The simple moving or 'rolling' average is a useful and uncomplicated method of forecasting the average expected value of a time series. The process uses the average individual forecasts (F) and demand values (X) over the past n time periods.

A suffix notation is used, which may seem complicated at first but is really quite simple: the present is referred to as time t, one period into the future by $t + 1$, one period into the past by $t - 1$, two periods by $t + 2$, and so on. This is perhaps best appreciated with reference to a time diagram:

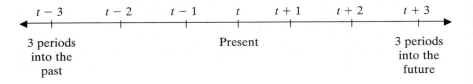

The simple moving average process is defined by the equation:

$$F_{t+1} = F_t + \frac{1}{n}\left(X_t - X_{t-n}\right)$$

where F_{t+1} is the forecast for one period ahead, F_t is the forecast made last time period for the present period, n is the number of time periods, X_t is the actual demand at present time, and X_{t-n} is the actual demand for period $t - n$.

Weighted average

The simple moving average has the disadvantage that all data in the average are given equal weighting, that is:

$$\frac{1}{n}$$

More recent data may be more important than older data, particularly if the underlying pattern of the data has been changing, and, therefore, should be given a greater weight. To overcome this problem and increase the sensitivity of the moving average it is possible to use **weighted averages**, with the sum of the weights equal to unity, in order to product a true average. In decimal form a weighted moving average can be expressed as:

$$F_{t+1} = 0.4X_t + 0.3X_{t-1} + 0.2X_{t-2} + 0.1X_{t-3}$$

(Notation as defined for the simple moving average).

Problems common to all moving average procedures still remain, the major ones being:

1 No forecast can be made until n time periods have passed, because it is necessary to have values available for the previous $n - 1$ periods.
2 The sensitivity or speed of response of moving average procedures is inversely proportional to the number of periods n included in the average. To change the sensitivity, it is necessary to change the value of n which creates problems of continuity and much additional work.

The methods of simple and weighted moving averages discussed so far are only suitable for reasonably constant (stationary) data – they are unable to deal with a significant trend. An example of a **stationary time series** is shown in Figure 5.5. It can be seen from the graph that over a period of nine months the time series fluctuates randomly about a mean value of 200 units which is not increasing or decreasing significantly over time.

In the times series shown in Figure 5.6, the underlying mean value of the series is not stationary. If a **line of best fit** is drawn through all of the points, you can see that while the actual values are fluctuating randomly, the underlying mean value is following a rising linear **trend**.

Double (linear) moving average

A method of moving averages designed for a reasonably stationary time series cannot accommodate a series with a linear trend. In such situations, the forecasts tend to lag behind the actual time series, resulting in systematic errors. To counter such error factors, the method of **double** (sometimes called **linear**) **moving averages** has been developed. This method calculates a second (or double) moving average which is a moving average of the first one. The basis of the principle is that a single moving average MA'_t will lag behind the actual trend series X_t and the second moving average MA''_t will lag behind MA'_t by approximately the same amount. The difference between the two moving averages is added to the single moving average MA'_t,

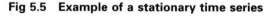

Fig 5.5 Example of a stationary time series

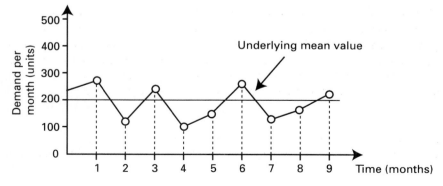

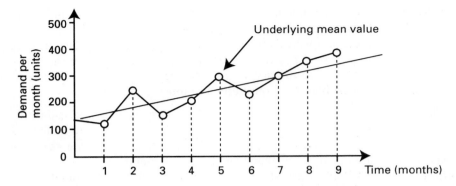

Fig 5.6   Example of a time series with a linear underlying trend

to give the level (a_t). The difference between MA'_t and MA''_t can then be added to the level (a_t) to produce a one-or m-period-ahead forecast.

The double moving average procedure can be summarised as follows:

1 The use of a simple moving average at time t (denoted as MA'_t).
2 An adjustment, which is the difference between the simple and the double averages at time t ($MA'_t - MA''_t$).
3 An adjustment for trend from period t to period $t + 1$ (or period $t + m$, if the forecast is for m periods ahead).

The **updating equations** for the double moving average are as follows:

Single moving average

$$MA'_t = \frac{X_t + X_{t-1} + X_{t-2} + \ldots + X_{t-N+1}}{N}$$

Double moving average

$$MA''_t = \frac{MA'_t + MA'_{t-1} + MA'_{t-2} + \ldots + MA'_{t-N+1}}{N}$$

Level component

$$a_t = MA'_t + \left(MA'_t - MA''_t\right) = 2MA'_t - MA''_t$$

Trend component

$$b_t = \frac{2}{N-1}\left(MA'_t - MA''_t\right)$$

Forecast

$$F_t + M = a_t + b_t M$$

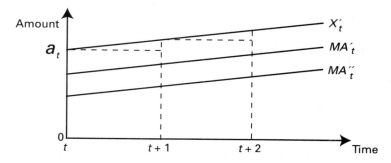

Fig 5.7　Diagrammatic representation of the principle of the double moving average

The general principle of the double moving average is shown diagrammatically in Figure 5.7.

Although the double moving average has the advantage of being able to handle data with a trend, it has the disadvantage of requiring extra data. N data points are required to update each MA'_t and MA''_t, i.e. $2N$ or twice the number required for the simple moving average must be stored. Clearly, the necessity for substantial data storage makes the double moving average less attractive in practice than other techniques which provide similar results from less data. This is particularly so if short-term forecasts were required on a routine basis (e.g. weekly) for a large number of items.

Exponential smoothing (time series)

The use of **exponentially weighted moving averages**, as the method is often called, was first developed from a number of unpublished reports by C. Holt of the Carnegie Institute of Technology. Such techniques overcome many of the shortcomings and limitations of the moving average method.

Simple exponential smoothing

When using simple exponential smoothing, weights used in the averaging process decrease exponentially over time, allowing greater weight to be given to more recent values. This is achieved by means of a **smoothing coefficient**, the value of which can be chosen to given the required weight to each piece of historical data used in the calculation of the forecast. To illustrate the principle, we shall let the weighting function used to smooth the random fluctuations from the time series, be denoted by α (alpha). A series can be constructed:

$$\alpha + \alpha(1-\alpha) + \alpha(1-\alpha)^2 + \alpha(1-\alpha)^3 + \alpha(1-\alpha)^4 \dots + \alpha(1-\alpha)^n$$

To illustrate how the technique is used in forecasting, we shall use the notation discussed in the earlier section for simple moving averages (that is, the one-step-ahead forecast produced in current time is denoted by F_{t+1} and the current demand value by X_t. Using this we get:

$$F_{t+1} = \alpha X_t + \alpha(1-\alpha)X_{t-1} + \alpha(1-\alpha)^2 X_{t-2} + \alpha(1-\alpha)^3 X_{t-3} \ldots$$

Transcribing the equation for F_{t+1} into F_t by substructing one from all the subscripts, we obtain:

$$F_t = \alpha X_{t-1} + \alpha(1-\alpha)X_{t-2} + \alpha(1-\alpha)^2 X_{t-3} + \alpha(1-\alpha)^3 X_{t-4} \ldots$$

This equation can be written as:

$$F_{t+1} = \alpha X_t + (1-\alpha)\left[\alpha X_{t-1} + \alpha(1-\alpha)X_{t-2} + \alpha(1-\alpha)^2 X_{t-3} \ldots\right]$$

Substituting F_t for the part of the above equation appearing in brackets we get:

$$F_{t+1} = \alpha X_t + (1-\alpha)F_t$$

More correctly, the process is a **geometrically weighted moving average**, the exponentially weighted moving average being its analogue in continuous (series) form.

The technique of simple exponential smoothing is historically very important, as it was the first type of **adaptive forecasting** method to be proposed. It is adaptive in the sense that the current forecasting errors are used to update the model. A more compact form of the equation can be achieved by noting that $X_t - F_t$ represents the value of the current **forecasting error**, e_t, and that the equation for simple exponential smoothing could be written as:

$$F_{t+1} = F_t + \alpha(X_t - F_t)$$

This section on sales forecasting does not give an exhaustive treatment of the subject, but it should give the reader a general understanding of the main methods and techniques. Some of the more advanced techniques such as Bayesian forecasting procedures, exponential smoothing techniques, multiple regression and other 'econometric' techniques are unfortunately beyond the scope of an introductory text such as this and a more robust treatment is given in the specialist texts available on forecasting.

5.9 Summary

This chapter has dealt principally with marketing information systems and some of the more commonly used techniques of sales forecasting. The general theme has been that in a purposeful, proactive marketing organisation the acquisition and management of information can not be left to chance. What is required is some form of formal system devoted to the entire information needs of the organisation, that is a marketing information system. We have examined the concept of such a system and how it can be effectively designed, established, monitored, controlled and managed. Marketing research forms part of the system but it is but part of a much wider collection of sources. We have examined these sources and the type of information available. It is important to remember that forecasting is the logical starting point for all business planning, so if the forecast is incorrect then all strategic and tactical plans will be affected. It follows that the most important link is with Chapter 15, which deals specifically with planning and control. Forecasting does, of course, impinge on other areas like marketing research (Chapter 6). Indeed, marketing research provides marketing management with a wide range of important forecasting techniques such as qualitative depth interviews and group discussions, the Delphi technique used for technological forecasting and the survey of buyers intentions, to name but a few. The subject of sales forecasting is linked to the topic of marketing information systems. It would be true to say of any information system or decision support system, that the end product usually contributes to a decision about the future usually made in the present and often based, at least in part, on information collected about the past. Hence sales forecasting is itself a very important function of a firm's integrated marketing information system.

Chapter Review Questions

Give a formal definition of a marketing information system.
A marketing information system consists of people, equipment and procedures to gather, sort, analyse, evaluate and distribute needed, timely and accurate information to marketing decision-makers.

Why do firms need a formal marketing information system?
Information is the very life-blood of successful marketing. Marketing, probably more than any other area of business with the possible exception of accounting and finance depends on pertinent, up-to-date information in order to make effective decisions. Management of a truly marketing-orientated firm cannot leave the collection, storage, analysis and dissemination of vital information to chance. A formal system is required to capitalise on information from a variety of sources, not simply marketing research. Such a system goes by the name of 'marketing information system'.

To manage a business well is to manage its future and to manage the future is to manage information (Marion Harper). Do you agree with this statement? If so/not, then give full reasons.
The general business environment is dynamic and constantly in a state of change. Political, economic, social, technological and demographic factors are constantly changing, some factors slowly, other abruptly and without warning. In order for

the marketing firm to stay abreast of these changes and to continue to offer bundles of value to its customers and shareholders it must attempt to anticipate these changes and use the resources of the firm to produce products and services that will be regarded as valuable in an ever-changing marketplace.

It is not a question of whether or not marketing management will make sales forecasts in order to make decisions merely how they will be produced. Is this statement true?

Managers have to make decisions. The present is already with us and whilst there are some operational decisions that need to be taken concerning the here and now, most of any manager's decisions concern the future. This is true of marketing and sales management just as much as it is true of any other form of management. Marketing and sales management are concerned with future demand for their products and/or services, and this means being concerned with sales at the end of the day. Marketing and sales management are forced to take some form of 'position' on the level and nature of future sales if they are to function as managers effectively. Whether they chose to produce such forecasts formally or informally, whether they choose to use qualitative or quantitative techniques is a matter of choice. What is certain is that sales forecasts of some sort form the very heart of decision-making in sales and marketing.

What are the main drawbacks in using a survey of buyers' intentions to produce medium-term sales forecasts?

Intuitively, actually contacting a selection of your customers or potential customers and asking them what their purchasing plans are regarding your type of products, seems eminently sensible. The information comes not from people at a second remove but directly from the 'horse's mouth', so to speak. One of the main problems is, however, that what people say they intend to do they do not always do. Business people tend to live in hope and are generally enthusiastic about their business and looking forward to future growth. They very often tend to be over-optimistic. When asked about their medium-term investment and other purchasing plans their reply can often be based on too rosy a picture of future business conditions. Consequently what they say they are going to do concerning their future purchasing intentions and what actually happens is very often quite different.

6 Marketing Research

6.1 **Introduction**

The marketing concept states that the very nature of the purposeful, marketing-orientated organisation, whether product or service-based, profit or non-profit-based, is the identification and genuine satisfaction of customers' needs and wants, more effectively and efficiently than the competition. The marketing concept can be defined as the key to achieving organisational goals and the marketing concept rests on market focus, customer orientation, coordinated marketing and profitability. In a profit-making business the firm obviously has to try and achieve this level of customer satisfaction as a way of staying ahead of the competition and making a profit. In a non-profit organisation (often referred to today as 'not for profit'), management substitutes profit for some other criterion such as maximum social or other benefits. A political party, for example, would be likely to substitute maximising votes for financial profit A public sector university on the other hand may substitute 'research excellence' or providing maximum opportunity, to purely financial profit. In order for organisations to be able to arrange their assets and resources in such a way that they are able to produce 'bundles of satisfactions' that satisfy the genuine desires of specifically defined target markets better than the competition, they need to know what the market regards as valuable. The concept of value is a subjective concept and lies within the mind of the individual prospective customer. Hence in a very broad sense marketing management needs to understand the 'minds' of their target markets, their attitudes and value-systems. They need a formalised, managerial approach to this very important task. This is the fundamental role of marketing research. We could go so far as to say that marketing research is the life-blood of successful marketing.

Without the information that marketing research provides, management cannot apply the marketing concept as an overriding business philosophy to their organisation. This text is intended to provide you with an introduction to the subject of marketing, and for some of you this book may be the first formal textbook you have read on this subject. It is not the intention of the authors to try and turn you into marketing research 'experts' by producing this introductory chapter on the subject. Many of the more arcane areas of the subject such as sampling theory or data analysis techniques can be covered only briefly. It is hoped, however, that you will get a general feel for the subject of marketing research after reading this chapter, particularly having also read Chapter 5 on marketing information systems and forecasting, subjects that are interrelated to marketing research and in fact have many marketing research aspects to them.

6.2 Definition of Marketing Research

Marketing research has been defined in many ways. Kotler (1997, p. 114) defines it as 'systematic problem analysis, model-building and fact-finding for the purpose of improved decision-making and control in the marketing of goods and services'. The American Marketing Association (1961) defines it as 'the systematic gathering, recording and analysing of data relating to the marketing of goods and services'. Whatever definition we choose to adopt, we can see that the emphasis is on the improvement in marketing decision-making. Marketing research is the 'scientific' approach to building value in the eyes of the firm's target market. The aim of research is to find, in a systematic way, reliable, unbiased answers to questions about the market for goods or services and to look at people's ideas and intentions on many issues. Marketing research is often concerned with the process of collecting, analysing and interpreting the facts to establish what it is that people want and why they want it.

Commercially, marketing research is employed by marketing management in the planning, evaluation and control of marketing tactics and strategy, but it is also of use in helping to make policy decisions in the non-commercial public sector. Research must be carefully planned with a disciplined and systematic approach, and a series of steps should be taken in the development, planning and execution of research. This chapter aims to give an adequate but general view of a number of topics without going into detailed methodological technicalities.

6.3 Marketing Research and Marketing Information Systems

Formal marketing research may provide a large proportion of the information requirements of the average firm, but not their total requirements. There are other valuable sources of marketing information beside formal marketing research. Philip Kotler, who over the years has innovated so much marketing theory and thought, states that the information requirements of the modern marketing firm should be professionally managed in a systematic way. What is needed is some form of formal system that will assist in the collection, storage, retrieval and analysis of various forms of marketing information, not simply the information collected using formal marketing research. Such a system is known as a marketing information system or MkIS for short. Various aspects of MkIS design, management and implementation have been covered in Chapter 5 and it is not intended to repeat what has already been covered. The concept of an MkIS and the role and place of formal marketing research within it is shown in Figure 6.1 in a slightly different fashion to that shown in Chapter 5.

We can see from Figure 6.1 that the MkIS is made up of basically four main component parts. Three of these component parts actually collect or 'produce' information of various sorts in its 'raw' form. These are the Internal Data, Intelligence Data and Marketing Research Data components of the system. The information from these three component parts is fed as 'input data' to the fourth component part, here described as Models and Statistics. This component of the system adds value to the data produced from the other three component parts by altering it or modelling it in some way. Using the data in a sales forecasting model would be a good example. Basically the Models and Statistics part of the system employs operational research methods and other management science techniques to the data derived from the other three component parts, and in doing so makes the information more useable and valuable to marketing management.

Activity

Explain the role of formal marketing research within the context of the firm's overall marketing information system (MkIS).

To manage a business well means managing its future, and to manage its future requires the effective management of information. In this sense information is viewed as the life-blood of successful marketing operations. Formal marketing

---

Fig 6.1 A marketing information system (MkIS)

research is a very important source of specific forms of marketing information. It is so important to the customer-oriented organisation that it is often referred to as the 'eyes and ears' of marketing. However, although formal marketing research is of paramount importance to the marketing-oriented firm, it does not provide all of the modern firm's information requirements. Information can be derived and obtained from other sources which have little to do with the collection of data through formal marketing research. For example, data generated internally as part of the firm's administration system may provide a rich source of data highly relevant to marketing management. Data collected 'informally' from company employees, particularly sales people, van drivers, van sales and service engineers constitutes a valuable source of marketing intelligence. The use of operational research techniques can enhance the value of information obtained from other sources. Formal marketing research provides a valuable source of marketing information, and along with information from other sources it represents input data for the overall marketing information system of the firm.

6.4 Types of Marketing Research

Market research activities can be classified by their purpose or general objective. For example, some market research exercises are intended to produce results that are purely **exploratory** in nature; such research is usually carried out at the beginning of the overall research project. Other research may produce data that are **descriptive** in nature or **predictive** or **conclusive**. Let us look at these general classifications of marketing research in a little more detail.

Exploratory research

As the name suggests, exploratory research is usually undertaken at the initial stages of the overall research process. Unless a researcher has experience of a particular industry or research area within it, then they will have to familiarise themselves with the general dynamics of that industry or research area in order to effectively carry out the main body of the research. Exploratory research is basically a 'lets have a look' type of activity. It is not designed to enable the researcher to draw firm conclusions about the research situation, but rather to enable him or her to establish its general parameters. The use of secondary data, that is data already in existence usually in printed form or on some kind of computerised data retrieval system, is an important part of the exploratory process. In terms of primary data collection, that is data collected for the first time specifically for a particular research exercise, then qualitative research methods are more often employed than quantitative methods. Depth interviews and group discussions allow the researcher to explore respondents' opinions and attitudes on key issues. Both of these interviewing techniques employ relatively small samples and hence by their very nature can only hope to provide general exploratory information. Nonetheless, information gained from qualitative exploratory research enables the market researcher to plan a more effective research programme than would be the case if the exploratory stage were missing. Exploratory research lays down the foundations enabling the rest of the research exercise to be built soundly.

Descriptive research

Again as the name suggests, descriptive research is intended to describe certain things that marketing management are likely to be interested in such as market conditions, customers feelings or opinions towards a particular company, purchase behaviour and so forth. Such research is not intended to allow the researcher to establish causal relationships between marketing variables and sales or consumer behaviour, or to enable him or her to predict likely future conditions. Descriptive research merely tells the researcher 'what is'. Such research, just like exploratory research discussed earlier, usually forms part of an ongoing research programme. Once the researcher has established the present states of affairs in terms of market-size, main segments, main competitors and soon, they may then proceed to types of research of a more predictive and/or conclusive nature. Descriptive research usually makes use of descriptive statistics to help the user understand the structure of the data and any significant patterns that may be found in it. All measures of central tendency such as the mean, median and mode are often used along with measures of dispersion such as the variance and standard deviation. Descriptive research result are often presented using pictorial methods such as graphs, 'pie charts', histograms and so forth.

Predictive research

Obviously the objective of predictive research is to enable the marketing researcher to predict something about the future. This might be future market conditions such as market growth or decline, increased competition, greater import penetration in a particular market, future price levels, or changes in consumer taste to name but a few examples. Many marketing research techniques can be used to generate information that might prove useful to the researcher in predicting future conditions. When using qualitative research such as depth interviews or group discussions, for example, the researcher can interview individual sales people or 'experts' in the industry. They may hold group interviews in order to arrive at a consensus as to what might happen within a certain market or industry in the future. Opinions can be elicited from respondents for various time periods into the future, for example the next few months, next year, next five years and so on. Similarly questionnaire surveys can be used to elicit the responses of a variety of people. For example the whole sales-force could be surveyed and asked for their opinion concerning future sales or market conditions generally. A survey of buyers' intentions is a very popular method of obtaining sales forecasting information. Formal statistical and mathematical techniques specifically developed for forecasting exercises can also be used. Secondary data obtained from existing printed or stored sources as well as survey information or information derived from qualitative interviews can provide the forecaster with valuable input data which can then be used in formal forecasting models such as exponential smoothing or regression models.

Conclusive research

When using conclusive research techniques the researcher is usually trying to establish causal relationships between marketing variables such as price, advertising or packaging to some other variable such as sales or patterns of consumption. In order to achieve this kind of test it is necessary to use a formal experimental design in order to be able to test a specific hypothesis. For example, assuming the marketing communications manager wanted to establish which set of merchandising materials, which price promotion and which shelf configuration would be most effective in achieving sales within a multiple grocery store chain, and also assuming that there were four different versions of each of the marketing variables – for example four merchandising 'sets', four price promotions that could be used in store and four different shelf configurations – the researcher would want to know which permutation of these three marketing variables is most effective. The researcher would set up an experiment where each permutation was randomly allocated to different retail stores. Differences between stores would be accounted for in the experiment which would be allowed to run until sufficient data had been generated. The results would then be analysed and used to see whether the hypothesis that one set of experimental treatments was more effective in generating sales than the others was in fact true or false. Statistically-designed experimental methods such as analysis of variance (ANOVA) would be used in such a situation. In particular, since the researcher is attempting to test for any interaction between marketing variables, a factorial ANOVA design would be most likely to be used.

All experimental exercises which enable the researcher to establish causation in tests have a number of things in common. The researcher starts with the marketing variables which are to be tested; these are known as the 'independent variables'. These variables are then applied to a given situation and certain effects are monitored. These effects are usually sales but might be something else such as behavioural changes of some kind, for example store loyalty. These effects are regarded as 'dependent variables' because they are dependent on the marketing variables discussed earlier. Experiments are set up with the purpose of trying to establish scientifically, using statistical tests, whether the effects seen in the dependent variables are in fact attributable to changes in the independent variables, that is the marketing variables, and if so what are the nature and strength of these effects. The marketing researcher want to know whether the experimental effects caused by the independent variables acting upon the dependent variables are in any way commercially exploitable.

6.5 **Stages in the Research Process**

Marketing research is a planned formal approach to the collection of marketing information:

1 **Problem definition** leads to a preliminary statement of research objectives to provide information, making this stage an identification of **information needs**. The information needed is:

- motivations, values, beliefs, feelings, opinions;
- evaluations, attitudes, intentions;
- knowledge, facts, behaviour, actions;
- demographic, socio-economic and soon (on/from people, stores, companies, brands, products).

This information is required for:

- exploration, description, prediction or evaluation.

It comes from:

- secondary data sources, both internal and external to a company; and
- primary data sources (that is from field work).

2 **Review of secondary data sources**

- Company records, reports, previous research;
- Trade associations, government agencies, research organisations;
- Advertising/market research agencies;
- Books, periodicals, theses, statistics, conference proceedings, and so on.

3 **Select approach for collection of new/primary information**

- Experimentation;
- Observation;
- Surveys – mail, telephone, personal;
- Motivational research techniques – depth-interviewing, group-interviewing, projective techniques.

4 **Determine details of research design** – methods, sample design.
5 **Data collection**.

6 Analysis and interpretation of data.
7 Evaluation of results and recommendations.

6.6 Tools of Marketing Research

Motivational research techniques

The aim here is to uncover the underlying motives, desires and emotions of consumers that influence their behaviour. These techniques often penetrate below the level of the conscious mind and there are two approaches: the **psychosociological approach** which relies on group behaviour of consumers and the impact of culture and environment on their opinions and reactions; and the **psychoanalytic approach** which relies on information drawn from individual respondents in depth interviews and projective tests. Freudian interpretations dominate such analyses.

Techniques used include:

1 **Depth interviewing** which involves interviewing and observational methods. Topics for discussion are chosen by the interviewer and indirect questioning leads the respondent to free expression of motives, attitudes, opinions, experiences and habits in relation to adverts, products, brands, services and so on. Depth interviewing is based on the psychoanalytical principle of 'free association'. It is not intended to be a formal question and answer session using a structured questionnaire; such an exercise would merely be the administering of a questionnaire by personal interview. A depth interview is intended to be something far more subtle and sophisticated. Such interviews fall under the heading of qualitative research. They are concerned with collecting information on people's beliefs, attitudes and opinions rather than more quantitative information that might more readily lend itself to statistical analysis. Depth interviews usually involve small samples, often only four or five interviews, and they are expensive and time-consuming to carry out. Although the interview may only take an hour or so to actually conduct, the research will take much longer than this in preparation, making the appointment, listening to tapes and making transcripts and analysing the information. Such an exercise can amount to more than a day's work for the professional qualitative researcher.

2 **Focus groups** in which the interviewer stimulates and moderates group discussion. In this method freedom of expression and interaction between individuals are encouraged. This is also known as **group interviewing**.

3 **Sensitivity panels** are a form of group discussion or focus group where the respondents are trained to take part in such groups. The members of the group are used time and time again for different research subjects such as

different products or packages, advertisements and so on. The technique was pioneered by the research firm Slackmans in the UK.

Activity

How, if at all, does the information gained by the market researcher from a depth interview differ from that of a group discussion?

If the information gained from these two methods was exactly the same then there would be little point in using two different approaches. As the name suggests, it is claimed that the individual 'depth interview' allows the researcher 'deeper' access to the respondents' feelings and thoughts. Topics of a highly personal nature, such as personal hygiene, borrowing and debt and sexual activities can only really be discussed in any great depth in a one-to-one situation.

A group discussion allows the researcher to take advantage of the phenomenon of 'group synergy' or 'group dynamics'. Whilst a group discussion may not enter the depths of exploration that is often experienced in a depth interview scenario, group discussion interviews often explore topics in substantially more breadth than can be achieved within a depth interview setting. Group dynamics often produce a 'snowballing effect' where topics are discussed and certain hitherto unknown aspects of the topic are identified and discussed by the group. In a sense a group seems to take on a life of its own with the conversation taking routes completely unexpected by the researcher at the start of the exercise. This process can often lead to a frustrating dead-end, but often it can produce qualitative research information of significant value.

Surveys (using questionnaires)

This is the most commonly used method of data collection which can be conducted by mail, telephone or personal interview. Questionnaires can be self-administered or used in an interview situation, depending on:

- Cost
- Timing
- Type of information needed
- Amount of information needed
- Ease of questioning
- Accuracy required

The practicability of any survey by questionnaire is best checked by a pilot survey. To check the questionnaire:

1 Use a non-probability 'purposeful' sample; it is not intended to use the 'results' in the final data set, and at this stage we are only testing the design of the questionnaire, whether it is of a suitable length, ordering of questions, whether the questions are easily understood and so on.
2 Pilot testing should involve the best-trained and most experienced staff

because it is very important to get the questionnaire right as the success of the entire survey depends on it. It is possible that three or four versions of the questionnaire will need to be tested before it is right. The last pre-test should use the final approved questionnaire.

Questionnaire design

The information collected must be accurate, and so the design of a questionnaire is of great importance. It should consist of questions that have the same meaning, a single meaning and the intended meaning to everyone. Questions should be numbered and have instructions to the investigator concerning the conduct of the interview in bold face, capital letters and underlined. Answer codes should be as near to the right-hand side as possible, and lines drawn at suitable intervals can bring clarity to the design.

The types of questions most commonly used are as follows:

1 **Open-ended questions** do not give the informant a hint of what answer might be expected. A question which begins 'What do you think of . . . ?' will bring forth large amounts of data which cannot always be satisfactorily summarised, but this type of question is useful in the pilot stage to show the range of likely answers.
2 **Unaided recall questions** do not mention the nature of the answer material and avoid asking leading questions; for example 'How did you travel to the station to catch this train?'
3 **Dichotomous questions** offer two choices of answer, usually 'yes' and 'no'.
4 **Multiple-choice questions ('cafeteria' questions)** offer a graduated range of possible answers, listed in order from one extreme to the other.
5 **Thermometer questions** ask informants to rate their feelings on a numerical scale, for example 0–10. This type of question seeks to minimise the disadvantage of discreet classification in the multi-choice question.
6 **Checklists** are a standard way of prompting the memory of a respondent without him being biased by the interviewer. However, brand leaders may be selected more frequently because of the weight of advertising.

General rules for question design

1 Use simple words that are familiar to everyone (that is, shop not outlet, shopkeeper not retailer).
2 Keep questions short.
3 Avoid asking double-barrelled questions (for example 'Have you a radio and/or television set?')
4 Do not ask leading questions (for example 'Do you buy instant coffee because it is the quickest way to make coffee?')
5 Do not mention brand names (for example 'Do you consider Hitachi to be the best audio equipment?')

6 Do not ask questions which may offend (for example 'Do you work or are you a housewife?')
7 Avoid using catchphrases.
8 Avoid words which are not precise in their meanings (for example 'Does this product last a **reasonable** length of time?')
9 Remember that direct questions will not always elicit the expected response – perhaps not all possible answers have been foreseen (for example the question 'Are you married?' does not cover the possibilities of divorce, separation, and so on).
10 Questions concerning prestige goods may not be answered truthfully. Careful rewording can avoid this (for example 'Have you a television capable of receiving teletext transmissions?' might be better asked by 'How many hours per week do you watch television?', followed by 'Do you watch teletext transmissions, that is Ceefax or Oracle?')
11 Only questions which the respondent can answer from knowledge or experience should be asked.
12 Questions should not depend on the respondent's memory.
13 Questions should only allow one thought to be created in the respondent's mind to avoid confusion and inappropriate answers. This particularly applies to questions beginning with 'Why. . . . ?'
14 Avoid questions or words with an emotional bias (for example use Conservative/Labour, not Tory/Socialist).

The first questions asked should gain the interest of the informant, and should be easy to answer in a factual way. More difficult questions should come later, with those of greatest importance being about a third of the way through. Transition from question to question should be smooth and logical. Details of the respondent (age, address, full name, occupation and so on) should appear at the end. The questionnaire must have a title and contain cross-references to others if needed. Standard information required includes the respondent's name, home address, sex, age (within a group), income group and occupation, the interviewing district identification, the place and date of the interview and the interviewer's name.

Answers should be recorded in one of the following ways:

• Writing a number.
• Putting a cross or a tick in a box.
• Underlining correct answers.
• Crossing out incorrect answers.
• Writing in a predetermined symbol.
• Ringing a number or letter.

Open-ended questions should be followed by enough space to allow for answers to be recorded word for word.

There are a number of basic questions which should be asked about any questionnaire:

1 Is each question clearly worded?
2 Does it break any of the basic rules of question design?
3 Is each question concerned with one factor only?
4 Are the questions ones which will elicit the answers necessary to solve the research problem?
5 Is each question unambiguous – will both the investigator and the informant have the same understanding of the question?
6 Are all the possible answers allowed for?
7 Are the recording arrangements foolproof?
8 Will the answers to each question be in a form in which they can be cross-tabulated against other data on the same or other questionnaires?
9 Will the answers be in a form which will allow at least some to be checked against established data?

Marketing experiments

An experiment is a way of gathering primary data in which the researcher is able to establish causation of effect amongst the variables being experimentally tested. It can be carried out in an artificial laboratory-type setting, or as a field experiment, the best example of which is the **test market** where researchers choose a representative geographical area or one where they can statistically adjust data to make them representative of a wider market area such as the UK as a whole. The test market is like a model of the total market. Test markets can be very expensive, but being a field experiment they have the advantage of realism or 'external validity' over laboratory experiments. Howard Schlussberg (1980) an American expert in the field, advocates 'simulated test markets' as a way of reducing costs. These are not full test markets and involve surveying a small sample of consumers and showing them pictures or samples of products and ascertaining their preference as if they were really shopping.

Other techniques include **extended user tests**, **blind** and **simple placement tests**. In addition, there are the techniques used in the pre- and post-testing of advertising themes and copy. Marketing experiments are one of the four main classes of research methods whereby marketing researchers collect primary information, that is information collected for the first time specifically for a particular research exercise. The other three classes of techniques are **interviews**, such as depth interviews and group discussions, **observation** such as retail audits and consumer panels, and **surveys** such as a postal questionnaire of telephone survey.

Observational techniques

Sometimes it only possible to collect the sort of data required by observation. It may be humans observing humans, humans observing things (for example cars, electro-mechanical devices such as cameras or tape recorders and so on). Retail audits and consumer panels are also classified as observational techniques. Retail audits are conducted by specialised firms such as Nielson's of Oxford in the UK, who conduct product audits in thousands of retail stores every month. A product manager can buy the retail sales data and other supporting information on a continuous month-by-month basis. Other related information on competitors' products is also made available at extra cost. The consumer panel is a home audit where a wide range of households are monitored as to their purchasing habits. Respondents are of different socio-economic groups, family size and stage in the family life-cycle. They record their purchases using a special bar-code reader and send the data to Nielson's down the telephone line using a coupler. In the retail audit most stores these days use electronic point of sale (EPOS) deving, and again can send retail sales information down the telephone line to the auditing company. Smaller shops that do not have the technology still have to be audited 'manually'. Observational techniques are a useful source of primary data and this method is often used in conjunction with other research methods.

6.7 Main Research Areas

Product research

This involves all aspects of design, development and testing of new products, as well as the improvement and modification of existing products.
    Activities include:

- Comparative testing against competitive products;
- Test-marketing;
- Concept-testing;
- Idea-generation and screening;
- Product-elimination/simplification;
- Brand-positioning.

Brand-positioning is particularly important when one considers the competitive pressures of the 1990s. Experts in this field are Professess Chernatony and Daniels of The Open University and Cranfield Business Schools, much of whose research examines the importance of marketing research in brand positioning.

Pricing research

Techniques such as the **buy–response model** can be used to:

- assist in establishing a more market-orientated pricing strategy;
- see what kind of price consumers associate with different product variations (for example packaging);
- establish market segments in relation to price.

Distribution research

Distribution research is concerned with two separate but interrelated facets of the subject, these are channels of distribution and physical distribution. In terms of channels of distribution marketers are continually attempting to create a competitive advantage by selecting innovative, creative and more affective channels. Channels of distribution are evolving over time and new channel formats are being developed. For example the Internet is supposed to hold out so much promise as a shopping medium particularly for services especially financial services such as insurance, mortgages and personal banking services. Other forms of 'non-shop shopping' are also growing in popularity such as the use of mail-order tied in with the phenomenal growth in direct mail as a communication medium. Television shopping is very popular in the United States and is gaining in popularity in the United Kingdom and other parts of Europe. It is now available on ordinary terrestrial television channels as well as on satellite and cable television. Other retail formats have become increasingly important such as the huge out-of-town shopping complexes like 'Meadow Hall' near Sheffield. Marketing research has an important role to play in evaluating the efficiency of existing channels and forecasting likely future retail developments both in terms of the actual channel formats likely to be used in the future but also the technology used within such channels.

Such techniques as the **retail audit** can monitor the effectiveness of different types of distribution channels and detect any regional variation. They can identify which channels are in relative decline in terms of their efficiency in retailing certain products. They can also tell which channels are likely to experience considerable future development and a growth in popularity. For example, the shopping areas within petrol stations have grown considerably in the last ten years in terms of turnover and especially the range of products on offer. Qualitative research such as depth interviews and group discussions as well as larger-scale sample surveys using questionnaires, can be used in the appraisal of existing channel efficiency and in predicting likely future developments. Techniques such as Delphi forecasting can be used to predict changes in retail technology.

New developments in the area of physical distribution can also be monitored and to some extent predicted using marketing research techniques. Many new developments originate overseas which necessitates an international dimension to such research. For example, the concept of just-in-time delivery systems which is used by a large number of organisations throughout the world originated in Japan. Materials handling and vehicle technology is developing all the time with obvious implications for the logistics industry especially transport. Computer technology has now made available 'tracking systems' so that customer can establish exactly where their order or delivery is in the order-processing cycle, and even establish exactly where a particular consignment is anywhere in the world.

Marketing communications research

Marketing communications research is concerned with the appraisal and evaluation of each element in the marketing communications mix. This will include advertising research, evaluation of below-the-line sales promotions, sponsorship evaluation and the evaluation of direct mail, trade journals, exhibitions, personal selling, corporate communications, telephone marketing, communication on the Internet and many others. Research is needed at many points in the overall marketing communications process. In the first instance a firm will need to research the characteristics of customers or potential customers for their product or service. These customers may form distinct groups or market segments. In terms of marketing communications planning these will represent the 'target audiences' for any future campaigns. Once the target audiences have been defined it is necessary to establish the most effective medium or media to use to send a marketing message to these audiences. What television programmes are the target audiences most likely to watch?. What newspapers, magazines, journals or commercial radio programmes will be most effective in getting the necessary message across? Marketing communications involves business-to-business communication as well as communicating with household consumers. Many consumer goods are sold through marketing intermediaries such as wholesalers or other 'middlemen', and people in these organisations need communicating to as well. Some products and services such as machine tools and haulage services are aimed entirely at the business market.

In business-to-business communications, personal selling is particularly important. In fact in many industrial firms up to 90 per cent of the overall marketing budget is spent on personal selling. Trade exhibitions, direct mail, sponsorship, transport livery, corporate workware, telephone marketing and trade journals are also important business-to-business marketing communication 'tools', although some of these 'tools' are also of use in consumer market communications, for example telephone marketing, exhibitions and sponsorship.

Once the target audiences have been identified and the most appropriate communications media have been established, further research is needed at the pre-campaign level to put the actual communications message together. A simple, one-way model of marketing communications is shown in Figure 6.2 to illustrate the points being made here. We shall see a similar model to this in Chapter 12 when we discuss above and below-the-line promotion. The model in Figure 6.2 illustrates the process whereby a marketing firm (the sender) develops a message which is then sent using a certain medium to the receiver (the target audience). The effectiveness of the communication is then evaluated via a feedback loop and future messages adapted accordingly. Marketing research has an important part to play at every stage of the communications process, identifying the target audiences, se-

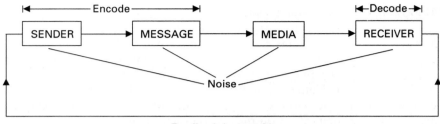

Fig 6.2   A sample one-way model of marketing communications

lecting the most effective communication media, developing the message, and evaluating how well the message has been communicated to the target audience and with what effect.

6.8 **Summary**

Marketing is the business process whereby business firms strive to create 'bundles of values' in the form of products and services which their customers will willingly buy. In the value creation process marketing firms attempt to at least meet, but preferably exceed, customers' expectations. To remain competitive, marketing firms have to create customer value more effectively and efficiently than the competition. Firms that are market-driven and customer-focused in this way are often said to be 'marketing-oriented' firms. However 'value' is somewhat subjective and lies in the minds of individuals and groups of people. Value changes all the time within people's minds. For example, what is regarded as fashionable in terms of clothing or popular music might not be so next year. What might be regarded as unimportant, say, ten years ago may become more important a decade later. For example 'green' and environmental issues were not something that concerned the majority of people ten years ago, whereas in the 1990s most people express some concern about such issues. This concern is reflected in a wide range of products that claim to be 'environmentally friendly', 'ethical' or 'healthy' and so on. In order to keep up with the changing tastes and changing value systems of customers, the activities of the competition and important changes in the external business environment, the marketing firm needs information. All long-term marketing strategy and marketing plans at the more tactical and operational levels need information. We can repeat that information is literally the life-blood of the marketing-orientated firm. Without the right kind of information effective marketing is impossible. Market research provides the marketing firm with a wide range of useful information, but on its own is insufficient; it must form an intrinsic part of the wider marketing information system.

Chapter Review Questions

Why is marketing research so crucial to the effective practice of modern marketing?

Marketing is the process of establishing what individuals, who collectively constitute a market, regard as valuable. Value is basically a subjective concept especially for the more sophisticated consumer products. In order to organise the resources of an organisation to create value, marketing management needs to understand the value-system of the individuals and organisations (which are themselves a collection of individuals). Market research, as part of an integrated marketing information system, helps provide the information management needs to carry out the marketing task effectively.

What is the role of exploratory research within the overall marketing research process?

A sound house is built on good foundations. Likewise when a painter and decorator decorates a room a large part of the job is in the preparation, making sure that all the woodwork is sanded and smooth and that all of the defects have been filled in the walls. In the same way, good quality marketing research is based on careful preparation. It too needs to be built on sound foundations if it is to have any true validity. Exploratory research, as the name suggests, enables the researcher to establish the general parameters of the research situation thereby putting him or her in a much better position to design a really effective research project.

Is the use of a census better than a sample when carrying out survey work?

Not necessarily. Some form of error is likely to occur in all forms of survey work. If you carry out a census it is true that every single member of a defined population will have been surveyed, thereby leaving no possible chance of any errors entering the results due to sampling. However, sampling error is but one source of error, and researchers also have to deal with the problem of non-sampling errors. In fact in many survey situations the error attributable to non-sampling error is greater than that commonly attributable to sampling error in situations where a sample rather than a census has been used. Sampling error is cased by a sample result being different from the true population values. Non-sampling error is error caused by everything else. If a sample is carefully chosen the result are likely to reflect the true population parameters within an acceptable and calculable degree of error. Size is not so important, although all other things being equal it is better to have a larger rather than a smaller sample. It is how the sample is selected that is really important. Sampling gives an acceptable degree of accuracy if properly carried out, and the money saved by using a sample instead of a census can be spent in reducing the risk of non sampling error.

7 Products and Services

For a marketing plan to be successful it is essential that all elements of the marketing mix should support each other. Marketing mixes will change between products, services and market situations and indeed this is what makes marketing dynamic; it is the skill of the individual marketing person in manipulating the individual mixes that can make a product or service a success or a failure. Different emphases to individual elements in the marketing mix are often called for. However, the product or service is particularly important in this calculation for this is the tangible element that will appeal to customers and it is upon this that customers' purchases and repeat purchases are based. This is what must provide the end satisfaction, for this after all is the practical application of the marketing concept.

A study of products and services is concerned with, amongst other things, its design, its appearance, how long it will last and how it is perceived by customers and non-customers alike.

7.1 **Defining the Product**

People purchase what marketing practitioners term a 'bundle of satisfactions'. This includes obvious things like the physical product itself or a less tangible service offering. If asked to state what they have purchased most customers will simply mention the product or service in its simplest terms. However, there is much more to a purchase than simply this.

Activity

What other satisfactions do feel customers purchase as part of this 'bundle of satisfactions' which make up what is called the 'augmented product'?

Additional trappings like image, shape and design, performance and value make up this extra 'bundle of satisfactions'. Added to this are such factors as price and value for money. Purchasers will not readily acknowledge this.

It is the task of marketing to take a more expansive view of what constitutes an augmented product or service and then combine the marketing mix in such a way as to present consumers with the 'bundle of satisfactions' which marketing research has identified as being most pertinent to their requirements.

The augmented product concept is sometimes called the extended product, and this definition includes the total marketing effort. Thus a view of the product or service is rather broader than the mere object or service offering; it is a satisfaction or a 'bundle of satisfactions' that provides satisfaction.

Activity

It is easy to envisage a product, but services are also discussed. Give three illustrations of service offerings.

- Insurance
- A holiday
- An educational course

7.2 Categories of Products

Given the background that has been presented, we are now in a position to present a formal categorisation system for products and services. Such a categorisation is needed in order that marketing planners can more easily formulate and design their strategies and tactics.

Industrial goods are separated from consumer goods as the first part of this categorisation.

Industrial goods

The mention of industrial goods conjures images of components and raw materials, but not all are as tangible as this. A number of additional items and services are important to ensure the smooth running of a factory.

Activity

Name three examples of goods or services that are industrial goods, but not required in the manufacturing process.

- Machinery repair services for the production line
- Computing equipment
- Fork-lift trucks

A classification exists to describe categories of industrial goods and services:

- **Installations** include the plant and machinery required for a company's manufacturing processes. These are very critical purchases and usually involve complex purchasing decision-making processes with price not necessarily being the deciding factor
- **Accessories** are also capital items but are less critical and depreciated over a shorter period of time. They include items like office equipment and materials handling equipment.
- **Raw materials** are the most obvious of industrial goods and this is the major task in a modern purchasing department. Here, buyers are specifically looking for a keen price coupled with quality and reliability of delivery.
- **Component parts and materials** are items that are required in the production process, but are not part of the finished product. They include such items as packaging, greases and oils.
- **Supplies** include items like cleaning and maintenance materials and stationery. Buying here tends to be more routine and it is often a matter of simply reordering with price being the major criterion consistent with a standard specification of quality.

This classification is linked to organisational buying behaviour where the fact that buyers are dealing with larger sums of money and larger quantities tends to make it a more professional and organised process than in consumer goods purchasing.

Consumer goods

These are the types of products and services with which we, as individuals, are familiar. Unlike industrial products, more irrational and emotional motives tend to be connected with their purchase and it is upon this factor that many manufacturers base much of their marketing effort. As with industrial goods, they also lend themselves to a number of sub-categories.

- **Convenience goods** are everyday items whose purchase takes little effort on the part of the buyer. They can be classed as everyday necessities which are purchased on a regular basis. Advertising plays an important role here in terms of attempting to persuade the consumer to take that particular brand. The techniques used by advertisers in this respect is the subject of Chapter 12. Staple convenience goods are products which are purchased virtually daily for consumption and here it is more difficult to differentiate one product from another and no pre-planning goes into their purchase. Many such products are delivered to the door like milk and newspapers.
- **Shopping goods** is the term used to describe durable products and their purchase tends to be at infrequent intervals. More planning goes into their purchase on the part of buyers and buyer behaviour is more complex as was illustrated in Chapter 4. The purchasing cycle is also much longer and, again, more complex models of buyer behaviour apply here. Further classifications relate to homogeneous shopping goods which are standard items like toasters and kettles, and heterogeneous shopping goods which are non-standard and where personal choice plays a far more important role.
- **Speciality goods** are major purchases which are made at infrequent intervals and much probing of the marketplace is undertaken by customers. Many more purchasing motivations are involved in the final decision and quite often the final purchase is a compromise between a number of purchasing criteria. Examples of such purchases are motor cars and a major item of relatively expensive clothing.
- **Unsought goods** are ones which the purchaser has not actively considered buying. Techniques used in their marketing are often rather dubious and this has led to much criticism of marketing. Consumers usually have to be persuaded that they need such products, as it would never occur to them to go out and actively purchase. Insurance typifies such a service – particularly life assurance – where the potential customer does not necessarily see an immediate need for this service. Methods of selling such goods and services tend to be the more directly targeted approaches like direct mail, telephone selling and even door-to-door methods are used.

Activity

Consider the sub-categories under each of the consumer goods divisions. Give an example of one product or service under each heading.

- Convenience goods – toothpaste
- Shopping goods – electric razor

- Speciality goods – dining room table and chairs
- Unsought goods – home insulation

7.3 Product Management

Organisational considerations

Larger organisations, especially those which produce consumer durables and fast-moving consumer goods (FMCG), often have what is termed a 'product management' system of managing single products or a line of similar products. In FMCG companies the term used tends to be 'brand manager' whose responsibility it is to manage the image and the marketing (but not the selling) of a single product line. This person will act as a liaison between the advertising agency and the company and will be responsible for the 'image' of the product and will commission marketing research when it is needed.

This kind of system has been criticised on the grounds that product managers have to rely upon others, especially the sales-force, to carry out their ideas. This has the potential for conflict, particularly on the part of the field sales-force who have to be sold the promotional idea with which they may, or may not, agree.

Where a system of product management is in operation, the typical organisation of the marketing function is that the marketing manager is in overall control and is directly under the managing director. Under the marketing manager is the overall products manager and under the products manager come individual brand managers. Alongside the products manager comes the sales manager and under the sales manager comes the sales team organised by various kinds of geographical or functional splits which are described in more detail in Chapter 11.

Strategic considerations

Under this heading of product management it is appropriate to discuss the possibilities open to product managers when devising strategies for their product portfolios. Igor Ansoff (1957) first introduced his idea of a simple matrix and it is described in Figure 7.1. Each of the decisions is looked at in turn under their respective headings:

- **1/1 decision**-takers are the true innovators, but the strategy is perhaps rather risky in terms of expenditure costs and the high failure rate of new products. This strategy is referred to as 'diversification'.
- **1/2 decisions** (new products into existing markets) comprise producers who like to stay ahead of their competitors or are able to provide some

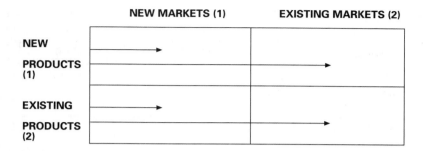

Fig 7.1 Ansoff matrix

sustainable advantage that makes their product unique in the minds of consumers. This is a strategy of 'product development'.

- **2/1 decisions** (existing products into new markets) relate to manufacturers who are seeking to expand their total sales volume by moving into an entirely new (to them) marketplace. An example might be an industrial adhesives manufacturer who decides to target the office stationery market by modifying the existing range of industrial adhesives. This strategy is known as 'market development'.
- **2/2 decisions** are taken by manufacturers who play it safe. It lacks imagination and there is a possibility of such manufacturers being left exposed if their particular market hits recessionary times. This is a strategy of 'market penetration'.

7.4 **New Products**

Different companies have different policies in relation to this subject. Many are happy to see others taking risks and will follow when new products are launched and proved. They are, however, very important for the thrusting innovative company, but there are certainly greater risks attached in terms of damage to the company's reputation if the new product fails, plus the attendant costs of development and launch. The product or service is the principal component of all marketing as it provides revenue without which commercial activity could not take place. Before we describe the formal development programme suggested for new products we have listed the types of new product categorisation used by marketing people:

- **Innovative products** are completely new to the marketplace.
- **Replacement products** are ones that provide a different slant on a traditional theme and might include well-known items, but with a new design and functions.
- **Imitative products** are quite common once an innovative product has

become successfully established. Marketing slang refers to them as 'me too' products. There is, of course, less risk involved in their launch.

- **Relaunched products** happen when an original product has gone into decline, but the company anticipates that there is sufficient potential sale if the image of the product is altered through manipulation of the marketing mix.

Activity

Give an example of a product or service under each of the new product categories cited above.

- Innovative products – the electronic wristwatch that acts as a personal organiser by downloading information from a computer screen.
- Replacement products – a new model of motor car.
- Imitative products – later personal computers that came out following their introduction by well-known personal computing manufacturers.
- Relaunched products – personal clothing products.

Organisation for new product development

How new product development is managed is a critical factor in relation to potential success or failure. There are a number of different organisational alternatives in this respect:

- **New product managers** are given the sole task of developing new products. Sometimes this task is part of the duty of a product manager or brand manager in a smaller organisation.
- **New product committees** receive new product ideas from marketing, or research and development, or indeed from any other source within the organisation and assess their viability in terms of potential success.
- **New product departments** exist in large innovative companies and their work cuts across a number of departments. When a new product idea looks to be viable they appoint a 'product (or project) champion' to see the development through from its design and development to its market launch.
- **New product venture teams** comprise people from different parts of the organisation who are brought together on an *ad hoc* basis in order that different views can be incorporated in new product decision-making. Their task is to develop products within predetermined budget and time-constraint parameters.

The process of new product development

The process of new product development goes through a logical series of steps from the inception of the idea to the actual launch of the product. These steps are now explained:

- **Idea generation** can come from a variety of sources. In innovative companies, such ideas tend to be research-driven. The notion of marketing orientation tells us that we should look to our customers first (through marketing research) before embarking upon new product development. However, in the case of companies producing 'breakthrough' products this might be difficult as customers will not necessarily be able to envisage what they require. However, as we shall see later in this section, ideas are not simply generated and made into products which are then marketed. Marketing research does come into the equation, but more through procedures like product testing which was explained in Chapter 6. A culture should exist within the organisation that encourages new product ideas amongst more than simply the research and development function. The sales-force should be a regular source of new product ideas, and such data can be gathered from the company's marketing information system as explained in Chapter 5. Brainstorming is a good method of producing new product ideas as long as it is chaired competently, but regular meetings of planning committees should have this at the head of their agenda. Venture teams can then be set up to progress likely ideas.
- **Screening** is the first stage of sifting viable ideas from less viable ones and obvious issues are addressed at this stage in terms of potential demand, the company's capability in terms of development and production and the profit potential. This is an important stage at which 'Go' or 'Drop' decisions are made. This screening process should have due regard to whether or not the new product will fit into range of products that the company produces and markets, for to start a completely new venture might mean expensive investment in not only production capacity and skills, but a completely new marketing team might be required.
- **Business analysis** is where the new product idea's financial viability is appraised. By this phase only 'serious' contenders will remain and here a critical stage has been reached. Such analysis needs to take into consideration total costs rather than simply development and production costs.
- **Product development** is the point at which the company has committed itself and indeed this is when costs start to increase sharply. Where appropriate prototypes will be developed and these can be assessed by marketing research through product appraisal tests. It is also here that product refinement and modification will be possible through feedback from marketing research. It might also be the point at which the product is abandoned if expectations do not match up to reality, rather than risk a 'high exposure' failure in the marketplace.
- **Test marketing** is the penultimate stage. This might be appropriate where the product is a fast moving consumer good when it can be tested in test towns or a television test areas before going 'national', but this is not always appropriate for more durable products. Here, product placement tests with members of the general public are probably more appro-

priate. The only problem with full-scale test marketing is that it allows your competitors to see what you are doing, so clearly this disadvantage must be weighed against the advantages of simulating a national launch before full-scale commitment. This indeed is why product testing, rather than higher profile test marketing, is better in terms of confidentiality.

- **Commercialisation** is where the product is to be launched on the market. All of the various filters have taken place, but even at this stage success is not guaranteed. However, there is a far greater likelihood of success if the procedure just described has been undertaken.

An American firm of consultants, Booz, Allen and Hamilton first put forward the notion of the decay curve of new product ideas which is illustrated in Figure 7.2. In their original research Booz, Allen and Hamilton found that it took 58 new product ideas to produce one potentially successful product. However, even during the 'commercialisation' stage there was still a 50/50 chance that the product would not be successful. Later research that they undertook suggested that it took considerably fewer new product ideas to produce a successful product. However, this might well have been a function of less 'outrageous' ideas being suggested at the evaluation and screening stage.

Factors for successful innovation

McKinsey & Co. conducted a consultancy research study in 1980 which investigated a number of large multi-national organisations. The research examined factors that were deemed to be essential in their successful operation and eight were highlighted:

Fig 7.2   Decay curve of new product ideas

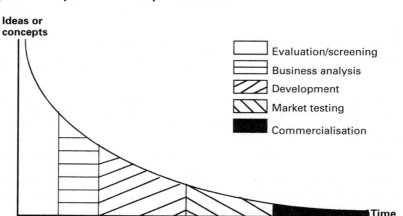

- a bias towards action;
- simple line and team staff organisation;
- continued contact with customers;
- productivity improvement via people;
- operational autonomy and the encouragement of entrepreneurship;
- simultaneous loose and tight controls;
- stress on one key business value;
- an emphasis on sticking to what it knows best.

This seminal piece of research has stood the test of time and it is still cited today as being the critical success formula for successful international enterprise.

7.5 **Product Mix and Product Line**

The above terms are used a lot within product management in addition to the terms 'depth' and 'width' of the product mix (or product assortment). This latter description means all of the product lines and items that a company offers for sale. Basically, the product line is a group of closely related product items. The width of the product mix denotes the number of product lines carried. The depth of the product mix denotes the range of items within each product line and is calculated by dividing the total number of items carried by the number of product lines. There is another term which is 'consistency', and this relates to the closeness of items in the range in terms of product and marketing characteristics.

Activity

Think of an example of a group of product lines. Then suggest the mix and depth and width of a separate line of products within the total portfolio of products.

A clothing manufacturer has four separate product lines which comprise: gents casual clothing, gents formal clothing, ladies casual clothing and ladies formal clothing.

In the ladies casual clothing product line there are eight separate styles of garment which represents the width of the product mix. There are also ten different sizes within each of these eight separate styles and this represents the depth of the product mix.

By attempting this kind of analysis, product management can look more objectively at its overall product mix and decide whether or not certain lines should be lengthened, shortened or deleted.

7.6 **Product Life-cycle**

The notion of the product life-cycle is almost as old as the subject of marketing. Various stages are proposed which show that a product passes through a number of stages in its life from the time it is conceived (the development phase) to the time it is deleted during the decline stage. Marketing people have found it to be a useful planning tool as we shall shortly discuss.

The principal problem with this theory is that it is so neat as to be totally 'believable', and some product managers tend to expect that every product will fit this neat curve. Marketing academics have therefore criticised the concept on the basis that when a product is launched it is often killed off prematurely because sales suggest that it has gone into a quick decline, whereas the reality is that what they are is probably only a slight hiccup in the growth curve of the product.

Figure 7.3 shows the theoretical curve of product life-cycle. On this diagram is superimposed the revenue curve, below and above the horizontal axis, which shows the product recovering its costs of development and launch and then moving into profitability. Naturally, all products will behave differently, but as a tool of planning this theory has much to commend it. The shape of the curve can alter and this is useful in illustrating the effect of different marketing conditions. A number of different patterns are suggested in Figure 7.4 together with appropriate explanations. It should, however, be emphasised that many more combinations are possible.

In Figure 7.3 the first diagram represents a 'fad' product which comes

Fig 7.3   The product life-cycle

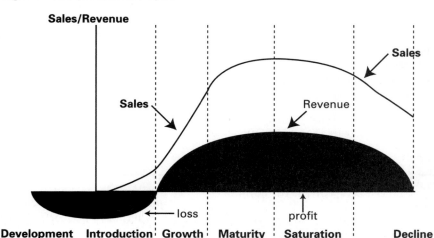

Fig 7.4 Different shapes of the product life cycle

quickly into the marketplace and is never seen again. The second diagram represents a 'fashion' product whose sales might go in cycles. The third diagram represents a product which passes through a number of phases, but where the product manager does not allow the product to become 'stale' after it has entered maturity. This is done by introducing a modification which builds upon the success of the original product.

As has been mentioned, the concepts as outlined in Figure 7.4 can be used as planning tools and such curves can be hypothesised which can fit almost any marketing situation. It is useful as a tool of product planning.

Activity

Consider a new 'pop' record which has entered the charts. Suggest a product life cycle curve that might equate to the life of this record.

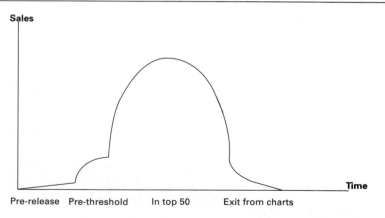

During pre-release the record is being sent to people who might play (and thus promote) the record – namely disc jockeys on the radio and in clubs. Pre-threshold is when it is first being played and small numbers of people begin to purchase. It starts its commercial life once it enters the 'top 50' and takes off. It then exits from the charts and sales quickly decline.

The product life-cycle is influenced by the nature of the actual product, changes in the competitive environment, and changes on the part of consumers who might display different preferences as the product moves through its life-cycle. The shape of the curve, from an individual manufacturers viewpoint, can also be altered as a result of competitive actions. The product-life cycle can thus be applied to the industry as a whole (which will include a summation of all manufacturers sales who are marketing that particular product), or it can apply only to the sales of a specific product for an individual company.

The time span of the product life-cycle can range from, say, a fashion season to many years. In this latter case the maturity and saturation stages will be considerably lengthened.

It is now acknowledged that different categories of life-cycle exist. We have used soap and shoes as our illustrations, so the curve is applicable within one of the following groups:

- **product category life-cycles** describe a generic product like soap or shoes. Life-cycles here tend to be long or infinite.
- **product form life-cycles** describe a type of product like perfumed soap or plastic shoes. Here the life-cycle is shorter.
- **brand life-cycles** describe the various manufacturers' brands of perfumed soap or plastic shoes. This might, in the case of plastic shoes, be linked to a single fashion season with a new brand coming out shortly afterwards, so this kind of life-cycle is the shortest of all.

Strategies suggested by each life-cycle stage

Successful use of the product life-cycle concept is being able to identify the passage from one stage to another. This requires that the company makes use of marketing research and marketing intelligence which form part of the company's marketing information system which was discussed in Chapters 5 and 6.

The product life-cycle can thus be used strategically to impart an anticipated course of product development for which strategies can be planned and which will ensure the company's long-term growth in the marketplace.

Marketing actions are now suggested which are normally appropriate to each of these separate stages. As you will see, many of the policies that are referred to during this next section are taken up in greater detail later in the text.

- **Development** is of course the pre-launch phase and it is during this period that confidentiality will usually have to maintained in terms of keeping information away from competitors. It is no secret that in many larger organisations the research and development function is housed entirely separately from the main production unit. In fact, in a lot of cases research and development is on an entirely different site. As the research and development process progresses from experimentation to the tangible product, so, in a marketing-orientated organisation, the involvement of marketing research will tend to increase. This is not to say that marketing research should not be involved at the earlier stages. For instance, focus groups/group discussions would be appropriate in terms of testing out the concept on groups of the general public at an early stage in the process before too much has been committed in terms of research and development expenditure.

- **Introduction** is the launch period and the product is slowly gaining acceptance. There are few (indeed sometimes zero) competitors at this stage, but this is where a number of new products fail. Figure 7.1 indicated that even after a new product idea had gone through its various filter stages there is still an even chance that it might fail. The product is seen to be innovative at this stage and potential buyers must me informed at to what it will do, so advertising tends to be of an informative nature. Buyers tend to be what are known as 'innovators' and this is explained later in this chapter. The product is new and can normally sustain a high initial price (known as skimming which is taken up in detail in the next chapter) as there are few or no competitors. Indeed, the product will probably have been expensive to produce and the marketing costs of creating awarenessh prior to, and during, its launch might have been high, so this is an opportunity to recoup as many of those costs as the market will sustain.

  Distribution is not widespread at this stage and is often exclusive within a particular geographical location. Even now, the product may not be totally appropriate in the marketplace in terms of its performance or design features, so product modifications tend to be more frequent at this stage.

- **Growth** is the period during which competitors will start to appear with similar offerings. Indeed, they might well have been conducting parallel research and development, but have been slower in launching their innovative products. Even now, the product is still exposed to failure, perhaps through competitive activity, as competitors have been able to learn from your mistakes during your launch. They will know your price and might undercut and they will know the perceived weaknesses of your product, so they can emphasise the strength of theirs. Although it might seem that being in the market first is a good policy, it is also a high-risk policy, and unless the company is large enough to sustain a costly failure at this stage, or has other products to fall back upon, then such a policy is very high risk indeed.

  This growth phase is sometime termed 'exponential', and it is during this period that sales begin to take off. If the company is small, then it might well be acquired by a large company. Such acquisitions are normally done on a mutually advantageous basis, but they can be aggressive if the company that has developed the new product is a public limited company and a larger company seeks acquisition through direct offers to shareholders, whilst the management disagree with the takeover terms.

During this phase, promotion tends to change from one of creating awareness to one of attempting to create an identifiable brand. Promotional expenditure is probably still relatively high. Distribution is also important during this phase. There are two parallel forces at work here. The first is in terms of powerful retail buyers attempting to rationalise the total number of lines they sell. The second is in terms of manufacturers attempting to secure as many distribution outlet possibilities as possible, as the product has now lost its innovative appeal. In distribution terms they move from exclusive, then to selective and finally to intensive distribution. The philosophy of the latter is that maximum exposure at the point of sale is probably as important as brand awareness. Distribution issues are dealt with in more detail in Chapter 9.

- **Maturity and saturation** are dealt with together, because the 'maturity' phase is the phase where the product's sales level off to a gradual peak over a longer period (often even years or decades) and the 'saturation' phase is from its peak, gradually downwards to the phase where sales start to decelerate towards the 'decline' phase. In fact, many marketing authors miss out the 'saturation' phase altogether and class all of this phase as 'maturity'.

During this phase sales slow down and repeat purchases are prevalent. There are attempts to 'differentiate' products through the addition of 'features'. Price competition is at its maximum as other manufacturers enter the market. These manufacturers come in with 'me too' products which have not had to sustain the heavy costs of research and development and promotional costs associated with their launch. Although their brands might not carry the same weight as the well established brands, price is the main competitive weapon, and price 'wars' between the established brands and these newer competitors is now uncommon. By now, the 'mystique' surrounding the product has dissipated and consumers feel confident in purchasing a product that bears a relatively unknown brand label. There is an increasing trend among retailers to trim their inventories, so unless the product can offer a sustainable product, brand or price advantage then there will be a reluctance to stock.

As market growth has ceased, marketing management must attempt to at least retain market share in the face of increased competition and it is at this stage than a number of manufacturers withdraw from the marketplace. If the brand is a sustainable brand name then advertising will be necessary to keep this in the mind of consumers and to keep them loyal to the brand. Promotion to the trade is also important as manufacturers will wish to retain their distribution outlets. Joint manufacturer/trade promotions are developed with costs being shared on an equitable basis. There is generally a move away from what is termed a 'pull' strategy of promotion towards a 'push' strategy, and these terms are explained more fully in Chapter 12.

* **Decline** is signalled by steadily and sustained falling sales after the 'saturation' phase. Marketing research should have told the company that this was due to happen in order that they could concentrate upon developing new product lines. However, company management quite often refuses to accept that its products are about to enter the decline phase and stay with it in the hope that the inevitable might not happen. Such a decline might be a function of a change in customer preferences, but more likely it is a function of a new product or process supplanting the existing one. In the United Kingdom, recent examples of industries that have entered such decline are coal and textiles.

The phase is characterised by competitive intensity and price cutting and sales falling continuously. Many producers decide to abandon the marketplace, or are forced to abandon because of financial difficulties. Thus, the decision to abandon the marketplace is a critical one and as can be seen from Figure 7.3 this should theoretically come when the product moves from a positive to a negative revenue situation.

However, a number of manufacturers do stay in business during the decline phase. It is only in relatively few cases that a product will decline completely and never appear again. There will usually be a residual or continued demand, but at far less volume than before. A good example is solid fuel which has largely been supplanted by gas and electricity and to a lesser extent oil for home heating purposes. However, there is still demand for solid fuel and as most of the solid fuel processors have now departed from the marketplace there is a vibrant market left for those who have remained.

Activity

Consider the product life-cycle concept. Try to cite a well-known product item that fits each of the stages within this life-cycle.

* *Introduction* – CD ROMs for personal computers
* *Growth* – personal computers for home use
* *Maturity* – refrigerators
* *Saturation* – traditional ovens
* *Decline* – black and white television

7.7 **Product Diffusion and Adoption**

The notion of product diffusion and adoption was first put forward by Everett Rogers (1962) p. 162. The diffusion process relate to the speed and extent of take-up of a new product and it considers the people who are the ultimate target of marketing efforts, rather than the marketplace itself which is the function of the notion of the product life-cycle. The diagram which forms the model suggested for the diffusion curve is very much like the model for the product life-cycle, and indeed there are similarities between them both. In the case of this theory, consumers do not necessarily fall into the same category for all purchases, and the theory very much describes consumer behaviour in relation to their individual needs and preferences. The theory is explained in Figure 7.5.

The figure represents the rate at which the product is purchased for the first time by single individuals who are categorised into adopter categories, depending upon when in the cycle of time the purchase was made for the first time. The process is termed the 'diffusion of innovations'.

- **Innovators** tend to be opinion leaders who are the first to purchase and these are basically the same purchasers as those who purchase at the introduction phase of the product life-cycle. They are likely to be younger and better educated from reasonably affluent high social status family backgrounds. Their knowledge of the product tends to come more from their own feelings than from the efforts of marketing people. They represent the first 2.5 per cent of the entire market – which is two standard deviations to the left of the mean.
- **Early adopters** possess similar characteristics to the innovators, but they are slightly more cautious and less gregarious. They tend to belong more

---

Fig 7.5   The product adoption process/diffusion of innovations

Source: Based on Rogers (1965).

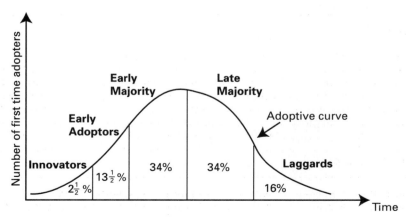

to 'local' groups, but as opinion leaders they are influential. These comprise 13.5 per cent of the entire market.

- **Early majority** purchasers tend to rate slightly above average in terms of their social class and now that the product has become more established, they rely principally upon marketing information before making their purchases. This group represents 34 per cent of the market.
- **Late majority** purchasers tend to be more cautious, but are more prone to social pressures to adopt the product for the first time. This group comprises 34 per cent of the total market.
- **Laggards** are the final 16 per cent category and they make up the cautious group. They tend to be older and more conservative, generally coming from a lower socio-economic class.

Diffusion is of course closely related to the adoption process of individual customers, and it has been found that five particular facets of products will lead to a more rapid and wider adoption:

1 **Relative advantage** in terms of the greater the perceived advantage of the new product to customers the faster it will diffuse.
2 **Compatibility** relates to the greater the extent to which the new product is compatible with existing products, the faster it will diffuse.
3 **Complexity** is a disadvantage, because the more complex the new product is, the more difficult it will be to understand in the marketplace and the diffusion rate will thus be slower.
4 **Divisibility** means the greater the ability of the new product to be used or tried on a limited scale before full commitment on the part of the purchaser, the faster it will diffuse.
5 **Communicability** means an ability of the new product to be demonstrated or communicated by early purchasers to later potential purchasers, then the quicker will be the rate of diffusion.

Activity

Think of a relatively new product, but one which has diffused up to say the 'late majority' first-time users. Then think of some of the people you know who have purchased this product. Then think of some people who have not yet purchased and include those who will probably never purchase the product. In which innovator category do you feel those who have purchased fell when they made their first time purchase, and into which innovator category will those fall who have yet to make a purchase? Is there anything about their individual behaviours and background that equate to the points mentioned against the innovator categories that have been listed?

This is really a question for which no answer can be provided, because it depends upon the individuals you have chosen. However, you might be surprised at the conformity between the people you have chosen and the descriptions that have been ascribed to each of the innovator categories.

Now reflect on the material that was covered in Chapter 4 when buyer behaviour was examined. The adoption process is very closely allied to the process that was cited in Figure 7.5, and indeed it links in very neatly in terms of the decision-making processes that take place prior to making the purchase of a new innovatory product or service.

Activity

Consider the adoption process. State what this, is and explain how it is related to the diffusion of innovations.

The adoption process can be described as:

Awareness → Interest → Evaluation → Trial → Adoption →
Post-adoption confirmation

It is related to the diffusion of innovations in that this is typically the process through which purchasers must go before making a major new product purchasing decision; more so in this particular case as they have never tried the product before.

Although Figure 7.5 adds up to 100 per cent, this is not to say that everybody will ultimately purchase the product or service. If we consider home telephones as an example it could probably be said that the country has reached saturation in terms of new subscribers. However, a number are not subscribers because they like privacy or have some other personal reasons for not wanting a telephone. A minority, of course, would like a telephone, but cannot afford one. In any case, the market for home telephones will never be 100 per cent of all households. The categories who never purchase are termed 'non-adopters'.

7.8 Portfolio Models

The first catalogued use of portfolio analysis was done by Alan Zakon who was working with the Mead Paper Corporation in the USA in the 1960s. He proposed a matrix as shown in Figure 7.6. The formula was very simple. Savings account meant no cash flow but growth; sweepstake meant speculative products; bonds were some cash flow and some growth and mortgage meant large cash flow but no growth. Products, or (SBUs) strategic Business Units, were simply assessed on a qualitative basis and then placed in an appropriate box. However, what the matrix did to was to allow management to look objectively at SBUs in terms of their current situation and allow management to make decisions as to their future.

However, since this first model, which is now of more historical interest

SAVINGS ACCOUNT	SWEEPSTAKE
BOND	MORTGAGE

Fig 7.6   Zakon's matrix

---

than for practical application, many models have been developed, the most important and well known of which are now described and evaluated in more detail.

'Boston Consulting Group (BCG) growth/share matrix'

The BCG matrix (sometime referred to as the 'Boston box') was an 'over-night success' but it had much to commend it, not least of which was the fact that it was underwritten by the Harvard Business School. It did, however, have much backing in terms of research which came principally from the Profit Impact of Marketing Strategy (PIMS) study which incorporated 57 large companies and 620 subsidiary companies in its database in 1974. By linking market-share with profitability, the PIMS study was found to closely correlate with the notion of the BCG matrix. It was also popular in that it was simple and by concentrating on the criteria of market growth and market share it was a tool to which the user could instantly relate. The BCG matrix is described in Figure 7.7.

Each of the circles in the figure represents the size of the overall market and the segment taken out of that circle represents the company's share of that total market. Each of the quadrants is now explained:

- **Stars** are SBUs with a high market-share in a high-growth industry and whirl have good earning potential. However, at what is probably an early stage in its life-cycle, the product is probably costly to maintain in terms of having to engage in aggressive marketing effort and this in all prob-ability means high advertising costs.
- **Cash cows** have a high market-share but have probably matured in a slow, or zero, growth market. They are typically well-established with loyal customers, and product development costs are relatively low as the initial research and development expenditure has been recovered. These are profitable 'safe' products and a strong company has many in its portfolio. Generally, stars move into this position when the overall market has stabilised.
- **Question marks** are sometimes referred to as 'problem children' or 'wild-cats'. Here, market growth prospects are favourable, but they have a relatively low market-share, so the SBU has only a weak foothold in an expanding, but probably highly competitive, marketplace. If the SBU is

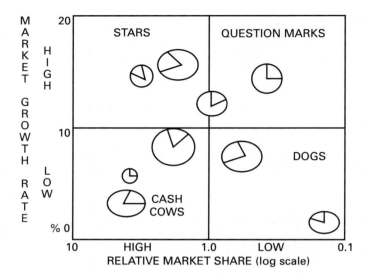

Source: *Long Range Planning*, February 1977.

Fig 7.7   BCG matrix

to become a star then substantial marketing or research and development expenditure might be needed and this is a problem that marketing
management must address.

- **Dogs** are sometimes referred to as 'pets' in this respect and this is an SBU
  characterised by low market-share and low growth. These are SBUs for
  potential liquidation, but as the 'pet' term implies they are probably still
  there for nostalgic reasons on the part of management. Indeed, when
  companies are in financial difficulties and the creditors take charge the
  first thing that is done is to prune the dogs from the portfolio. However,
  it is accepted that in some circumstances the retention of dogs might be
  necessary in order that the company can provide a comprehensive portfolio of products that it offers as part of its overall product mix.

In practice companies tend to have a balanced portfolio, but those with a
preponderance of 'dog' products are clearly in difficulty. Stronger companies will have a preponderant mixture of 'stars' and 'cash cows'. It does not
follow that SBUs must progress around each of the boxes in a sequential
manner. However, the matrix is dynamic and will change over time as
market conditions get better or worse and indeed as products move through
their product life cycle stages. Marketing management must attempt to
ensure that 'star' and 'cash cow' SBUs remain in their respective positions
for as long as possible, for these are the ones which provide most of the
company's profits and such SBUs are indeed the company's insurance for

the future. Clearly 'question marks' must be looked at in terms of pushing them into the 'star' category through marketing actions. 'Dogs' clearly need careful evaluation to see whether any pruning of the range of products might be called for.

Activity

If you work in a company, or if you are closely associated with one, try to put each of that company's products or services into their respective quadrants on a BCG matrix.

This, again, is an activity for which no answer can be given, because it will depend upon the company and its portfolio of products. Surprisingly few companies attempt to analyse their SBUs in this manner, so both pleasant and unpleasant surprises can be expected.

The General Electric (GE) business screen

This matrix was developed by the management consultants McKinsey & Co. when they were working with General Electric (USA). It was an attempt to try to overcome some of the difficulties encountered when attempting to apply the BCG matrix by using a broader range of company and market factors when assessing the position of a particular SBU.

The technique uses market attractiveness and business position as its two criteria (Figure 7.8). Different weights are attached along each axis along the parameters of 'low', 'medium' and 'high'. For the 'market attractiveness' axis, measurements like market growth rate, market size, difficulty of entering the market, numbers of competitors, profit margins and technological requirements should be taken into consideration. The 'business position' axis considers matters like the size of the SBU, the strength of its position compared to that of the competition, capabilities of the organisation in relation to production and research and development, and the strength that is displayed within the management of the SBU.

The matrix uses nine boxes, in whirl, similarly to the BCG matrix, the circles represent the size of the overall market and the segments within each represent that SBU's share of the total market.

Activity

As with the activity on the BCG matrix, try to put each of the company's products or services into their respective positions on the GE matrix.

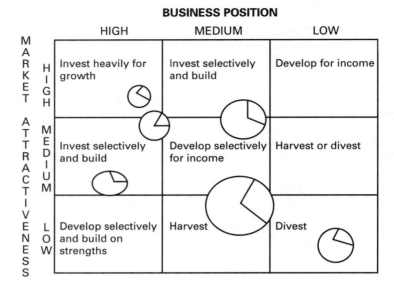

Source: Porter, M. E. (1980).

Fig 7.8   General Electric (GE) matrix

Again, no answer can be given here, but you might find that this is an easier matrix to visualise and apply. It is also perhaps more plausible in that a nine-box matrix gives a greater degree of precision.

Porter's generic strategies and the industry/market evolution model

Michael Porter identified three generic strategies for achieving success in a competitive market:

- **Overall cost leadership** which means producing a standard product at low cost to undercut competition or through engaging in heavy advertising.
- **Differentiation** which is selling at a higher price than average something that consumers will then see as having some unique feature of quality or image or design.
- **Focus** which concentrates on a specialist product range or a unique segment of the market or a combination of them both.

Figure 7.9 illustrates the profitability implications of these strategies. It can be seen that financial success does not necessarily mean that a company has to have a high market share to be successful. The figure illustrates the profitability implications of the three strategies. It can be seen in this model

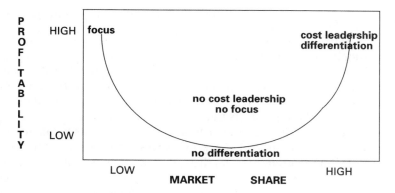

Source: Porter, M. E. (1980).

Fig 7.9   Based on Porter's generic strategies

that financial success does not mean that a company has to have a high market-share. Companies can have a small market share and still be profitable (upper left) through specialised product offerings. The upper-right sector is also profitable because products can be differentiated or they can have a large market as a result of economies of scale which can be reflected in appropriately lower prices to customers. Companies that are 'stuck in the middle' have problems as a result of low profits and a modest share of the market.

Activity

Think of a range of products with which you are familiar, for example, compact hi-fi systems. Perhaps you could visit your local electronic superstore just to remind you of the manufacturers who produce this equipment – especially the names that do not immediately spring to mind. With this list of manufacturers in mind, try to put them on the scale as shown in Figure 7.9.

This will be a subjective listing, but as in the hi-fi example this is a product that is now in the maturity phase of its life-cycle, it is more than probable that you will have listed the names that come quickly to mind (that is, the heavily branded popular products that are competitively priced) in the top right-hand corner and the specialist producers (those with unique product features or high-quality images) in the top left-hand corner. A few will probably be 'stuck in the middle' which, in the case of the very competitive hi-fi market, is not a place in which they will be able to remain for very long.

In 1985 Porter developed a model which furthered this earlier research. This work was reported in his book *Competitive Advantage*: *Creating and*

Sustaining Superior Performance. His model was based upon three broad stages in the evolution of and industry/market:

- **Emerging industry** which is portrayed by hesitancy on the part of buyers over the likely performance of products, the function of these products, and the possibility of obsolescence as manufacturers leapfrog each other in terms of technological improvements at the early stage of the life of the industry and the products that are being produced.
- **Transition to maturity** is distinguished by reduced profits throughout the industry and a general slow-down in growth. Customers become more confident with their purchases as they are more familiar with the range of products and manufacturers. The industry settles down in terms of technological breakthrough and most product offerings are relatively similar. Emphasis moves away from product features towards non-product features like branding and advertising.
- **Decline** is where substitute products begin to make inroads into the marketplace, and customer-needs change because of social or demographic reasons. The product is basically becoming 'stale' and other products begin to supplant it.

Each of these stages were then looked at in terms of whether the company was a leader or a follower in the particular industry, and the resultant matrix is illustrated in Figure 7.10 which also suggests strategies for each individual sector.

In summary, emerging industries should be developed in order to coun-

Fig 7.10   Strategic position in industry life-cycle

Source: Porter, M. E. (1985).

	GROWTH (emerging industry)	MATURITY (transition to maturity)	DECLINE
STRATEGIC POSITION — LEADER	Keep ahead of the field	Cost-leadership; raise barriers to entry; deter competitors	Redefine scope; divest peripheral activities; encourage departures
STRATEGIC POSITION — FOLLOWER	Imitation at lower cost; joint ventures	Differentiation; focus	Differentiation; new opportunities

teract rivalry between competitors, with the possibility of substitute products being developed to put the producer in a powerful bargaining position. Transition to maturity means developing new markets and focusing upon specific market segments as well as attempting to become more efficient. A decline strategy suggests either divesting the product or profitably supplying residual demand.

Shell directional policy matrix

This matrix was suggested by Shell Chemicals (1978) and its scope covers the organisation's competitive capabilities against the prospects for profitability. There is a suggested strategy for each of the boxes that comprise the matrix which is illustrated in Figure 7.11. Shell contend that whatever strategy is selected, it should be 'resilient' and viable in a diverse range of potential futures. It is important, therefore, that each strategy is evaluated against all possible future contingencies.

In the matrix, both of the axes look at the criteria for market growth, market quality, the industry situation, plus environmental considerations. Sector profitability, however, specifically looks at these from an overall industry point of view, whereas company competitive capability looks at each from a more specific company-based point of view on the basis of market position, product research and development and productive capability. On each of these factors, a product (or SBU) is given from one to five

---

Fig 7.11   Shell directional policy matrix

Source: Porter, M. E. (1985).

PROSPECTS FOR SECTOR PROFITABILITY

		Unattractive	Average	Attractive
COMPANY / **COMPETITIVE CAPABILITY**	**Weak**	disinvest	phased withdrawal	double or quit
	Average	phased withdrawal	custodial	try harder
	Strong	cash generation	growth	leader

stars. For example, the factor of 'market quality' might be estimated on the basis of past profit stability in that sector. This evaluation is then converted into a quantified rating (although such a rating has been qualitatively assessed). A similar procedure is undertaken for each of the other three factors, so the overall score on sector profitability is then a total of the ratings on all factors.

Arthur D. Little industry maturity/competitive position matrix

The American consultants Arthur D. Little developed this matrix which looks at 'stage of industry maturity' alongside 'company's competitive position'. The 'stage of industry maturity' axis is, or course, similar to the various stages in the product life-cycle concept. The resultant matrix is illustrated in Figure 7.12.

A number of factors are used to assess the stage that an SBU or an individual product is in. These relate to their rate of market growth, their future potential in the industry, the product or line of products themselves, the number and relative efficiency in marketing terms of competitors, purchasing patterns by consumers, the ease of competitive entry, and the complexity or simplicity of the technology.

Barksdale and Harris portfolio analysis/product life-cycle matrix

Many textbooks do not quote this matrix. However, it is felt that it is good in that it successfully combines the product life-cycle concept with ideas from the BCG matrix. A commonly made criticism of the BCG matrix is that new products and declining products are ignored, and this model overcomes this problem as we now illustrate in Figure 7.13.

The assumptions inherent in the model are that products have a finite

---

Fig 7.12   A. D. Little competitive position/industry maturity matrix

STAGE OF INDUSTRY MATURITY

		Embryonic	Growth	Maturity	Ageing
COMPANY'S COMPETITIVE POSITION	Dominant				
	Strong				
	Favourable				
	Tentative				
	Weak				

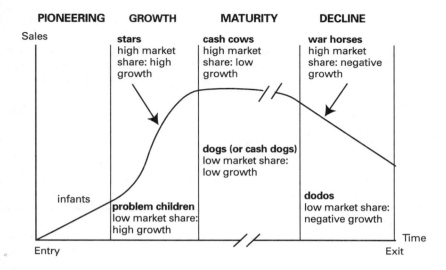

PIONEERING   GROWTH   MATURITY   DECLINE

Sales

stars
high market
share: high
growth

cash cows
high market
share: low
growth

war horses
high market
share: negative
growth

dogs (or cash dogs)
low market share:
low growth

infants

problem children
low market share:
high growth

dodos
low market share:
negative growth

Time

Entry   Exit

Fig 7.13   Barksdale and Harris combined portfolio

lifespan, that cash generated and profit margins are positively related to market-share, and that costs of production are related to volume and units costs decrease as volume increases. Each of the categories listed in the model is now explained.

- **Infants** appear in the pioneering stage and they are products that carry risk. Their profits will be very little or even negative because they consume a lot of promotional costs informing customers of their function and existence at this early stage.
- **Problem children** are the same as for the BCG matrix with a low market-share but high growth, so they are costly to maintain.
- **Stars** are the products to nurture, but they are probably high cost in marketing terms. Although they have a high market-share and high growth rate marketing expenditure in the form of informative promotion in a relatively new market will he high.
- **Cash cows** as with the BCG matrix are steady income-earners with a high market-share in a low-growth mature market.
- **Dogs** in this matrix are sometimes called 'cash dogs' because they are placed in a low (or even zero or marginally negative) growth sector of a saturated market. However, even though their market-share is still low, they might make a marginal amount of money for the company – hence the term 'cash dogs'.
- **War horses** are sustainable products in that they are in a declining market, but possess a high share of that declining market. They have probably been cash cows, but the overall market trend has worked against

them. They should clearly receive the attention of management in terms of sustaining them for as long as possible in this declining market, but little should be expended on promotional expenditure. Once the time is right they should be withdrawn from the marketplace before they become 'stale' as this could adversely affect the image of the company in the minds of consumers.

- **Dodos** have a low share of the total market in a market that is in decline with little opportunity for cash generation. The only way they could be made profitable might be if many competitors exit from the market and they are turned into 'war horses'. The most probable answer is to prune them at this stage.

Activity

Think of a typical household product in each of the stages represented in the Barksdale and Harris portfolio.

- Infants – waste disposal units.
- Stars and problem children (where they are depends upon the particular company) – automatic washing machines.
- Cash cows and dogs (again, where they are depends upon the marketing efforts of the particular company) – refrigerators.
- War horses and dodos (similar again, in terms of how the company is marketing the product) – black and white television.

7.9 **Packaging**

This final section on packaging is often classed as part of promotion, and indeed reference is made to it again in Chapter 12. However, packaging is the 'end' part of the product, because the external appearance and finish of a product will have an influence on its ultimate acceptability. Packaging has a number of functions to perform:

- Protect and preserve its contents;
- Distribution in terms of helping transfer the goods from where they were made to the ultimate customer, through a number of logistics intermediaries;
- Selling in terms of its promotional appeal insofar as design and information conveyed on the pack is concerned;
- For the convenience of users and an aid to storage of the contents;
- To conform to statutory and voluntary regulations in terms of providing a list of contents or weight.

Packaging is an important aid to selling and indeed many products that cannot be differentiated on product features can be differentiated through packaging and associated branding. As well as appealing to customers, packaging must of course appeal to those who retail the goods. This will include packaging in relation to 'outers' (the bulk packaging that bundles together a number of individual products) as well as the individual packages in which the goods themselves are packed. Well-packaged products, both in relation to 'outer' and 'inner' packaging will thus be an extra inducement for distributive intermediaries to display and promote a specific brand as opposed to the brand of another manufacturer.

7.10 **Summary**

This is the longest chapter in the book and probably the most important one, for without a product or service a company could not function: the product or service is indeed the rationale for all trade and commerce. The chapter has traced the product or service from its simple categorisation under each of the headings of industrial goods and consumer goods and then examined product management issues. New products were examined in terms of the categories of new products and suggestions made for new product organisation. The process of new product development was examined and factors for successful innovation discussed after which product mix and product line was explained. The product life-cycle was dealt with in detail including suggesting strategies for each of its stages. Product diffusion and adoption was then examined in terms of innovator categories. A detailed examination was then made of portfolio models from the very first one to the BCG, GE and Shell matrices, plus the work of Porter and Arthur D. Little management consultants. The Barksdale and Harris combined portfolio was finally examined in this section and a relationship established between the BCG matrix and the product life-cycle. Finally, packaging was considered in the context of the product with a reference to a later chapter which will look at the implications of promotion in relation to packaging.

Chapter Review Questions

In relation to each of the quadrants in Ansoff's matrix, what strategy is suggested by each of the following:

- New products into new markets
- New products into existing markets
- Existing products into new markets
- Existing products into existing markets

The answers are: Market intensification (or market penetration); Market diversification; Product development (or product diversification) and conglomerate diversification.

What alternatives exist for the management of new product development?
New product managers; new product committees; new product departments (sometimes appointing a product/project champion); new product venture teams.

What are the logical steps in the process of new product development?
Idea generation; screening; business analysis; product development; test marketing; commercialisation.

List all the stages in the product life-cycle.
Development; introduction; growth; maturity; saturation; decline.

List the categories in the diffusion of innovations process.
Innovators; early adopters; early majority; late majority; laggards.

List the quadrants in the BCG matrix.
Stars; question marks (or problem children or wildcats); cash cows; dogs.

The GE matrix has as its measurements 'high', 'medium' and 'low'. What are the two axes on the matrix?
Market attractiveness; business position.

In the Shell directional policy matrix the measurements are: 'unattractive', 'average' and 'attractive' and 'weak', 'average' and 'strong'. What axes do each relate to?
Prospects for sector profitability and company competitive capability in that order.

What categories of products are referred to the Barksdale and Harris combined portfolio?
Infants; stars; problem children; cash cows; dogs (or cash dogs); war Horses; dodos.

What are the functions of packaging?
Protection; an aid to distribution; promotional appeal; storage of contents; to display statutory regulations.

8 Price

8.1 The Importance of Pricing

Price is the means whereby an organisation covers the costs of its research, manufacturing, marketing and other activities, and in a profit-making organisation the surplus is profit. Price is also important in 'not for profit' organisations where services or products are sold or dispensed. Here, the organisation must work within budget constraints, so that any revenues that might be accrued from the sale or dispensation of services must be within the constraints of the agreed budget. Organisational goals and objectives are determined through market conditions, so price is a function of such conditions. These organisational objectives are sometimes compromised by the realisation that certain levels of profit cannot be achieved.

As an element of the marketing mix, price is of course the source of revenue for the organisation, whereas the other elements incur costs. Its importance will vary according to market conditions and the type or product or service being marketed, but only in rare cases is price the only criterion when purchases are made. Other elements like the brand name, service and warranty considerations, the sales routine and sales promotion all have their part to play but, as we shall see in Chapter 11 which examines the selling process, the final consideration usually rests upon price so its importance should not be underestimated. As price directly determines the amount of profit (or loss) an organisation makes it is important that it is approached in a reasonably scientific manner. Organisations should consider pricing in conjunction with marketing objectives and these too should be quantified in terms of reaching the organisation's goals which is the subject of Chapter 15 which deals with marketing planning. Therefore, pricing is the means through which marketing objectives are reached. However, prices should be set at a realistic level which infers that marketing (and pricing) objectives should be attainable through the organisation's marketing efforts.

As individuals, the level of prices in the economy affects our individual standards of living as well as the functioning of the economy as a whole. In a market-driven economy the goal must, therefore, be to provide products and services that we need, but at good value for money, which will be a reflection of prices charged. However, competition between providers of such goods and services will tend to drive prices down as purchasers look for value, and this principle is at the very heart of marketing thought.

8.2 **Pricing Perspectives**

Pricing theory distinguishes three separate approaches and philosophies. Among these, marketing propositions have been put forward as being the most sensible. However, since marketing theories were the last to be developed, it is perhaps not surprising that these are more sustainable than the other approaches in a modern commercial environment. Each of the three approaches is dealt with later in this chapter in terms of the theories they deal with, but the general philosophy pertaining to each is dealt with now:

- **The economist's approach**   This approach contends that price is the means through which supply and demand are brought into equilibrium. The mechanism operates along a range of markets from perfect competition, through imperfect competition, to monopoly. The assumption is that profit will be maximised and the only input to purchasing decisions is the relationship between demand and price.
- **The accountant's approach**   Here the thrust is upon recovering costs in order to make profits, and this is often expressed as a required rate of return. The accountant's approach thus emphasises the importance of identifying and classifying different costs. The principal disadvantage with this approach is the tendency to ignore the volume of demand and prevailing market conditions.
- **The marketer's approach**   This approach emphasises the effect of price on the organisation's competitive market position. This includes factors like level of sales, market-share and levels of profit. Value is emphasised as well as price, and the notion is to set prices at 'what the market will bear'.

These approaches have been briefly explained at this early stage in order to provide an understanding of the various views to follow. Each philosophy is expanded and elucidated in detail later in the chapter.

8.3 **Pricing Decisions**

Prices play an important part in the buyer/seller relationship. As we edge towards the era of 'relationship marketing', which is examined in more detail later in the text, the significance of price is perhaps reduced as factors like quality and reliability of delivery are emphasised as being of equal or even greater importance. There is a mutual trust between seller and buyer which contends that prices will be set at a 'fair' level. Indeed, there is a notion of what is termed 'open accounting' whereby in such long-term relationships, price bargaining does not enter into the negotiation equation. Here, suppliers typically provide component parts to a main manufacturer, and are then shown how this customer's price is arrived at for the end product. Equally, these customers see their suppliers' price make-up and calculations in terms of labour, material, expenses and overheads that are attributed to the component parts in question. (The entire process is termed 'supply chain integration', SCI.) An acceptable price is then agreed based upon relative profit margins. However, open accounting is perhaps an idealistic situation which may be appropriate for component manufacturers supplying large manufacturing plants, but not for the vast range of products on the market. In general commercial practice, the buyer will always view price as a cost which is paid for in return for a series of satisfactions, and the seller sees price as a means of cost recovery and profit.

The principal inputs to pricing decisions are customers, competitors, costs and company considerations.

Activity

Under each of these four Cs – customers, competitors, costs and company considerations, what do you feel will be appropriate criteria that should be examined under each 'C' in terms of pricing considerations?

- **Customers** – what they will be willing which will be affected by price levels in the marketplace; the effect of price on long-term relationships; their loyalty to your particular product (brand loyalty in the case of FMCG).
- **Competitors** – the nature and extent of competition; their numbers (how many or how few for the type of market being supplied); how aggressive they are in terms of marketing activity, which will include pricing; the prices they charge.
- **Costs** – materials; labour; overheads; considerations as to whether, in a highly competitive market, the goods might be produced on a marginal cost basis (where overheads have been recovered on other product manufacture) and where the only costs in the equation are direct costs of materials, labour and a margin for profit.
- **Company** – its objectives in terms of growth; whether it wishes to be the market leader or a market follower; company image; resources of the company.

In addition to these four 'C' factors, there are also a number of macro-considerations that will affect price including: legislation – corporation tax and VAT; tariffs and duty where appropriate; the effect of government on pricing (for example if the company is becoming a powerful player in the industry, perhaps through merger or takeover, any suspicion of prices that are, or might become, too high would probably attract the attention of the Monopolies and Mergers Commission or action might be taken under the Restrictive Trade Practices Act).

8.4 Concepts of Pricing

Economics is the starting point from which an understanding of pricing commences. Economic theory looks at the ideas of utility and value in relation to price. Utility means that aspect of a product or service which makes it capable of satisfying a want or need. Value is the term used to quantify utility and price is the monetary unit that this value represents.

Accounting provides a more pragmatic approach which contends that costs, competition and demand are the prime factors that relate to pricing decisions, but that price should always recover a company's fixed costs (for example rent, rates, heating) and variable costs (direct materials, labour and expenses), plus a margin for profit.

Marketing's view holds that 'prices shall be set at what the market will bear', which is the cornerstone of marketing thought. In reality this is not as stark as it seems, for factors like competition, costs, long-term goodwill towards customers and even the potential for government intervention have to be considered. Indeed, in the interests perhaps of gaining entry to a market, or maintaining a product line in times of intense competition, there might be situations when the company markets its products anticipating a loss in the short term.

We have put forward three views from the theoretical to the logical to the realistic. Each view is now examined in turn.

The economist's approach

This approach commences with the notion of supply and demand, where these are expressed as demand and supply schedules or curves as in Figure 8.1. In Figure 8.1(a) it can be seen that the lower the price, the greater will be the amount demanded and, conversely, the greater the price the lower will be the amount demanded. Conversely, in Figure 8.1(b) the lower the price, the lower with be the amount that suppliers will be willing to produce, and the higher the price, the more suppliers will be prepared to supply.

In Figure 8.2 we superimpose the two curves and where they intersect is the market price. In economic terms, where the two curves intersect at the market price defines the price P and the quantity, or amount demanded, Q.

Elasticity and inelasticity of demand are terms used by economists to describe how price changes affect the level of demand. The term elasticity

Fig 8.1   **Supply and demand curves**

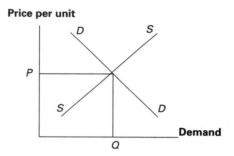

Fig 8.2   The law of supply and demand

is better described as 'responsiveness'. 'Inelastic demand' is less sensitive to price changes and 'elastic' demand is very responsive to price changes. The concepts are shown in Figure 8.3.

In Figure 8.3(a) we can see that a large reduction in price from P to $P1$ will hardly affect demand which only moves from Q to $Q1$, and this is known as inelasticity of demand. In fact, when the demand curve is vertical this is known as infinite inelasticity. In the case of Figure 8.3(b) a small reduction in price from P to $P1$ will have a big effect on demand which moves from Q to $Q1$.

Activity

Think of a product that has inelastic demand and a product that has elastic demand.

Salt or soap for inelastic demand, and colour televisions or hi-fi units for elastic demand.

Price per unit

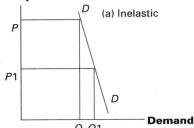

Price per unit

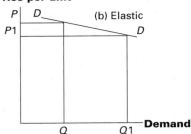

Fig 8.3   Inelastic and elastic demand

It can be seen that the incline of the demand curve, or the elasticity of demand for the product, will very much affect pricing decisions. However, in practice measures of total elasticity or inelasticity of demand are unrealistic. Even when demand is elastic, there is usually some point on the demand curve where a further price reduction makes little or no difference to demand. Determining the exact position of this point is important in demand analysis, because it would make little sense to reduce the price if this would not result in an increase in sales sufficient to offset this price reduction.

Companies market their products in a market situation which ranges from what economists call 'perfect competition' to 'monopoly' – each representing an extreme on the continuum. Perfect competition is a market in which there are a large number of fully informed buyers and sellers of similar products, and where there are no obstacles to exit or entry on the part of companies. Monopoly is where there is a single producer of a product for which there are no substitutes.

A theory developed by economists that has great relevance to marketers is the notion of 'oligopoly' which falls between the extremes of monopoly and perfect competition – towards the monopoly end of the scale. This concept has particular relevance for marketers of fast-moving consumer goods (FMCG). Here we find a market dominated by a few sellers where each company must weigh the effects of its own policies on the behaviour of its rivals.

More specifically, the theory maintains that these few sellers are interdependent and the goods they produce are basically similar (or homogeneous). Companies competing in this situation are very sensitive to price changes between the various players, because as goods are similar then customers will tend to purchase at the lowest price, so if one company lowers prices then the remaining players have to do the same in order to market their products. Therefore, price as an instrument of competition tends to be less effective than competition that is based upon such non-price factors as branding through advertising and sales promotional activities. All players produce below their maximum and the price of entry to the system can be prohibitively high through either the amount of promotion that must be done to establish a foothold or because of the costs of setting up manufacturing activities in terms of investment in plant and machinery and research and development costs. Therefore, in perfect competition, which is typified by a preponderance of small companies, each player is striving to perform at a personal best, whereas in oligopoly the actions of each player very much depend on the actions of other players.

Activity

Although the views put forward by economists tend to be theoretical ones, and are sometimes difficult to envisage in reality, they are useful to relate to in marketing terms because they tend to relate to certain kinds of marketing behaviour. With this background in mind, think of an example of an industry or service provision that more or less equates to perfect competition, oligopoly and monopoly.

- Perfect competition – the restaurant trade.
- Oligopoly – motor cars.
- Monopoly – the coal industry.

Figure 8.4 explains the theory of oligopoly: At price P the law of demand states that quantity Q will be demanded. If the price is then reduced to $P1$, then $Q1$ will be demanded, so $Q - Q1$ will be the additional amount

Fig 8.4   Oligopoly

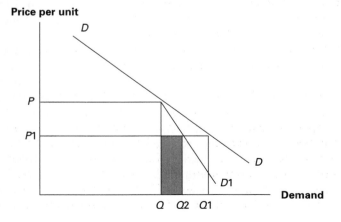

demanded. However, in a situation of oligopoly where price as an instrument of competition is less effective, then the demand curve will kink to $D1$ and the dark area covered by $Q - Q2$ will be the additional amount demanded. A price reduction in these circumstances is less effective as customers will have been 'pre-sold' their existing products through non-price factors like advertising and branding, and indeed this is termed 'non-price competition'.

The subject of economics is vast, comprising the entire structure matter of many first and higher degrees with hundreds of books having been written on the subject. In this very brief section we have attempted to put the economist's view of pricing. The view is devoid of sociological and psychological influences that might influence purchasing decisions, but it is an essential starting point when attempting to understand the market. The next approach to pricing that we investigate is the accountant's approach.

The accountant's approach

The philosophy underlying the accountant's approach to pricing is to achieve a targeted rate of return on investment from a given level of sales. Once total costs have been determined, the company then decides on the percentage of profit it requires. To accomplish this objective consistently, the company must be a market leader, otherwise fluctuations in demand will affect the value of profits made. In such a situation, companies have a clear idea of the volume of surplus they wish to achieve and can then estimate the profit margins needed to realise this. This approach is termed 'cost-plus' pricing.

This, however, is a rather mechanistic approach which is not usually used in practice, although mark-up pricing which simply adds a fixed percentage onto the cost of goods and services is still used a lot in the more traditional sectors of the retail trade. The reality is that the overall profit margin is normally the result of several pricing strategies applied to a variety of products in response to changes in the marketplace. Therefore the percentage of 'plus' that is applied in respect of each contract or product line is a function of market conditions and individual customers which means that it is more a decision that marketing should make rather than finance. However, the target rate of return that is expected in such circumstances should equate to the overall percentage that has been agreed with finance, so if certain contracts are agreed with customers at less than this target rate of return, then this shortfall should be made up on other contracts which will be priced at more than this target rate of return. This technique is more flexible than simple cost-plus pricing in that it allows marketing more flexibility when dealing with customers, and for obvious reasons this pricing technique is termed 'target pricing'.

Activity

Under what circumstances can you envisage cost-plus or target pricing as being particularly appropriate?

In a manufacturing situation where the company has to make and perhaps install something that is unique and purpose-designed. Such a product might be for the design, manufacture and commissioning of an oil refinery; here the client is probably asking for tenders from a number of companies so the company must estimate the likely costs of such a project and then add a margin on top of this for profit.

The accountant also has to control the flow of cash in an organisation and there is normally a need to recoup the often high costs of development as early as possible in the life-cycle of a product. However, it is through the financial function that a balance is kept between a variety of other demands on the company's limited resources, which means that a fine balancing act has to be performed when attempting to meet the often conflicting demands and requirements of, for instance, production, research and development, training and marketing. It can then be seen that the accountant's view of pricing is more governed by the internal workings of the company than with the vagaries of the marketplace.

In any manufacturing concern there are fixed costs like depreciation and maintenance of plant and equipment, rent and rates for factory buildings and the costs of a minimum labour force which the company has to pay regardless of the level of output. Variable costs have also to be added and these are a function of the level of output which includes direct labour, materials and energy costs. The total costs are the sum of fixed and variable costs. This is shown in Figure 8.5 which explains the concept of break-even analysis.

In the figure it can be seen that variable costs increase in direct proportion to the volume produced or sold, and the sum of these is total cost. The break-even quantity (BEQ) occurs when a certain number of units sold at a given price generates sufficient revenue to exactly equal total costs. Total revenue is of course the amount of money that the company receives and this will increase with output. Therefore, the gap between total revenue and total costs prior to the break-even point will represent a loss to the company and the gap between these after break-even will represent profit. Figure 8.5 then represents a straight 'cost-plus' approach to pricing which assumes a balanced fixed and variable cost element and an unchanging profit margin. In reality things do not work as neatly as this, as there are elements of extra costs and reduced revenues that must be considered. As output and sales increase to a certain level, there will be additional costs like the commis-

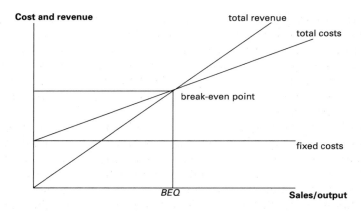

Fig 8.5   Break-even analysis

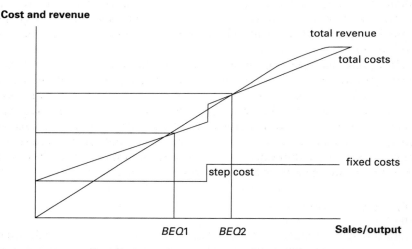

Fig 8.6   Break-even analysis showing step cost and revenue reduction with increased sales

sioning of a new production line which will incur a 'step cost'. As sales grow there will be a tendency to trim profit margins in order to attract more customers. This is explained more fully in Figure 8.6.

Here it can be seen that *BEQ*1 represents the normal break-even concept as seen in Figure 8.5, and after this point total revenue exceeds total costs. Between *BEQ*1 and *BEQ*2 there is a step cost which is a reflection of another production unit being established to cope with increased output, and it is at this point that total costs exceed total revenue for a short period.

At *BEQ*2 the second break-even occurs and once again total revenue exceeds total cost. However, shortly after this total revenue begins to tail off as a result of price reductions which have to be made in order to sustain increasing levels of sales, and ultimately this moves to a point where total revenue and total costs are again equal. What Figure 8.6 infers is that demand must be taken into consideration when deciding the amount of 'plus' in cost-plus pricing decisions.

Demand-orientated pricing might be viewed as being preferable to cost-based pricing, but we should be aware of certain practical limitations when it is related to break-even analysis. It assumes that costs are static, whereas they can vary considerably (both up and down) in reality. Revenue is over-simplified as market conditions can change rapidly, and even if they return to the condition on which the analysis was originally based, the actual revenue may not be as predicted. With these provisos taken into account, break-even analysis related to demand can be an effective price computational technique, especially if costs and demand levels are comparatively stable, even if only in the short term. It should, however, be appreciated that accurate demand estimation is difficult to achieve despite an organisation's best efforts when attempting to provide accurate forecasting as shown in Chapter 5.

Now that we have considered economists' and accountants' relatively disciplined views of pricing, we are now in a position to look at the marketer's approach. It should be emphasised here that what has been and is going to be put forward are relatively theoretical constructs, and the purpose of theory is to enable the world of reality to be viewed in a more ordered and disciplined manner. In reality, if an accountant and an economist were faced with price-making decisions, it would be unlikely that they would personally take their respective theories too literally.

The marketer's approach

An organisation should have to hand as much information as possible to use when setting prices and this will depend on the overall marketing strategy. The pricing techniques we have examined pay less attention to demand and concentrate on cost. Marketing techniques place more emphasis on the combined elements of the marketing mix as well as aspects of consumer behaviour in relation to the way price is perceived.

Improvement or maintenance of market-share is a common pricing objective and this is market-based. When a market is expanding, existing prices being charged by a company may not encourage a corresponding improvement in market-share. A downwards price adjustment might increase sales in an expanding market to a level where the return-on-investment increases in monetary terms although the percentage return on each unit sold might have fallen. Market-share is a key to profitability and this is an indicator of an organisation's general health. Price levels and profit margins carry much of the responsibility in a marketing mix designed to maintain or improve market-share.

Smaller firms generally have little influence over the level of prices in a given market and organise their businesses so that costs are at a level which will allow them to fall in line with the prices charged by the market leaders and price leaders. This is sometimes termed 'going-rate' pricing. Prices tend to be market-led with little scope for any deviation from the established price structures. As long as returns are considered to be adequate, there is justification for keeping things as they are by conforming with prices that have been established by the leaders. It should, however, be noted that price leadership does not equate to total authority in the marketplace. Many price leaders are not necessarily market leaders. Non-price competition can improve a company's market-share through manipulation of the marketing mix, so the group with the final influence in price setting is indirectly the end-consumers who react to a company's manipulation of its marketing mix through their individual purchasing actions.

If a company desires a rapid growth in sales then, if clear product superiority cannot be sustained, price is the component of the marketing mix that must be manipulated. In such circumstances the firm must appreciate the competitive conditions in which it is operating and a price-cutting action should always be made with caution. This caution is not only in terms of competitors' reactions, but a sudden price reduction might also affect the balance of other elements in the marketing mix.

Activity

In relation to the last statement, cite the circumstances that might prevail where a substantial price reduction in relation to the company's products might adversely affect its position in the marketplace.

In the case of a strongly-branded line of perfumes.

Profit maximisation is a natural policy for any business organisation to pursue. However, market conditions can make it impossible to maximise profits on all products, in all markets, at the same time. For this reason, companies employ pricing techniques which can promote sales, but reduce profits on certain products in the short term. The overall objective is to maximise profits on all goods that are to be sold over a period of time. The company's product mix should, therefore, be considered as a complete entity, rather than as a range of products whose profits have to be maximised individually. This idea might run counter to the product/brand manager system that was put forward in Chapter 7, and which looked at product issues with the premise that each product or brand manager was in control of a specific SBU whose objective was to maximise profits. However, a more global view like the one expressed here sometimes has to be taken by the marketing manager or director which might mean that certain product lines be held back in the interests of maximising the overall profitability of the company.

Break-even analysis has already demonstrated that to ensure profitability, prices must ultimately exceed costs. It is logical then to consider cost as the first step when planning price levels. However, market-based pricing strategy should begin with the consumer and then work backwards towards the company. Pricing decisions must be consumer-orientated for it is the customer who will ultimately decide whether the product is purchased or not.

When making market-based pricing decisions, a number of sequential steps should be taken:

- **Customer or market identification** is to focus the marketing decision-maker's mind on the market from the beginning. It prevents price from being perceived separately from other marketing mix elements.
- **Demand estimation** or, more technically speaking, sales forecasting, is a skilled process that should provide the company with a series of potential demand levels at different selling prices. The potential sales volume will directly affect costs, and the price necessary for profit maximisation can then be calculated. The price a company is able to charge will vary according to market conditions and the chosen market segments in addition to less tangible criteria like the value customers place on a given product.
- **Assessing competitive reactions** assumes great importance when products are easily inaugurated and markets are easy to enter. Even when a company's products or services can be differentiated in some way, it is not usually too long before competitive offerings appear. This competition appears from three sources:

  - Direct or 'head-on' competition from similar product offerings;
  - Competition from substitute products or services;
  - Competition from products that are not directly related, but which compete for the same funding sources or disposable income.

Activity

Give an illustration of two products or services that might compete for the same funding.

Expensive perfume manufacturers and jewellery manufacturers might sometimes be in competition, as these items are often purchased as gifts.

- **Market-share analysis** is to consider production factors against the anticipated share of the market. If a large market-share is envisaged, then the
price will probably need to be competitive. If production capacity is
insufficient to meet the demand that the anticipated market-share will
produce, then there is little point in setting a low price that will bring in
orders that cannot be fulfilled.

We shall now explain two pricing strategies, backed up with appropriate
figures, that have been developed by marketers and to which reference is
frequently made. The strategies are called 'market penetration' and 'market skimming' and they relate very much to new products that are being
introduced to the marketplace. It is at the start of a product's life-cycle that
such pricing decisions should be taken, for that decision will help to determine the volume of sales for that product over its life.

A market penetration strategy relies on the economies of large-scale
production to allow the product to be introduced to the market at a price
low enough to attract a large number of buyers as quickly as possible. This
will tend to constrain possible competitors by creating a low price barrier to
market entry. If product design and manufacture is costly to set up and
operate and is also conducted on a large scale, then this too will deter
competitors. The aim is to attain a high, or even total, initial market-
share and keep this share high during the later stages of the product's life-
cycle.

Figure 8.7 explains this idea, and it can be see that the product is introduced at an attractively low 'penetration' price at the beginning of its life-
cycle. As a result, demand for the product is high at the early stages,
whereas the product life-cycle concept shows a slowly rising trend at the
beginning which only begins to rise substantially during the growth phase.
This policy is particularly suitable for products that have a high demand
elasticity and where reductions in unit costs can be attained through large-
scale operations, and indeed where a large volume of sales is essential from

Fig 8.7   Penetration pricing

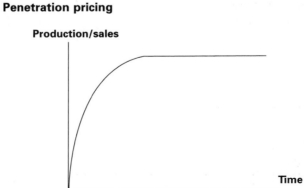

the outset in order to keep production levels high, as high production is a function of the manufacturing process.

Activity

Name a type or class of product where a penetration pricing strategy tends to be used.

New mass produced models of motor cars

A market skimming policy infers that a company will initially charge the highest price that the market will bear, and promotional effort is directed at a small percentage of the potential market. These customers are likely to be the innovators who will purchase during the introduction stage of the product's life-cycle, followed closely by the early adopters who are also more receptive to new concepts and products. Their income levels and generally higher social status make them less sensitive to high initial prices.

To be able to reach a wider group of customers once the innovators and early adopters have purchased, the company reduces its prices progressively thus skimming the most advantageous prices from each successive adopter group. Price reductions are successively brought in as sales slow at each phase, until the product has reached all of the target market. Figure 8.8 illustrates market skimming and here it can be seen that individual 'skims' have been taken at certain times. The explanation that follows is for illustration purposes, for the timing of skims does not necessarily relate to social class, for the innovator categories for, say, a home computing

---

Fig. 8.8   Market skimming

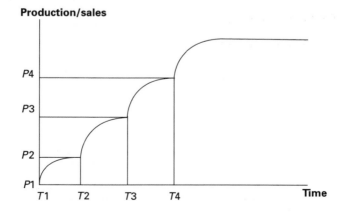

system will be 'technically minded people', whereas the innovator category for an expensive new brand of perfume might well be the 'A' and 'B' social grades.

In Figure 8.8 the new product is introduced at time $T1$ at a high initial price $P1$. The product is meant to appeal to the AB social grades at this stage. They make their initial purchases and the market then begins to tail off, so prices are reduced to $P2$ which brings in the C1 social classes at time $T2$. The same thing happens again at time $T3$ when the C2 social classes are brought in by bringing down the price to $P3$. The final skim is brought in as price $P4$ at time $T4$ which brings in the DE social grades and this is when the product has reached its maturity/saturation phase.

Activity

Think of a product or service that has used market skimming as its pricing policy.

Personal computers have already been mentioned and this is the obvious example. However, products like micowave ovens and pocket calculators have gone through this process.

A modification on the model described is to initially introduce a refined 'de-luxe' version of a new product, with simpler versions appearing later at appropriately reduced prices.

In order to be successful, a skimming strategy must relate to a product or service that is distinctive enough to exclude competitors who might be encouraged to enter the market in the early stages through the high prices being attained. Other elements of the marketing mix must assist this skimming strategy by advancing a good quality, distinctive image.

A skimming strategy is particularly relevant for new products because at the earlier phases of the product's life-cycle, competition is minimal and the uniqueness of the new product can create opportunities for non-price competition. In addition, as we have seen from the example, the market can be effectively segmented or 'cherry picked' on the basis of innovator characteristics who will be willing to purchase regardless of the initial costs. At a more practical level, high initial prices can lead to quicker recovery of research and development plus production set-up costs, and it can keep demand within the capacity of production whilst production levels are building up.

We have now looked at the three approaches to pricing and it has been demonstrated that it is the marketplace rather than the company that exerts the greatest influence in prices determination. Marketing may be faced with a general level of demand for a given product or product type, but inside this level of demand there are opportunities for tactics to be developed which centre principally on the customer. It is upon such tactics that the next section now focuses.

8.5 Tactical Pricing Issues

Some consumer goods purchasers attach a great importance to prestige when making purchases. This prestige element is rarely admitted, and in some cases it is never consciously acknowledged, for the buyer does not always realise that it forms part of the purchasing decision. It does, however, allow for psychological pricing techniques to be applied. In such cases the customer sees value in exclusivity, and if he or she has the ability to pay high prices, the image projected as a result of this kind of purchase might enhance that person's lifestyle. When we consider prestige pricing this produces a demand curve as shown in Figure 8.9. Here it can be seen that price reductions below a certain level can decrease demand since the product loses its exclusive image if price becomes too low, and this produces what is termed inverse demand.

In the case of certain products there are psychological price bands within which price reductions have little effect. If, however, the price is reduced so that it falls into the next psychological price bracket, then demand will increase, resulting in a step-like demand curve. This thinking is also at the basis of what is termed 'odd/even pricing'. Here prices like £9.99 are applied which means one penny change out of £10.00, and it somehow looks a lot less expensive than £10.00 because this is a sum that is in the next psychological price band. 'Price lining' is a variation of this and is used a lot in the USA by retailers who sell all of their products in a number of distinct price bands like $49.95; $59.95 and $69.95 for such merchandise as trainers.

A company's discount structure is also a major factor in pricing decisions and in some industries a 'trade discount' for members who belong to a certain profession is the accepted norm. Such professions are usually the trade professions like building or plumbing. Customers who purchase in

---

Fig. 8.9 Prestige pricing

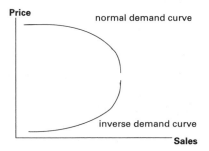

large volumes may also reasonably expect to pay a lower price than would be the case for smaller purchases, and discounts are sometimes offered to encourage large purchases. Discounts can also be offered to encourage sales of a new product or increase demand for a slow-moving product. A rebate policy may also be applied to payment terms to encourage prompt payment.

In easily segmented markets, companies sometimes charge different prices to individual segments for a product which is basically the same and this is referred to as 'price discrimination'. In such cases it often takes only a minor modification to allow a discriminatory price to be charged. Such a discriminatory price may even be based on the individual customer or the location in which the product is being marketed.

Activity

Give an illustration of price discrimination.

Reduced rates offered to students on bank charges, whilst they are students, in the expectation that they will become permanent customers.

8.6 Summary

An organisation's willingness to adapt and modify price levels according to the needs of its customers and the market conditions which prevail is a pointer to the level of marketing orientation that prevails. Marketing management has, therefore, to devise pricing strategies that are compatible with other elements of the marketing mix.

A knowledge of economic and accountancy theory is an essential precursor to understanding the wider issues involved when making pricing decisions, and to this extent these approaches have been given full consideration. Marketing approaches have also been discussed, for it is recognised that price embodies more than simply money which is exchanged for a product or service. To this extent the psychological and behavioural implications of price have also been investigated as well as the more practical issues of market-based pricing theory.

Chapter Review Questions

What are the three basic philosophies of pricing?
The economist's, the accountant's and the marketer's approaches.

What is the difference between elastic and inelastic demand?
In a situation of elastic demand a small downwards of upwards movement of price will greatly affect levels of demand, whereas in a situation of inelasticity of demand large price movements have very little effect upon demand levels.

What are the principal characteristics of oligopoly?
Few sellers of basically similar goods; all produce below their maximum; there is emphasis on non-price competition; entry to the marketplace might be artificially high through the high costs of seeking to establish a branded product.

What are the principal features of cost-plus pricing?
Fixed costs and variable costs are added, onto which is added a margin for profit.

How does target pricing differ from cost-plus pricing?
The percentage of 'plus' can be manipulated by the marketing department, as long as the 'plus' at the end of the period equates to what was agreed at the beginning of the period.

In break-even analysis what is a step cost?
An extra fixed cost at a certain volume of production that is incurred as a result of a new factory or production line or other capital item being brought into commission to cope with increased demand.

Explain the principal characterises of penetration pricing.
A low initial price that captures market share very quickly in order to keep out competition and allow the company to produce at high volume from the outset.

What is market skimming?
When a product is being introduced, a high initial price is charged to skim off certain segments to which the product will initially appeal. The price is then lowered by successive stages to attract further groups of purchasers.

What is prestige pricing?
Where the customer sees value in exclusivity and is willing to pay a higher price in the interests of 'image'.

Describe price lining.
Normally used in retail outlets where a similar range of merchandise is offered to the public at a limited number of specific prices.

9 Channels of Distribution

9.1 **Introduction**

The subject of distribution has been described by Peter Drucker (1973) as the 'economy's dark continent'. What he meant by this statement is that out of all the areas of the marketing mix, the subject of distribution is perhaps the least researched and developed. It is often regarded as the 'poor relation' of modern marketing. This is a very strange state of affairs when we consider that distribution is an intrinsic part of any commercial organisation's marketing mix, with a strategic role within that mix of absolutely paramount importance. The correct choice of distribution channels is of great importance to the success of any business enterprise, and often strategic and competitive advantage can be gained by using innovative and imaginative channels. For example, the home magazines *Living* and *Family Circle* are distributed almost entirely in supermarkets and hypermarkets and, what is more important, unlike the majority of other magazines on sale in the store these two are sold on the shop side of the checkout till. There are a number of other publications which have copied the example of these two magazines, but for many years these two highly innovative publications have managed to carve out a strategic competitive advantage simply by their choice of distribution channel. When examining the flow of goods and/or services through a distribution channel, it is often helpful to use an analogy and think of the system as a pipeline with main pipes, subsidiary branches, free flows and blockages. In fact marketing communicators working in the field of sales promotions think of distribution channels as a kind of plumbing system or pipeline. For example, they talk of consumer promotions as 'out of the pipeline' or 'pull' promotions, whereas promotions aimed at company employees or marketing intermediaries are referred to as 'into the pipeline' or 'push' promotions. In this context they are referring to products or services either being pulled through the distribution pipeline by consumer demand, or 'pushed' into the pipeline by sales persons or dealer incentives.

The two components of distribution

The overall subject of distribution is made up of two components, channels and physical distribution, and it is the important subject of channels of distribution that is covered in this chapter. The term 'distribution system' refers to that complex of agents, wholesalers and retailers through which manufacturers move products (and services, for example financial services such as life insurance) to their intended markets. Marketing channels are usually made up of independent firms or individual and independent entrepreneurs who are themselves in business to make profit. These are known as marketing intermediaries or middlemen. Distribution channels may also include some combination of owned and independent outlets, or arrangements such as franchising. Along with physical distribution, which today is part of the total business logistics function, channels of distribution contribute to what economists often refer to as 'time and place utility'. Goods and services may be manufactured or provided but to be of any real economic value they need to be made available for consumption in a certain place, for example a public house in the case of beer, and at a certain time, for example right now. The correct choice of channels can add significant real and perceived value to the product or service offering and consequently are a very important area of the marketing mix, in fact the 'P' designating 'place' in McCarthy's categorisation of the '4Ps' actually refers to channels of distribution and physical distribution. The subject of physical distribution is covered separately in Chapter 10.

9.2 Channels of Distribution and the Marketing Concept

As mentioned above, channels of distribution are often organised and serviced by firms or individuals that are separate and independent from the manufacturing firm or service-provider, for example a mutual fund for investment purposes is often sold through independent financial advisors. These firms or individuals act as channels in order to make a profit. In a very real sense the manufacturing firm relies on the effectiveness of the channel member to market their products. The manufacturer is often attempting to achieve business objectives such as market-share, return on capital, growth and profit margins through third parties. If their channel members are not successful then they will be unsuccessful also. As separate, independent businesses with their own set of aspirations and objectives, they too must be viewed by the manufacturing firm as having their own set of needs and wants. Hence the marketing process of addressing the satisfaction of specific needs and wants is not simply confined to the end-users of the product, but must also be applied to all intermediaries in the distribution chain.

Activity

How would you describe the term 'channel of distribution system'. Use examples to illustrate the points made.

Remember that the term 'distribution system' refers to the total system that has two separate but interrelated parts, that is physical distribution (logistics) and channels of distribution. This activity is asking you to consider 'channels of distribution' only. Generally speaking, the term 'channels of distribution system' refers to a complex system of agents, factors, wholesalers and retailers through which marketing firms move their products (and services) to their intended markets. Marketing channels or marketing intermediaries as they are sometimes called, are usually made up of independent firms who are themselves in business to make a profit and who consequently have needs and wants of their own. Distribution arrangements differ in their length and complexity. For example Avon cosmetics are sold and delivered to customers through direct agents who receive stock direct from the manufacturer. Kleeneze use a network of agents and distributors on a hierarchical 'multi-level marketing' basis. Hallmark Greeting Cards use independent agents to sell stock to wholesalers who then in turn split bulk and sell on to small retailers, who in turn sell to the general public. Distribution outlets may include some combination of owned and independent outlets or semi-independent outlets such as those found under franchising arrangements.

Direct customers rather than 'end-users'

One of the central tenets of the marketing concept is that organisations need to really understand their customers. In situations where a manufacturer delivers goods on site direct to the user, the definition of who the customer is usually straightforward. However, where a sophisticated, multi-layered distribution system is used there can be a hierarchy of customers. Often it is a raft of marketing intermediaries that are the immediate customers of the manufacturing firm. Hence being 'customer-focused' also applies to their immediate customers in what Philip Kotler calls the 'task environment', this includes another very important group of 'customers', suppliers as well as their marketing channel members.

9.3 Indirect versus Direct Systems

The choice of a distribution system depends upon whether a manufacturer decides to sell directly to customers, employing salespeople, or uses intermediaries such as agents, wholesalers and retailers. Generally speaking distribution channels in many industrial and business-to-business markets tend be direct or at least more direct than in consumer markets. Many products in industrial markets are buyer-specified rather than suppler-specified. That is, products are often a unique 'one-off' made specifically for the client from the client's own specifications, or are standard products which have been adapted in some way to meet the specific client's needs. In such cases products are manufactured or adapted and then delivered directly to the customer. In the case of products such as machine tools, they are often also installed and tested before being officially handed over to the client. That is not to say that marketing intermediaries are never used in industrial and other business-to-business markets. Products such as elec trical equipment and cable are often sold to the trade through a kind of wholesaler referred to in the United Kingdom as a 'factor', rather than being supplied direct from the manufacturer. Commercial vehicles and standard small machine tools such as drills and welding equipment and supplies are often marketed through agents or distributors sometimes on an exclusive basis. The three most common channel configurations are illustrated in Figure 9.1.

Direct distribution is less common in consumer markets particularly for fast-moving consumer goods (FMCG) such as packaged grocery. There has, however, been a move towards direct distribution within the consumer durable and consumer services sectors. For example firms such as Kitchens Direct allow consumers to order their fitted kitchen direct from the manufacturer rather than go through a retailers like MFI, B&Q or Wickes. Direct

---

Fig 9.1 Example of different channel configurations

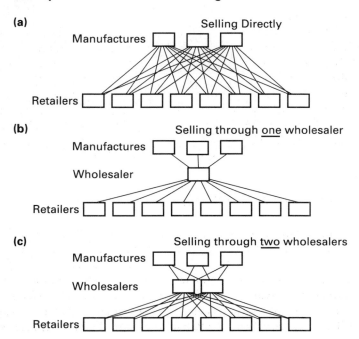

distribution has also developed at a remarkable pace within the UK financial services sector. First Direct, now a subsidiary of the Bank of Scotland led the way by offering consumers low-cost insurance by telephone. This use of direct telephone marketing has now spread throughout the financial services sector and it is now possible to order a pension, a mortgage or even open a conventional bank account by telephone directly with the supplier or provider. Direct distribution of goods has also been pioneered in the United Kingdom by such companies as Avon Cosmetics and Betterware who market household cleaning and maintenance products. The growth in what is often referred to as 'network' marketing or 'multi-level' marketing (MLM) has also accelerated the use of direct distribution. A good example is the company Kleeneze which uses the MLM approach applied to a team of independent, self-employed agents and distributors at various managerial levels within the MLM hierarchy. Kleeneze is perhaps the most successful firm of its kind within the UK. The decision to use direct or indirect distribution is usually based on cost factors, taking into consideration the following:

1 the number of potential customers in the market;
2 how concentrated or dispersed they are;
3 how much each will buy in a given period;
4 costs associated with the practical side of the distributive operation, including transport, warehousing and stockholding.

Selling direct through an employed sales force is viable when there is a large enough potential sales volume. Industrial goods manufacturers tend to use direct selling and direct delivery, although many use wholesalers or factors. Consumer goods manufacturers generally use a network of marketing intermediaries because of the dispersion and large numbers of potential customers. Most often, manufacturers will sell to wholesalers who break bulk, mark-up and sell to retailers. It is common nowadays for manufacturers to sell direct to large multiples, particularly in the packaged grocery market. Whichever method is used, the important point is that the manufacturer relies on these middlemen for ultimate marketing success, since they have the responsibility of taking the product to the ultimate consumer.

Activity

What do you understand by the term 'multi-level marketing'?. Using examples distinguish between the use of multi-level marketing systems such as those employed by the Kleeneze group, to direct agent distribution such as that used by Avon Cosmetics Ltd.

Multi-level marketing is a form of distribution which uses a hierarchical 'cascade' of agent and distributors. Many people are suspicious of this form of arrangement as it evokes thoughts of 'pyramid selling' which is illegal in the United Kingdom. Basically an agent is recruited by another practising agent and then sells the product door-to-door usually using catalogues posted through the door and then following these up in an attempt to secure an order. The agent can make money by selling products 'retail' by this method. However, the real money is made by recruiting further agents who in turn go out selling 'retail'. The commissioning agent gets a percentage of their sales revenue as well as his or her own retail selling commission. If agents at this second level also recruit further agents, the agent at the first level also gets commission from their sales also. Eventually, if all goes well, the original agent concentrates on managing the network of agents and gives up selling retail himself/herself. A successful agent may receive commissions from literally hundreds of agents at different levels in the multi-level marketing structure. Like many marketing innovations, multi-level marketing originated in the United States where today it is a very successful and very popular distribution system.

Direct marketing using dedicated agents door-to-door, on the surface seems very similar to multi-level marketing, but in fact it is a much simpler form of distribution. There is no building up of a hierarchical team of agents and no cascading-down stream of commissions from various levels within the system. Direct marketing systems such as that used by Avon Cosmetics is a sort of precursor of multi-level marketing in that they only use the first level.

9.4 **The Nature of Distribution**

The nature of channels of distribution is often subject to considerable change over time, and such change is often slow and barely noticeable. At least this has been true in the past. There is now evidence that the rate of change is accelerating over time, as new channels for products and services are being developed all the time. Consider the explosion in the range of goods offered for sale in petrol stations within the UK. There is also the growth in availability and popularity of television shopping, particularly in the United States where it now forms the major channel for some goods and services. Because of the changing nature of channel formats over time and the introduction of completely new formats, often due to technological developments, marketing management must continually scan the business environment and try to identify likely changes and developments and act upon their research in order to stay competitive. Consider the likely impact of shopping on the Internet over the next 25 years as more and more households get 'wired up' to use the new technology.

The rationale for choosing one channel system design over another is its superior effectiveness in assisting the distribution of product from the producer to the final customer. Marketing management tend to think of this process in terms of the concept of 'flow'. Product 'flows' through the distribution 'pipeline' rather as water might flow through a pipeline distribution system. As with the water system, products too can face blockages and other problems which may hinder the free flow of goods. This idea of flow within marketing channels is illustrated in Figure 9.2.

A firm does not tend to change its channel policy very often. Setting up a distribution arrangement, particularly if the arrangement is selective or exclusive, requires extensive discussion, negotiation and legal agreements. Because such arrangements are often relatively long-term in nature, they are classed as strategic rather than tactical or operational decisions, for the following reasons:

1 Channel decisions have a direct effect on the rest of the firm's marketing activities. For example, the selection of target markets is affected by, and in turn affects, channel design and choice.
2 Once established, the channel system may be difficult to change, at least in the short term. Because the optimal channel arrangements for a given product are likely to change over time, albeit relatively slowly, manufacturers need continually to monitor the distributive environment and reassess their existing channel structure with a view to exploiting and capitalising on any changes.

The actual word 'channel' is derived from the French word for canal. In marketing terms this can be interpreted as meaning the route taken by products as they flow from their point of production to points of intermediate and final use. Marketing is the primary factor in a continuous cycle that starts and finishes with the needs and want of consumers. Marketers must identify the needs and want of potential consumers and then organise the organisation's resources to produce goods and services that meet or exceed the desires and expectations of customers. On completion of the manufac-

Fig 9.2   The 'flows' in marketing channels

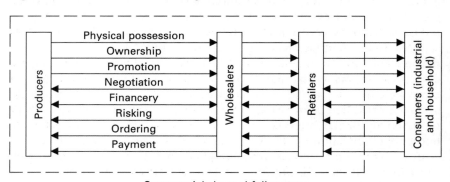

Commercial channel full system

turing process, the finished product is moved through an often complex system of marketing intermediaries and finally in to the hands of consumers. Channels of distribution provide a means whereby the product can be made available to consumers and this availability itself provides value in the form of time and place utility.

9.5 **Strategic Elements of Channel Choice**

The degree of market exposure sought by the company dictates the formulation of channel policy and how many marketing intermediaries are used. Choice of channel strategy will depend on a number of factors including the nature of the product or service, the technical complexity of the product and/or its servicing arrangements and the desired perceived image the marketing firm wishes to portray in the minds of consumers. Three distribution strategies can be distinguished:

1 An intensive distribution strategy is used by producers of convenience goods and certain common raw materials aiming to stock their products in as many outlets as possible. The dominant factor in the marketing of such products is their place utility. Producers of pens, cigarettes and confectionery try to enlist every possible retail outlet, ranging from multiples to independent corner shops. With such products, every exposure to the customer is an opportunity to buy, and the image of the outlet used is not a significant factor in the customer's impression of the product.

2 Exclusive distribution to recognised official distributors will enhance the prestige of a product and develop a high-quality brand image. Exclusive distribution, a policy of granting dealers exclusive rights to distribute in a certain geographical area, is often used in conjunction with a policy of exclusive dealing, where the manufacturer requires the dealer not to carry competing lines, as in car dealerships. By granting exclusive distribution, the manufacturer gains more control over intermediaries regarding price, credit and promotion policies, greater loyalty and a more aggressive selling effort.

3 Selective distribution lies somewhere between the extremes just described. Instead of spreading its marketing effort over the whole range of possible outlets, the manufacturer concentrates on the most promising of profitable outlets only. Selective distribution is also used where the facilities, resources or image of the outlet can have a direct impact on customers' impressions of the product, as in the case of expensive brands of perfume. Some products may require certain storage and marketing facilities, for example frozen food intermediaries must have adequate deep freeze display facilities.

Activity

What kind of distribution strategy might you choose for a high-priced, reasonably prestigious brand of perfume?

Products can be viewed as a 'bundle of attributes' in the minds of consumers. Some of these attributes are real such as colour, weight, taste and so on. Many will be implied by using packaging, branding, pricing and distribution. Choice of distribution channel can have a significant effect on the perceived quality and value of a brand. There are some perfumes that are so prestigious that they cost literally thousands of pounds for a few ounces. Such products are usually purchased by the very rich and are to be found in exclusive outlets in major cities such as Paris. This activity asks you to consider an appropriate distribution strategy for a reasonably prestigious brand of perfume. There are many such brands that spring to mind but perhaps the most universally recognized prestige brand is Chanel No. 5 perfume, which is popular all over the world. Chanel have decided to use selective distribution for this particular product. The perfume is positively high priced in line with the desired brand image, and a lot of attention is paid the packaging of the product which includes the glass container, label and outer packaging. It is advertised in appropriate publications as a luxury, prestige product. The brand is not as expensive as some of the exclusive Paris perfumes, in fact it is positioned at the top end of the 'popular' perfume market. You will not see it for sale in Kwik Save or other limited line discount stores because they would not maintain the correct positioning for the product. You will see it for sale in stores that have a facility for the demonstration and selling of cosmetics; such stores range from Boots to Harrods.

Changing channel systems

Individual changes in channels may be very small, but cumulative change can be very significant. Like many other areas of our lives the speed of change within many channel systems seems to be accelerating. We discussed earlier the tremendous growth in the use of direct marketing channels by companies such as First Direct and Kleeneze. A period of approximately ten years, from the mid-1980s to the mid-1990s saw what can only be described as a revolution in the distribution of financial products and services. The next change in distribution channel systems is already underway, although at present few people in Europe realise it. The potential magnitude of this development is in the way they are likely to order and receive goods and services. The technology driving this change is based on the fibre-optic cable which provides many thousands of communication channels which can be used simultaneously. The United Kingdom is currently in the process of being 'wired up' with such optical fibre cables being fed into every home, businesses and other establishments such as hospitals and public sector offices.

The Internet and world wide web (WWW) is the latest marketing tool. In the USA cable television shopping channels are very popular and well-developed; orders can be placed via a television hand-set and the goods are delivered to the customer's door. Payment is by tapping in a credit card number to a hand-set, or by ringing toll free (an 0800 number in the UK) to order and give the credit card details. Cable television and satellite television are allowing such shopping channels to be established in Europe. Technical forecasters and 'futurologists' are fairly certain that 'web site' technology is going to be an even bigger marketing tool than cable and satellite television. The world wide web is currently growing by about 40 per cent compound a month. All kinds of organisations, from universities advertising courses to banks advertising mortgages and personal equity plans (PEPS), are using the WWW to create the direct marketing channel of the next century.

As mentioned earlier, when planning long-term channel strategy companies need to monitor such change and attempt to anticipate future macro-developments. It is no use waiting for things to change and then be forced to react to such changes in an attempt to catch up with competitors. To gain a strategic competitive edge a firm must embrace change and if possible be a part of that change. It needs to be at the centre of things influencing events in its favour and not be merely a passive bystander watching others forge ahead into a more competitive future.

Change occurs at all levels, but it is perhaps most noticeable at retail level where significant changes in practice have occurred over the past 30 years. This period has seen an increasing polarity in the turnover distribution of retail firms. At one end of the spectrum are the very large-scale operators: multiples, discount chains and the Co-operative movement. At the other end there are still a large number of small shops, some completely independent and others linked to wholesalers. Generally speaking, in the UK during the period 1950 to date, the actual number of shops has declined with an increased concentration of market-share in the hands of a relatively small number of large multiples. This concentration is particularly marked in the grocery sector with the large multiples holding a 66 per cent market share in 1979. In general, the large multiples have grown at the expense of Co-operatives, independents and other small multiples.

Activity

How do you see the development of 'non-stop' shopping developing over the next ten year period?

This is a very interesting question and the answer will depend on a number of factors. The first thing to discuss is the nature of shopping itself. People go shopping for a variety of reasons not simply to obtain a certain product or service. If we take the big out-of-town shopping centres such as Meadowhall in Sheffield or the Metro Centre in Tyneside, shopping is an occasion, an experience even a leisure pursuit. The first question to answer then is how popular will non-shop shopping become? Do we really want to buy all our goods and services from the Inernet, from catalogues or from television shopping channels? Has shopping become simply another chore to get done in the simplest way possible? Is shopping more than just obtaining goods? People go shopping for a complex array of psychological and sociological reasons and that there will always be a need for people to engage in the physical act of shopping. In this sense the successful development of non-shop alternatives may be more limited than futurologists would have us believe. Looking at the technological trends it would seem that dedicated television shopping channels will grow in popularity over the next decade; such channels are very popular indeed in the United States and are growing in popularity in Europe with the increasing adoption of satellite television channels. Direct distribution systems such as multi-level marketing are also growing in popularity. The real technological breakthrough is of course the development of the world wide web. This system is still in the development stage as a distribution channel, but has enormous potential for the future.

The structure of industrial marketing channels

Industrial marketing channels are relatively complex structures with two basic components:

1 The placement of intermediary types in relation to each other;
2 The number of different intermediary levels or stages included in the channel.

Within industrial marketing, firms tend to use a more direct approach. Many products in industrial markets are 'buyer specified' rather than 'supplier specified'. This means that products are often made or at least modified to a particular customer specifications and such products are usually delivered direct to the customer. Manufacturers of machine tools and industrial vehicles make use of distributors and agents whilst manufacturers of such goods as electrical equipment make use of wholesalers, often referred to as 'factors'. Basically, the same principles of channel management apply as in consumer markets. The main difference between the two sectors is that generally speaking consumer markets use more channel layers in the distribution system than is the case in industrial markets.

Types and classification of channel

Marketing channels can be characterised according to the number of channel levels. The number of intermediaries involved in the channel operation determines on how many levels it operates. There are four main types of channel level existing in consumer markets as shown in Figure 9.3. The first three levels are quite straightforward. The three-level channel usually constitutes three intermediaries, a merchant wholesaler or 'jobber' who intervenes between the other two, the wholesaler and retailer. As mentioned in

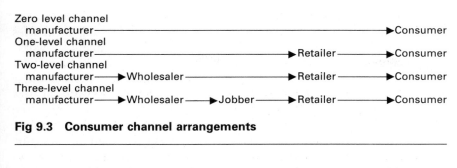

Fig 9.3 Consumer channel arrangements

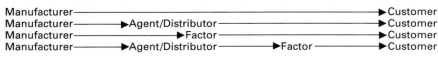

Fig 9.4 Industrial channel arrangements

the previous section industrial channels are usually more direct as Figure 9.4 demonstrates.

Many consumer markets are becoming more like those found in industrial markets. The trend in consumer markets seems to be a more direct form of marketing which often removes the need for any kind of middleman and allows the manufacturer or service provider to deal directly with the end-users. This trend has been particularly marked in the financial services industry. In the past if a customer wanted a financial product such as insurance, a mortgage or a personal equity plan (PEP) they would have probably visited a bank manager, an insurance broker, an estate agent or an independent financial adviser. Today it is possible for the customer to deal directly with the firm offering the financial product often by telephone or the world wide web. There seems to be less need for a complex array of intermediaries all taking their share of the mark-up. This form of direct distribution has allowed the providers of such financial products to improve their profit margins and at the same time reduce the cost of such products to customers and provide a more convenient and efficient service.

Channel conflict and co-operation

When the management of a manufacturing firm sets out to plan and design a distribution channel system for their products there are a number of factors they need to take into consideration. Channel strategy must be derived from overall marketing strategy. Because of the long-term, strategic nature of channel decisions, channel arrangements tend to be changed infrequently. This is all the more reason for the marketing firm to select marketing intermediaries with great care as the decision is likely to have a long-term effect. In planning a distribution system, management tries to achieve a smooth running system where all channel members are working together towards the same ends. Such relationships should be seen by all members of the channel team, at whatever level in the system, as being mutually beneficial. The reality is often quite different as we shall now examine. Channel members are often independent businesses and often have conflicting goals and aspirations. This often leads to tension, hostility and inefficiency within the channel system. This can be damaging commercially for all parties involved and not just for the original manufacturer.

Conflict

Each member of the marketing channel system should ideally be part of an integrated system. They should all be working together towards a common end which is profit through customer satisfaction. A manufacturer who does not deal directly with customers is placing the responsibility for commercial success in the hands of third parties (that is marketing intermediaries). These are usually independent firms with their own sets of aspirations, needs and wants. These are not always the same for every channel member and this can result in channel conflict. The overall channel system should be a set of interlocking and mutually dependent elements and it is in the interests of all the channel members for there to be a high degree of cooperation between each.

Channel conflict is a situation in which one member of a distribution channel system views another as an adversary. As a result such a channel member might act towards the perceived 'enemy' in a hostile way and may even attempt to cause commercial harm to this 'foe'. Such actions may upset the finely-tuned distribution structure and have adverse consequences for other members of the channel system; many of them are likely to be independent businesses in their own right. It might also have commercial consequences for the manufacturing firm which is relying on channel cohesion to achieve satisfactory distribution objectives. Conflicts in distribution channels may take different forms. Three conflict types are described as follows by Cespedes and Corly (1990):

1 **Horizontal conflict**   Horizontal conflict relates to marketing intermediaries who are at the same level in the channel system and of the same type, for example two cash-and-carry wholesalers working in the same town or two retail stores in the same area stocking a similar range of goods. This type of conflict is illustrated in Figure 9.5.
2 **Vertical conflict**   Unlike horizontal conflict which takes place amongst marketing intermediaries in the same level in the channel system, vertical conflict takes place amongst marketing intermediaries at different levels

Fig 9.5   Diagrammatic representation of horizontal conflict

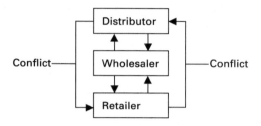

Fig 9.6   Diagrammatic representation of vertical conflict

or layers in the channel system. This type of conflict is potentially more damaging to the manufacturing firm as it can destroy the free flow of goods through the channel pipeline and cause a blockage which may have serious consequences for the commercial interests of the manufacturing firm and other channel members in all levels of the system. The principle of vertical conflict is illustrated in Figure 9.6.

3 **Intertype conflict**   'Intertype Conflict' refers to competition among different types of intermediary at the same level in the channel system. This sort of competition has increased in recent years especially with the growing practice among intermediaries of 'scrambled' merchandising, a practice which involves intermediaries dealing with products that were previously outside their normal product range. Intertype conflict can be seen as a sort of Darwinian evolution taking place among different sorts of channel intermediary at the same level within the channel system, for example cash-and-carry wholesalers verses conventional wholesalers. Over time the most profitable, most efficient and most popular type of channel configuration will emerge and dominate until further configurations evolve and compete against the established order of things, and the whole cycle starts all over again. This third type of channel conflict is illustrated in Figure 9.7.

Coordination

It is important that marketing channels are organised and coordinated in a proper manner. Without such coordination the activities within the overall

Fig 9.7   Diagrammatic representation of intertype conflict

---

channel system will not operate efficiently causing commercial problems to the manufacturer and the channel members themselves. Channel members are often independent businesses that have to make a profit to survive and consequently have commercial needs and wants of their own which need to be taken into consideration. The long-term objective of channel management is to achieve the maximum level of service for final customers in the most efficient manner. At the same time this has to be achieved in such a way that individual channel members, often independent businesses themselves, can obtain commercial returns which are satisfactory to them and which adequately compensate them for their contribution to the efficiency of the channel system as a whole.

Once marketing management has identified their target market and desegregated segments from these target markets, and established the marketing mix to produce the right kind of goods and services for them, they must then decide how and where these products and services can be made available for consumption by customers in the most efficient manner and in a way that fits in with the rest of the company's marketing strategy in terms of company and individual brand image. Lancaster and Massingham (1993) recommend four major steps in the coordination process. The first is to determine the level of service outputs demanded by the final users of the channel system. The second is to determine the level of service outputs and which channel members have the capability to perform the necessary tasks. The third step in the coordination process is to determine which strategies should be used to bring about the required results. The fourth step is concerned with possible channel conflict which we have already discussed. Figure 9.8 clearly identifies four major steps which represent the coordinative process.

Ideally, channel members should attempt to plan their objectives together so that they are mutually beneficial, avoid harmful and potentially unprofitable arguments and conflicts, and work together as a harmonious integrated system. A channel system as a whole should aim to add value by way of exploiting a 'synergistic dividend'. Synergism is a phrase often used in strategic planning which refers to certain situations where the sum of all the parties acting together produces an effect greater than simply adding up the effects of each individual component part working in isolation. Channel members should attempt to coordinate their objectives, plans and activities with other intermediaries in such a way that the performance of the total distribution system to which they belong and play an important role, is

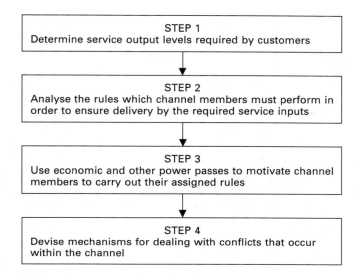

Fig 9.8   Stages in the channel coordination process

enhanced. In reality such cooperation among channel members is rare; there seem to be two principal reasons for this:

1 Channel members are often independent businesses that have to make a profit to survive. They are too busy looking after their own affairs to pay attention or even to care about what goes on in other different levels of the channel system.

2 Channel members tend to only show any real interest and concern in those other channel members that impact directly on their business for example those intermediaries immediately above and below themselves in the channel system from whom the buy and to whom they sell.

   The concept of a unified integrated channel system is thus more of an idealised theory than a practical reality. Channel members do not on the whole function as components of a well-ordered system. Quite to the contrary, in fact, they tend to behave as independent businesses and have little regard for other members of the channel system unless they immediately impact on their own business affairs. This is what makes the day-to-day management of any channel system such a managerial challenge.

9.6 Changes in the Structure of Retailing

The dynamic nature of the changing business environment impacts on all marketing intermediaries at every level in the channel system. In Chapter 2 we examined the subject of Marketing and the Macro-environment, and saw how changes in the external business environment are largely, but not totally, outside the control of the individual firm and how these have an impact on the marketing policies and practices of the marketing organisation. Factors in the external environment, whether political, social, legal or technological, all have a consequence for a firm's future marketing actions. These external environmental factors are driven by many complex interrelating forces which bring about change. Sometimes the resulting change is quick and dramatic, for example the unification of Germany after the fall of the Berlin Wall. Usually change takes place at a slower pace, in fact so slow that it is imperceptible and can only be appreciated in retrospect. Nothing illustrates this principle more than the changes that have taken place within the retail environment over the last 30 years.

The 'wheel-of-retailing'

This concept refers to evolutionary changes in retailing. The wheel appears to be turning with ever-increasing speed with each retailing innovation taking less time to achieve maturity. It took around 50 years for department stores to reach maturity, supermarkets took around 25 years, and hypermarkets and now megastores only 10 years. This concept can be compared to Charles Darwin's theory of evolution which states that a changing environment leads to adaptation and hence evolution. Environmental changes that have occurred which have caused this evolution can be summarised as follows:

- Economic factors have compelled retailers to increase their scale of operation in order to achieve economies of scale in both size of establishments and buying power. This has resulted in retailing hypermarkets and megastores. Retailing has also become more concentrated with only a small number of retail multiples controlling over 70 per cent of fast-moving consumer goods (FMCG) trade.
- Resale price maintenance (RPM) was abolished in 1964 by the Resale Prices Act and this practice meant that retailers had to sell at manufacturer-stipulated prices with the threat of having supplies withheld. Prior to 1964, protection was afforded to small retailers from price competition from growing organisations like Cohen Stores (which later became TESCO). Indeed Cohen Stores, it has been contended, deliberately sold at below manufacturers' stipulated prices, with a subsequent cutting-off of supplies, for the publicity of 'selling too cheaply'. As a result of the restriction of having to sell at manufacturers' stipulated prices, retailers relied on non-price competition, resulting in the level of personal service in many stores being higher than needed. Customers might have preferred to sacrifice service in the interests of lower prices. With the abolition or RPM and bigger stores going for cut prices as the principal

medium of attraction, many smaller shops went out of business together with a number of the wholesalers who supplied such outlets. Multiples expanded into the freed-up market, and used their purchasing economies to compete on price, passing savings on to customers. This led to the self-explanatory phrase: 'Pile it high, and sell it cheap'. Thus, multiples expanded at the expense of independents. At the same time, the Co-operative movement, although being collectively large enough to take advantage of this environmental change, was too slow to react, principally as a result of having too many individual democratically-controlled societies (Co-operative retail societies which were owned by members who shopped there) each with their own management structure. There was no centralised control so it was not possible to impose policy from the centre to take advantage of this environmental opportunity. The irony is that it was Co-operative stores that pioneered the notion of self-service during the Second World War to free up labour to help in the war effort, but they failed to capitalise on this saving at the end of the war and reverted to personal service.

- Selective employment tax (SET) was a tax on selected occupations which was introduced in 1966. Retail shop workers were seen as being 'non-productive' so a tax of 7 per cent was imposed on employers with a view to encouraging companies to automate to save labour costs. As labour became more expensive, capital investment became comparatively cheaper and many retailers were attracted to labour-saving checkout systems which gave more impetus to the introduction of self-service. These large capital investments meant that operators needed a faster turnover and the consequence was that the shelf-life of consumer goods became shorter. Multiple chain retailers of fmcg produce were able to sell fresher merchandise which fact they exploited in their advertising, so this tax indirectly helped them to expand at the expense of independents.

Growth of multiples

As has been explained, multiples have been able to eliminate wholesalers from commercial transactions through central buying direct from the manufacturers, in effect acting as their own wholesalers. Bulk purchases have meant advantageous prices from producers, whilst independents have still to purchase through wholesalers, so there are immense difficulties for small retailers in terms of price competitiveness. Some groups of wholesalers attempted to counteract this growing competition from multiples by setting up their own groupings called 'voluntary groups', and here retailers were invited to affiliate and display the group's logo and accept the rules of operation. Notably, Spar is still a successful voluntary group operator nowadays, but many groups have now ceased to trade in the light of competition from the larger multiples.

The 1970s witnessed the introduction of 'economy' lines by multiples. These were no-frills products which carried no advertising or promotion and were wrapped in plain factual containers. To a large extent this exacerbated the 'pile it high and sell it cheap' image of the multiples.

However, during the early 1980s retailing witnessed the introduction of own-label products which were brands commissioned by particular multiple chains from manufacturers, and which bore the chain's own logo. Specifications on such products meant that they had to be perceived as being amongst the best of traditional branded lines; not to be associated with economy-line products of the 1970s. The first multiple to do this was Sainsbury's, with others quickly following. The outcome has been that power in retailing has passed from manufacturers' brands to retailers' own-label brands. The problem for manufacturers was that they would in effect become the production arm of the multiples with no power in the market-place in terms of heavily branded products. Many producers resisted this move to own-label by refusing to supply. However, such was the purchasing ability of multiples that very few manufacturers still refuse to supply with notable exceptions being Kelloggs and Nestlé. These producers make a virtue of not supplying own-label by clearly stating in their promotion that they do not manufacture products for anyone else. However, despite these exceptions, in the UK (unlike many other countries) power within retailing has moved from manufacturers to retailers.

'One-stop' shopping

The motor car is the principal reason for the fact that customers tend to shop less frequently, with once a week or longer periods between shopping trips becoming the norm. Shopping is also becoming more of a family occasion, especially amongst the middle classes, so that many husbands along with other members of the family tend share in this task. This has accounted for the growth of out-of-town shopping centres where most of a family's needs can be bought within the same complex. It is not uncommon to see that the well-known multiples are set up in certain centres with a number of satellite establishments supplying goods they do not market. Such stores tend to be hypermarkets or megastores and the principal reason why this trend might slow down is because of planning restrictions and a recognition that such out-of-town centres will lead to the decay of traditional town centres.

As well as increased mobility, most people own freezers which enables them to transport and store large quantities of frozen food. Increased ownership of microwave cookers has also increased sales of 'instant' meals, many of which are cooked from frozen.

A final point related to the growth of one-stop shopping is the movement in population from urban to suburban centres. Congestion in towns discourages car drivers who prefer to shop in large out-of-town establishments where parking is convenient and normally free.

Activity

Has the concept of one-stop shopping reached its natural limit in terms of development, or can it go further? If it has further to go, how do you see its future development?

Over the last 30 years or so we have witnessed the growth of one-stop shopping in hypermarkets. These stores have been concerned mainly with grocery products. Basically we can now go to any of the large multiple retail stores such as Asda and carry out, say, one month's total grocery shopping all under one roof. This is a one-stop grocery shop, and the idea seems to be developing for shopping as a whole. In the United States we have seen the development of stores such as Sears where it is possible to buy virtually anything in one store. America has also been at the forefront of shopping-mall development where there is a wide range of different shops in an enclosed 'mall'. In the United Kingdom we have seen the development of very large out-of-town retail developments such as Meadowhall near Sheffield. Despite the worries expressed by certain town planners about the decimation of conventional town-centre shopping, these huge shopping 'cathedrals' point the way to future developments. The exact course of such developments is difficult to predict, but worldwide retail trends seem to point to the Meadowhall-type model.

Scrambled merchandising

The consumption of food products in an industrialised society is relatively income-inelastic, in that customers do not buy more food when they have more money. They tend to 'trade up' to better quality foods. Multiples have consequently diversified into non-food items to advance their turnover and profits. Many now sell clothing, electrical goods, plants and flowers and have extended their traditional range of food products. A number have, however, become even more diversified (for example, gone into publishing) and recently some have moved back to their core business of food retailing because of a confusion of image associated with retailing extraneous products.

Franchising

This is a system of selling and distribution organised through a contract between a principal seller (franchiser) and distributive outlets (owned by franchisees). It is sometimes referred to as 'business format' franchising.

Such a scheme depends on the franchiser having an idea, a name, a 'secret process' or specialised equipment or goodwill that will be attractive to customers. If this is the case, then the franchiser will grant the franchisee a licence, for some kind of commercial consideration, for the franchisee to exploit that name, idea or product. Such a licence agreement might include rules for operating the business which might be a royalty, an initial fee, a share of profits, the obligation to make bulk purchases from the franchiser, to abide by certain 'rules' of hygiene and presentation possibly involving training, and many more considerations depending on the type of product or service being considered.

The business format franchise was developed in America, but it has increased in strength in the UK since the early 1960s. It is a contract between a franchiser and each independently-owned establishment of the franchisee. The franchiser's brand and reputation is used for marketing a product or service and the support received by the franchisee from the franchiser will depend on the initial agreement. The contract is usually written so as to minimise the risks in opening a business. What attracts new franchisees is that others have successfully followed the 'blueprint'. The larger franchiser supplies the franchisee with a business package or 'format', a trade name and specific products or services for sale. Examples of such franchise agreements are Dynorod, Little Chef and Mister Minit.

Miscellaneous

There has been a growth in other forms of selling over the past 30 years including:

- Party Plan is popular for products like cosmetics, kitchen-ware, jewellery and linen. A 'party' is organised, usually in the home of a hostess who invites friends, and then receives a 'consideration' in the form of cash or goods based based upon what they purchase.
- Door-to-door direct selling is relatively expensive, but wholesaler and retailer margins are eliminated. As long as the salesperson can build up a regular list of clients for relatively frequently purchased items then it can be successful. Avon Cosmetics and Betterware are two examples of companies who are successful in this respect.
- Automatic vending has grown a lot since the 1960s and is now used for beverages, cigarettes, chocolate, and many other products. Vending machines are placed in convenient locations like bus stations, colleges, public houses and factories. They have been used since the 1950s to provide entertainment through juke boxes and more recently arcade games. Cash-dispenser machines are relatively new and in addition to dispensing cash they can answer balance inquiries, take requests for statements and cheque books and accept deposits.
- Mail order business is through catalogue or non-catalogue sources. The first relies on expansive catalogues to obtain sales, sometimes using

agents to deal with order-collection and administration for a commission. Products can be purchased interest-free and extended credit terms are available. There are some specialist mail order houses that deal with a limited range of lines that are difficult to access in shops (for example clothes for very large people). Non-catalogue mail order depends on press and magazine advertising and is often used to sell a limited range of products.

- Other direct marketing techniques include using direct mail, where a promotional letter and instructions on ordering are sent through the post. Such methods are used by book and record clubs. Television can also be used with orders often being placed by a telephone call to a free number with the request for the quotation of credit card details to an answering machine. Telephone ordering is sometimes combined with press advertising, especially in colour supplements.
- Television shopping via on-line computer is still at an early stage, but it should become more popular if companies invest enough in the development of appropriate software and hardware. This very direct form of retailing is economical as orders are often placed direct with manufacturers.
- The world wide web (WWW) on the Internet is a medium that encourages customers to search for the seller rather than the other way round. Academics working in this area now talk about the 'virtual value chain' and the 'market space' rather than the conventional marketplace. The WWW is still in its infancy as a marketing tool but it is growing in importance, particularly in the area of marketing communications.

9.7 Summary

The overall subject of distribution is made up of two separate but interrelated components, channels of distribution and physical distribution management. Physical distribution management, which forms part of the wider subject of 'logistics management' is covered in Chapter 10. In this chapter we have concerned ourselves with channels of distribution which refer to an often complex arrangement of agents, wholesalers and retailers through which marketing firms move products and services to their intended point of purchase. The correct choice of channel is of vital importance to the commercial success of any company. A strategic, competitive advantage can be gained from such choices. When examining the flow of products or services through a distribution channel system it is useful to use an analogy and think of the distribution system as a pipeline. The pipeline has the main pipes, subsidiary pipes, free flow and blockages. In consumer markets marketing channels can be made up of a complex array of marketing intermediaries. In some situations direct marketing is used which aims to cut out the middle-man from the system. In industrial marketing channels direct distribution is much more common especially when the products being ordered by the customer are 'buyer specified' rather than 'supplier specified'. Wholesale-type firms are used in industrial distribution channels although they are often referred to as 'factors'. Likewise, industrial marketing firms also make use of agents and distributors just as do their counterparts in consumer markets. Overall, the subject of channels is a major marketing subject and together with physical distribution forms a major area of strategic marketing management.

Chapter Review Questions

Explain the 'wheel of retailing' concept.
The wheel of retailing concept is similar in many ways to the idea of the product life-cycle, but it is applied to retail configurations and formats rather than products. Basically the idea is that retail formats evolve and change over time and in this sense have a life-cycle.

Under what conditions might you choose to employ a selective distribution strategy?
There are many possible conditions under which you might decide to employ a selective distribution policy. The product may require special storage facilities so you only allow distributors with these facilities to stock it. Another would be if the product required a particular skill or expertise to demonstrate and market it effectively, staff may require a certain type of product training and so on. It could also be that you want the type of distribution channel to reflect the type of brand image you have carefully built up for your product so you only distribute to selective channels.

Explain the term 'retail concentration'.
Retail concentration refers to a measure indicating how many separate retail firms control the retail market. In the packaged, branded grocery market for example, three or four of the major players such as Sainsbury's and Asda have the bulk of the market-share.

What do you understand by the term 'non-shop shopping'.
Consumers today can shop for many goods and services without actually visiting a real shop. Typical examples of non-shop shopping are ordering goods by mail order, ordering from a satellite television shopping channel, and ordering goods via the Internet or world wide web.

Do you agree that channels of distribution and physical distribution (business logistics) are two separate but interrelated business areas?
Channel management is concerned with the selection and management of marketing intermediaries and final channel selection and management. Physical distribution is concerned with all of the processes that get the final product to the point of purchase; this involves materials handling, stock control, transport, warehouse location and design among other things. Both management areas are concerned with providing time and place utility or value for the final customer. It is true that the overall subject of distribution can be divided into two component parts for the purposes of study, but from a management point of view channel decisions and logistics decisions must be made in relation to one another.

10 Logistics Management

As we mentioned in Chapter 9, from a marketing standpoint the subject of distribution management is divided into two separate but closely interrelated subject areas – channels of distribution and physical distribution management. Having carefully chosen a network of intermediaries who will take over the management of goods as they move along the channels of distribution, the company next has to think about how these goods can be efficiently transferred from the manufacturer to the consumer. This activity falls within the scope of an area of management known as physical distribution management (PDM), which is a critical area of overall marketing management owing much to the adoption of logistics from the military. However, the term physical distribution management is somewhat outdated. Today the subject is often referred to as 'total business logistics' management. This technique is concerned with far more than simply delivering finished products to customers in an efficient manner. It is actually a total system which starts with sourcing and finishes with how transport for outward delivery is planned. In fact logistics management is concerned with the entire process of obtaining materials from suppliers, storing, processing, retrieving and delivering them to the customer.

10.1 Scope of Logistics Management

As we have said, logistics management is concerned with more than just transport. It covers every stage of the physical distribution process, from raw materials and component parts being ordered and delivered to the factory, materials handling and storage, stock control, sales forecasting from which the forecasts of individual components parts, transport and storage requirements are derived, order processing, the purchasing and replenishment of stock, packing, delivery, achievement of set service levels, warehouse location, fleet management and scheduling, and the management and operation of a logistics information system which acts as a recording system, aids forecasting, scheduling, model building and produces the myriad of documentation needed for the efficient management of the system.

Marketing has many definitions, one of them being the process of getting the right goods to the right place at the right time. This is an over-simplistic definition but in a way it encapsulates the importance of time and place. We stated in Chapter 1 that it is the mission of the marketing-orientated firm to produce goods and/or services that satisfy the needs and wants of specifically defined target markets more efficiently and effectively than competitors. Products can be viewed at a 'bundle of attributes', many of which are implied attributes created by branding, packaging and advertising. The core product or service is just a part of the total product offering. In order for the value of goods and services to be fully realised they need to be available to customers and consumers at the right place and at the right time.

What the right place and the right time is will of course depend on the nature of the product or service. The importance of time and place will also depend on the nature of the product or service and the situation or occasion in which they are used. For example, if we walk into a public house or a cafe for a drink of beer, we expect the beer to be available there and then. A Christmas present really only has maximum value on Christmas day. If we order flowers by telephone to send to someone on Valentine's day they are of little use if they are delivered the day after. On the other hand, if we are ordering a new car from a showroom we may be prepared to place an order and wait several weeks in order to get exactly the car we want delivered from the factory in terms of colour, engine size, trim and other specifications. In the case of the Valentine's day flowers or the glass of beer, the time and the place of consumption form an intrinsic part of what the customer perceives to be the 'total product offering'. For other types of products and services time and place are less important. Hence, for some product and service categories time and place produce a great deal of value or utility to the consumer. Business logistics plays a key role in the creation and delivery of this notion of time and place utility.

Activity

Do you agree that customers take a holistic view of product and service offering and in fact see them as a total 'bundle of attributes'. Fully explain the reasons for your agreement or disagreement with this proposition.

You should start by defining the nature of a product or service. In particular you should examine the concepts of real, tangible product attributes and those that are less tangible and more implied to the customer through the use of marketing. An example or two here may well illustrate precisely the points that you are trying to get across. For example, Perrier water is basically water containing a few trace elements and minerals and some natural carbonated gas. However, it is marketed as much more than a bottle of water. The implied attributes include sophistication, style, cleanliness, health and many other positive qualities. The shape and colour of the bottle, the brand name and design of the label, even the place where it is sold all contribute to the image the consumer has of Perrier. It is viewed holistically as a bundle of total product attributes. Having made your case through the use of examples you must now go on to agree or disagree with the notion in the light of the evidence you have examined.

In many industrial markets, factors such as stock availability and reliability of delivery are just as important, if not more important, than price. The speed at which a supplying firm can process an order and deliver goods to the necessary location at the required time with the desired level of reliability over the long term may well be the deciding factor in awarding a contract even if the supplying firm is less competitive on price. Different industrial sectors and segments have differing service sensitivities. The level of service offered by the supplying firm is often the key marketing variable in obtaining business. You can see from this example that logistics management is much more than simply managing transport and distribution. It can provide the marketing firm with a long-term competitive advantage and as such must be viewed for what it really is, a long-term strategic tool.

In order to be truly effective all of the functions within the logistics function must be fully integrated, which is what is at the heart of 'total business logistics'. Because the activities making up logistics management are often complex and highly specialised, they need to be managed by professional staff. To illustrate this, the use of fork-lift trucks, cranes, gantries and lifts can be a very dangerous business; such equipment forms the tools of materials handling, and its improper use can result in serious injury and damage or even death. Consequently, the people in charge of such operations must be fully qualified and professional.

Likewise, those in charge of transport must have technical expertise. The proper loading of vehicles, the securing of loads, the correct weight distribution of loads, the handling of dangerous and hazardous material all require specialised knowledge and expertise. No one would expect the marketing manager or marketing director, no matter how experienced, to be qualified in all of these specialist areas. Although it is becoming increasingly likely that senior marketing staff might have come from a physical distribution background, specialist staff will still be needed. It is not intended that marketing should dictate the day-to-day management policy of the logistics function. This should be left to those individuals who are qualified to make the correct decisions and judgements. However, because logistics has such an important long-term strategic dimension within marketing strategy it is necessary for overall logistics policy to emanate from senior marketing staff. Overall logistics decisions must form part of the overall strategic marketing plan. Logistics management does not operate in a vacuum, but has a vital, intrinsic part to play in the long-term marketing strategy of the firm.

Activity

Why in your opinion is it necessary for all of the functions making up logistics management to be fully integrated?

Customers do not necessarily differentiate between the various 'component parts' that go to make up a product or service offering. Research into consumer and organisational buyer behaviour has shown that customers view the product or service offering in its entirety, as a 'bundle of product attributes' some of which are real and tangible and some of which are implied and intangible. The total product or service offering is the result of the imaginative and creative formulation of an appropriate marketing mix. In a sense, the '4 Ps' of the marketing mix are put together in such a way as to create the desired product/service perception in the minds of specifically defined target markets or market segments. Logistics falls under the 'Place' heading of the marketing mix, and along with channel selection and management produces the time and place utility dimensions of the total product and/or service offering. The level of customer service which logistical activities provide is in turn unlikely to be 'split up' into its component parts such as materials handling, invoice processing, stock availability, delivery availability and so on. Each one of these elements, on their own, are of little importance to the customer. In fact the majority of customers, especially in consumer markets, are totally unaware and indeed care little for the plethora of logistical expertise that eventually brought their product or service to their point of consumption at the desired time. To have any real value as a business function logistical functions need to be fully integrated and form an intrinsic part of the rest of the marketing programme. In turn, the other marketing mix elements, along with logistics, must themselves be fully integrated if the overall marketing programme is to have any chance of achieving the desired commercial impact.

10.2 History and Development of Logistics Management

In the Second World War, the Korean war and Vietnam war, supplies officers were faced with the task of moving a diversity of materials across seas and continents. Marketing management saw that these skills could be applied to physical distribution management (PDM). Military planners had used the developing science of operations research, often involving sophisticated statistical and mathematical techniques, to work out logistical strategies, and such techniques have since enabled logistics managers to optimise operations in terms of time, materials cost and manpower. It was seen that distribution could be analysed and organised in a scientific way and this led to the development of business logistics. Wars are costly and the Second World War made the UK virtually bankrupt; the country had to rely on financial help from the United States to keep going during the war and to help it to reconstruct after the war. During the war, factories were converted to war production from civilian production as was illustrated in Chapter 1. Operational researchers and production planners realised that war production could be made more efficient through scientific organisation which maximised the use of scarce wartime resources, much of which had to be imported from overseas which was expensive in terms of money and in loss of life protecting British convoys. These new scientific techniques were applied to the distribution of war-time production, to where it was most needed during the conflict. This greatly reduced costs and increased the effectiveness of the war effort.

Staying with the military analogy, battles and wars have been lost, not because an army could not fight or because of lack of manpower or equipment, but often through lack of ammunition, lack of food and drink, or lack of blankets and warm clothing. It has been said that armies 'march on their stomachs', meaning that a well-fed army has the strength and endurance to fight. Without proper nourishment even the most skilled and highly trained army will eventually weaken. Likewise, it is no good having highly trained troops with the latest rifles if they are not constantly supplied with ammunition. It is often seemingly small things that matter in the success of military campaigns. Successful armies organise themselves to have a wide range of vital supplies in the right place at the right time, and get supplies there more effectively and efficiently than their enemies. They can thus seal a strategic, competitive advantage which may possibly decide or at least influence the outcome of the battle.

As with war, so with business which is a form of non-violent commercial warfare. Competitive firms are involved in the 'battle for the customer'. A firm's strategic objective may not be to take a hill or town from the enemy; strategic concerns are more likely to be market-share, turnover or profit margins. However, the principles are the same and the commercial battle for business is more likely to be won in the battlefield of the marketplace with the aid of effective logistical back-up than without such support.

With the increasing sophistication of marketing analysis has come a greater awareness of the costs of physical distribution. Businesses must aim to provide customer satisfaction in order to make profits, and to achieve this goods must be in the right place at the right time. There is a balance that must be struck between the costs of physical distribution and customer satisfaction. Greater levels of service usually mean greater costs and the balance is the task of physical distribution management.

PDM has also increased in importance as a marketing function because of the more demanding nature of the economic environment. Twenty years ago many companies held large stocks of raw materials and components, but today stocks are generally held to a minimum with the responsibility for carrying stock falling on the supplier. This move has been dictated by interest rates and the emphasis on an analytical approach by management, and its effect is felt throughout the marketing channel with each member committed to a high level of service.

Just-in-time management (JIT) has been widely adopted by companies with large purchasing power who impose stringent delivery conditions on their suppliers. This type of regime involves them carrying only a few hours' stock of raw materials which has to be replenished regularly in order to keep production running. They therefore demand a very high level of service from suppliers. JIT has been extensively taken up by the automotive industry, where very large companies need to operate strict delivery controls. They can make large financial savings in stockholding costs when JIT is employed.

The logistical process involves much more than merely transportation. PDM covers the movement of goods from the receipt of an order to actual delivery to the customer. It involves close liaison between the production planning department, the purchasing department, order processing, material control and warehousing. These areas must work together in order to serve the customer efficiently, without involving the company in any more cost than necessary.

Activity

In your opinion how valid is the analogy between military logistics and total business logistics? Explain your position by using specific examples to illustrate the points made.

This question should be answered by first of all explaining what is meant by the term military logistics. This is best illustrated by means of example. You can then go on and make the comparison between the role and importance of logistics in military campaigns and in commercial 'campaigns'. You need to compare and contrast the two situations and clearly state your opinions. In the 20th century, modern wars have been fought either globally, for example the First and Second World Wars, or in distant lands, for example the Korean War, Vietnam War, Falklands War and the Gulf War. In the Second World War the UK had severe resource constrains, so a great effort was expended in trying to find more efficient methods to organise inward transportation of raw materials, production of war supplies, usually munitions, and outward distribution of a whole range of products including rations for the troops fighting at the front line, ammunition and small arms, transport, bridges, clothing and a host of other materials. In the Falklands War the task was to get thousands of troops, aircraft, ammunition, food, fuel, hospital supplies and so on to virtually the other side of the world to fight a war. Again, this operation had to be meticulously planned using the latest operations research and management science techniques, aided this time by the use of powerful computers to carry out the millions of calculations required in the planning of operations.

Today many businesses are global and global competition is extensive. Component parts are often made throughout the world and then assembled in one particular country. Such products are marketed and distributed worldwide. In a sense, firms operating in the global marketplace really are at war with one another and are fighting for their very survival. The production and distribution complexities are just as difficult and important in today's commercial war as they have been in the past in military conflicts. The same basic principles apply and the scientific techniques that were used with such great effect in past military campaigns can be just as effectively employed in helping to solve logistical problems in peace time commercial 'conflicts'.

10.3 Definitions

As we have already discussed, modern management theory and practice takes a holistic approach to physical distribution management and today this managerial function is often referred to as 'total business logistics'. The five main elements are:

1 Order processing;
2 Stock levels/inventory;
3 Warehousing;
4 Transportation;
5 Service levels;

Business logistics management integrates these functions, ensuring each element is used to maximum effect towards a common objective. This is known as the systems approach to distribution management.

As PDM has a clearly defined scientific basis, we can now present some of the analytical methods which are employed by management when developing a logistics system. A clear understanding of the two core themes is important:

1 The attainment of an effective distribution system is based on solidarity of effort. The overall service aim can be achieved, even though it may look as if some individual elements of the system are not working to optimum efficiency.
2 The best service cannot be provided at the lowest cost, since costs increase with the level of service offered. After deciding on the level of service that should be offered to customers, the company must then explore ways of keeping costs to a minimum without jeopardising the agreed level of service.

10.4 The Distribution Process

This is initiated upon the receipt of an order by a supplier. The customer placing the order has no practical interest in how the supplier's distributive system is structured, nor in any problems the supplier might have in distribution terms. The customer's only concern is that the distribution system is effective, resulting in the goods ordered being in the right place at the right time. The period of time between the placing of the order and actual receipt of the goods is known as the lead time, and this varies for different types of products and type of market and industry. Two extreme examples are in the

shipbuilding industry where lead time is measured in parts or multiples of years, and the retail sector where days or hours are more prevalent measures. The JIT concept eliminates the idea of lead time.

The lead time quoted by the supplier is the base used by the customer when planning production. Customers do expect the quoted delivery time to be met, and suppliers not adhering to their quoted lead time run the risk of earning customer dissatisfaction.

Order processing

This is the first stage of the logistical process, and an effective order processing department has a direct influence on lead times. Orders come from the sales team via the sales department, arriving only rarely on an *ad hoc* basis, most companies preferring to build up regular supply routes with an efficient supplier which remain stable over a period of time. Contracts are frequently set up and regular repeat orders are made throughout the duration of the contract.

Fast and accurate order processing systems are essential in order that other departments in the company are aware of the order and can pass on rapid confirmation to the customer, along with an exact delivery time. A company's image depends upon a high level of office efficiency, and slow reaction to orders is an often overlooked route to ill-will and dissatisfaction. Effective order processing can make the difference when buyers are making decisions about their preferred suppliers.

Order processing has been made much more efficient by the use of computerised systems which allow automatic updating of stock levels and delivery schedules, thus accurately illustrating the sales position. Such accuracy is essential in the order processing department, but this must be combined with speed of processing.

Inventory

This is a critical area of PDM, since customer satisfaction depends on the company not running out of stock and being able to deliver orders. An optimum stock level must be operated whereby stock-out situations do not happen. However, stock levels should not be too high as this is costly to maintain. Techniques for ascertaining optimum stock levels are examined later in this chapter.

Stocks mean cost – the **opportunity cost** which exists through constant competition for the company's resources. If a high stock level has to be maintained then the profit contribution must be larger than the costs associated with carrying extra stock. Some companies may have to carry high stock levels to meet short lead times in a particular market, and these companies must look to reduce costs in other areas of the PDM mix.

Warehousing

Many firms dispatch goods direct to the customer from their own on-site warehouse. However, if a firm sells goods which are taken off regularly, but in small quantities, strategically located warehouses around the country may be used. Large retail chains use this type of system, in which goods are transported in bulk from manufacturer to retail warehouse, where stocks are stored before being distributed to individual stores belonging to the retail chain. Level of service and costs will increase with the number of warehouses used and, again, an optimum strategy should be laid down which enables operation of the desired level of service. The factors which must be taken into consideration are the location of customers, the size of orders, frequency of deliveries and desired lead times.

Transportation

This is usually the greatest cost in distribution, and is simply calculated according to numbers of units or weight. However, it must not be thought that management of the transportation function is an easy task, since costs must be carefully controlled and type of transport chosen, and these must be kept under review. Many companies now have transport managers, illustrating the importance of the PDM function.

Road transport, with its advantages of speed and door-to-door delivery, has become the most popular method of transportation over the past 50 years. Indeed, its flexibility is essential for many companies operating on low stockholding and short lead times. Some firms purchase their own vehicles instead of using sub-contractors where large volumes of goods are moving, although some very large retailers like Tesco, Sainsbury's and Marks and Spencer now leave all their warehousing and transportation to companies like BOC, Excel Logistics and Tibbett and Britain who are specialists in logistics.

Rail transport is often used when lead time is not of such paramount importance, or when attempting to bring down transport costs. Hazardous, or very bulky, goods are also often transported by rail, but it is also suitable for light goods which must be delivered quickly, for example letter and parcel post which use an integrated system of rail for transport over longer distances and then road for shorter distances.

Air transport is not widely used for distribution within the UK, although overseas long-distance routes do justify the cost. It is used for transporting goods which are highly perishable or valuable in relation to their weight. It also has the advantage of being less of a problem in terms of packaging as less is needed than for ocean transport, coupled with the fact that insurance premiums are less costly for air than for sea freight. Air freight is quite popular in the USA because of the great distances involved, and its use in export markets can be cost-effective.

An alternative method of transportation in export markets is the roll-on roll-off (RORO) cargo ferries. These serve the European and near-European markets, but 'deep sea markets' like Australasia and South America are served by traditional ocean-going freighters. This method of transportation has been made more effective with the development of containerisation.

Whatever mode of transportation is selected, goods should be protected during transit and this relates particularly to ocean transport where longer times and more robust handling methods mean that more protection is needed.

Service levels

If we aggregate the effects of the previous four elements of the logistics system then we arrive at the total output of the system; in the eyes of the customer this is the level of service they receive. As mentioned earlier, customers are likely to view the products and services that they buy in their entirety, in fact Lancaster's theory of demand takes the position that customers view products and services as a 'total bundle of attributes'. Stock availability, the speed at which purchase orders are processed, the stock control, storage, materials handling procedures employed, location of warehouses and delivery reliability are rarely examined by customers individually, even in industrial markets. The logistics component of the 'total bundle of product attributes' is seen as a particular level of service. Some customers or market segments are likely to attach varying levels of importance to the level of service they receive, and some will be more-service sensitive or 'service-elastic' than others. From this point of view, service sensitivity can be used by marketing management as a basis for market segmentation.

10.5 **A Systems Approach to PDM**

We have already emphasised that various marketing activities need to be combined to form a single marketing effort. Managers are now becoming more conscious of the potential of PDM and that logistical systems should be designed with the 'total' function in mind. A disconnected approach to PDM will result in a firm failing to provide satisfactory service and involve it in excessive costs. It should also be noted that within the PDM structure there will be possible conflict between individual managers aiming to achieve their personal goals to the detriment of the overall PDM objectives. For example, production managers will favour long production runs and standard products, whilst sales and marketing management will look towards high stock levels, special products and short production runs. At the same time, transport managers may want to lower costs by selecting a slower transportation method or waiting for a full load, and financial managers will prefer reduced inventory and dislike extensive warehousing networks. Each department may appear efficient when they realise their individual goals, but marketing strategy might not be effectively served.

Companies aim to provide customers with an acceptable level of service at optimal cost, and Burbridge (1987) has suggested how this might be achieved. Essentially, senior management must ensure that overall distribution objectives are communicated and understood throughout the management structure, making it clear that company objectives should be considered before departmental objectives. If senior management fails to make objectives clear, this can cause organisational problems when implementing the systems approach. This should encircle production and production planning, purchasing and sales forecasting, and involve the concept of total cost, where individual costs are held to be less important that the total cost. For example, the total cost of holding high stocks may look unacceptable, but if it enables the company to provide a service leading to higher sales and profits then the total cost of all the PDM activities will be justified.

PDM has now come to be recognized as a marketing tool in its own right. In a market where products are similar and price variations small, service counts as a major force in competition. It may even be possible to command a higher price for products which are always delivered on time. A sales-person in a company which provides a large spare parts and service facility for needy customers has an advantage in price discussions. It can therefore be seen that far from being merely an adjunct to marketing, distribution has a full place in the marketing mix and indeed is a fundamental part of marketing strategy. A well-coordinated business logistics system can help to discover marketing opportunities and improve the overall marketing mix.

Activity

Explain the 'total systems' approach to logistics management and examine how the position of the final output from such a system is perceived by potential and actual customers in 'level of service' terms.

In order to answer a question such as this you need to explain the concept of a system and the fact that most systems are made up of a number of sub-systems. The output from each sub-system contributes to the achievement of objectives for the system as a whole. Each sub-system must be fully integrated to achieve its individual objective. The objective for a logistics system is likely to be a particular level of customer service. You need to explain this service concept and how an integrated logistics system can help to deliver customer service. The marketing mix has been variously described over the years, but perhaps the most enduring and most widely used definition or 'model' is that of McCarthy's 4Ps. It is a somewhat simplistic model, but it serves its purpose. One of the 'Ps' is of course **place**. The place component is made up of two separate, but nonetheless highly interrelated sub-components, channels of distribution and business logistics which are sometimes still referred to as physical distribution management. The 4 Ps marketing mix system can and should be viewed as a total system. Many management scientists and managerial economists have been working on ways to optimise the marketing mix in terms of resources allocation and marginal return by using a systems approach. Each 'P' of the marketing mix can be viewed as a sub-system and treated in its own right. This system can then be split further; for example, the logistics system can be viewed as a system in its own right. The objectives set for each sub-system are not set in isolation, but in terms of how they contribute to the achievement of objectives for the marketing mix system as a whole. For example, the objective for a logistics system is likely to be a given level of customer service. This service level is likely to have been set by marketing management, as the level of service offered to customers is an intrinsic part of the product or service offering and hence an important marketing variable.

10.6 **Monitoring and Control of PDM**

Getting the right goods to the right place at the right time for least cost is the objective of PDM. The basis of monitoring and control is to provide definite measures of operational effectiveness, giving management objectives which point to criteria which allow useful assessment of performance.

The output of a physical distribution system

The level of customer service is the key output from any system of physical distribution and this is a competitive benefit that can be offered to customers to keep existing business or to attract new business. The level of service offered should be at least comparable to that of major competitors; it is often perceived as the time it takes to deliver a customer's order, or how many orders can be met from stock. Technical assistance, training and after-sales service is also involved. The two most fundamental areas are reliability and frequency of delivery and the ability to meet orders quickly from stock. If a company sets a service policy of delivering a certain percentage of orders within a set number of days from the receipt of the order, this is a useful and specific objective which offers strict criteria for evaluation. From this, a simple delivery delay analysis, showing number of orders received, days late and relating this to the percentage of total orders can be prepared, making it clear to management whether such objectives are being reached or whether any adjustment of service level is needed. This analysis can be updated upon receipt of a copy of the dispatch note, and will indicate any over or under-provision of service.

Elasticity of service

The cost of providing service is measured in time and money, especially in industrial markets where service can often take precedence over price when potential customers are deciding on a supplier. Companies operating JIT manufacturing are particularly conscious of this factor.

Marketing firms wishing to raise their service levels can face diminishing returns. Figure 10.1 shows a hypothetical example. Here, 80 per cent of the total possible service can be provided for about 45 per cent of the cost of 100 per cent provision. An increase of 10 per cent in general service levels means a cost increase of approximately 25 per cent.

For a company to offer 100 per cent service provision, every eventuality would have to be covered, which is costly. Maximum customer satisfaction and minimum distribution costs are not compatible and there has to be some compromise in other areas. This depends on the degree of service sensitivity or service elasticity in the particular market. Two industries which use the same product from the same supplier may have differing criteria for choosing that supplier. As an example, both the oil exploration and the sugar processing industries use large high pressure 'on-line' valves in their processes. The oil industry is highly service-sensitive because of the very high cost of operations and potential breakdowns, and therefore price is not as important as service, whereas the sugar processing industry is more price sensitive. Much of the processing is done within two months, and as long as service levels are adequate to avoid disruption during this period they can be given a lower priority for the rest of the year.

Fig 10.1   An illustration of possible diminishing returns to service level provision

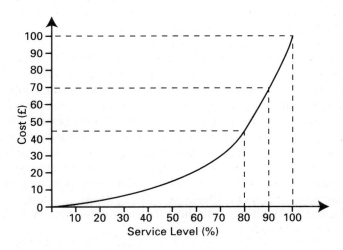

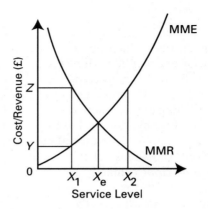

Fig 10.2   Service level versus cost/revenue

Service levels should be increased to the point where marginal marketing expense equals marginal marketing response. This follows the economist's profit maximization criterion of marginal cost being equal to marginal revenue. Figure 10.2 illustrates this point. The marginal expense (MME) of level of service provision X_1 is Y, and the marginal revenue (MMR) is Z. It would pay the firm to increase service levels since the extra revenue generated by the increased services (MMR) is greater than the cost (MME). At service level X_2, however, the marginal expense Z is higher than the marginal revenue X – service provision is too high. Clearly, the theoretical point of service optimisation is where the marginal marketing expense and the marginal marketing response are equal, at service level X_e.

Inventory management (stockholding)

Inventory gives cover against what may happen tomorrow. Inventory is kept to increase profitability with the support of manufacturing and marketing. Manufacturing support comes through two types of inventory, that of the materials for production, and that of spare and repair parts for maintaining production equipment. Marketing support is provided through an inventory of the finished products, and of spare and repair parts which support the products. Stocks are accumulated because supply and demand cannot be perfectly coordinated, and because of the uncertainty of future demand and reliability of service. They ensure that raw materials, spare parts and finished goods are available when needed.

Inventories are kept because they act as a 'hedge' against such events as unexpected demand or machinery failure. They can assist production, transportation and purchasing economies. They also act as a 'hedge' against

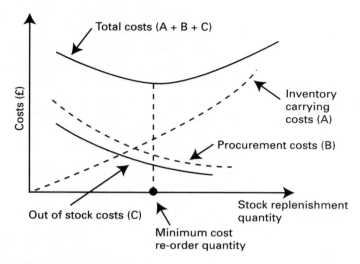

Fig 10.3   Cost trade-off model

inflation, price or exchange-rate fluctuations. In addition, inventories can enhance customer service levels by providing greater stock availability.

Different types of cost need to be balanced when planning inventories, weighing the cost of holding stock and procurement against the cost of running out of stock which could result in stopping production and loss of business and goodwill. Larger inventories reduce the possibility of this happening, but it means that more money is tied up in working capital. However, if quantity discounts are offered for large orders, then fewer orders being placed will reduce purchasing administrative costs.

When these conflicting costs are combined, the total cost thus formed can be plotted as a U-shaped curve. Management must establish a plan of ordering which results in an inventory level involving the lowest possible total costs. This is illustrated in Figure 10.3.

Economic order quantity (*EOQ*) assumes that total inventory costs are minimised at some definable purchase quantity. This method assumes that inventory costs are a function of the number of orders processed per unit of time, and the costs of maintaining an inventory over and above the cost of items included in the inventory (for example warehousing). It takes no account of transportation costs (which may greatly increase for smaller shipments) or the effects of quantity discounts. These factors limit the usefulness of the *EOQ* concept in inventory management, but increasing use of business computing has allowed the operation of more sophisticated versions. Such models are beyond the limits of this text, but in order to give a general understanding of the principles there follows an example of the traditional *EOQ* method.

EOQ can be calculated using the following formula:

$$EOQ = \sqrt{\frac{2AS}{I}}$$

where A is the annual usage (units), S is the ordering costs (£), and I is the inventory carrying cost as a percentage of inventory value.

For example, for an annual usage of 2000 units, ordering costs of £10, inventory carrying costs of 15% (=0.15), and unit cost of £1.50:

$$EOQ = \sqrt{\frac{2 \times 2000 \times £1.50 \times £10}{0.15}}$$

$$= \sqrt{\frac{60000}{0.15}}$$

$$= \sqrt{9000}$$

$$= £94.87$$

The *EOQ* concept and its variations basically seek to define the most economical lot-size when considering the placement of an order. The order point method can be used to determine the ideal timing for placing an order. The relatively simple calculation uses the following equation:

$$OP = DL + SS$$

where *OP* is the order point, *D* is the demand, *L* is the lead time, and *SS* is the safety stock.

For example, for a demand of 200 units per week, a lead time of 4 weeks, and a safety stock of 400 units:

$$OP = (200 \times 4) + 400$$

$$= 800 + 400$$

$$= 1200 \text{ units}$$

A new order should be placed when inventory levels decrease to 1200 units. The size of the order placed when stock reaches this level can be computed using the *EOQ* formula.

This order point method assumes fixed lead times that can be evaluated accurately, which is not often the case. Despite certain limitations, *EOQ* and order point methods are basically valid and form the basis of the more meaningful computer-based inventory models.

10.7 Summary

An understanding of physical distribution is equally important to suppliers and purchasers. As well as an appreciation of the distribution tasks facing the supplier, the purchasing department must also understand logistical techniques for inventory control and the order cycle. PDM is therefore closely associated with purchasing, as well as with operations management. A logistical system should not be inflexible, but should have established routines for certain functions which will facilitate the distribution process.

PDM is firmly linked to all the marketing sub-functions, and in this way a coordinated marketing effort is offered to the customer. The marketing manager should not necessarily have day-to-day hands-on control of every element in the physical distribution system. Such expertise would most likely be beyond the scope of most marketing managers; the logistics function has many highly technical and specialised areas of expertise which necessitate the employment of specialist staff. Purchasing and supply is a profession in its own right. Likewise, materials handling, warehouse management and transport and distribution all have their own professional bodies and qualifications. The logistics function plays a vital part in delivering value and satisfaction to customers. It is a long-term strategic tool which can be used to gain a competitive advantage. It delivers a level of service and time and place utility to customers. Because of this, it must ultimately come under the influence of senior marketing staff. Specialist staff are needed to carry out the complex tasks that make up the logistics function, but strategy and policy formulation for logistics management must be woven into the fabric of the strategic marketing plan if logistics is to play its full part in achieving marketing orientation within the firm.

Chapter Review Questions

Why is a specialist area like physical distribution management of such strategic concern to marketing management?

Physical distribution or logistics provides time and place utility to the customer which is encapsulated in the concept of level of service. The delivery of a certain 'level of service' is an intrinsic part of the product or service offering; that is, it is part of the marketing mix. Success or failure in meeting agreed service levels will impact on the customers' perception of the firms product or service offering. As such, the logistics function is of vital strategic concern to marketing management.

Why is the physical distribution function often referred to as 'total business logistics'?

The concept of 'logistics' has been derived from the military. There is a strong similarity between running complex military campaigns and running equally complex commercial campaigns. The military developed a total systems approach to the arranged procurement of stores and equipment, its storage and transportation. Firms have adopted the same sort of integrated systems approach to their purchasing, warehousing, materials handling and transportation needs.

Explain the concept of 'service elasticity' and show how this concept can be applied by management when setting levels of service or pricing strategies in different sectors.

A firm may be supplying the same, or similar, products to different industries. The product offering is more or less the same, and what differentiates the needs of one industry or sector from another using similar products is the level of service demanded. This service level forms part of the total product or service offering and contributes to what is often called the 'augmented product (or service)'. The marketing firm can offer different service levels and different pricing structures to reflect this difference, in line with the service sensitivity of different customers.

Examine the idea that 'diminishing returns' can be faced by marketing firms when attempting to raise their level of service to certain customer groups. People, whether in their capacity as individual consumers or in their working lives as part of an organisation, will only pay for something if they consider that the utility that they will get from the purchase is at least equal to the price they are prepared to pay. If the perceived utility for a particular good or service is less than the utility to be gained by holding on to your money, you are unlikely to buy it if you are acting rationally. If a high level of service is very important (for example, if you are a contractor operating out in the North Sea for an oil company), then you will be prepared to pay a premium price for an enhanced level of service. If you are in a less service sensitive industry then a level of service offered in excess of what you would be prepared to pay for has little or no value. As marketing firms increase their service levels they are likely to approach the level that some of their customers regard as being adequate. Any further increase will have little or no effect. In this way the marketing firm may experience diminishing returns when increasing service levels.

Explain the concepts of 'time and place utility' with respect to the output of the total logistics concept. Where and when a product or service is used or consumed also has a value to the customer. For example if you are going out at night to the pub for a drink with some friends, you expect to be able to get a drink of beer when you arrive. The beer should not be somewhere else or only available at a different time. Consuming the beer at the right place and at the right time is part of the 'consumer value' of consuming the beer. If you use a special delivery firm such as TNT, Group 4 or Parcel Line in order to get an important conference paper to the United States for next-day delivery, it is of little use if the package ends up in France three days later. For the service to be of any value to you, your package needs to be delivered in the right place at the right time. If you purchase flowers through an Interflora agent to send to a funeral two days later, the flowers must be there on the correct day and in the correct cemetery. Actually owning a product can give an individual 'possession utility', but as we have seen the time and place when many products or services are purchased or used also has significant value to the customer.

11 Managing Selling

11.1 The Importance of Personal Selling in the Organisation

Selling is part of the promotional, or the communications mix, whose other elements are: above-the-line promotion (for example advertising), below-the-line promotion (for example sales promotion) and public relations as it applies to marketing. These areas are the subjects of Chapters 12 and 13, and these themes will be explained in further detail then. However, personal selling is a very important element of marketing and by categorising it as a sub-function of promotion perhaps devalues its importance. The way personal contact is managed with customers is critical to the success of any organisation, and it can only be carried out competently by people who adopt a professional attitude towards their training and their approach to the business of looking after customers in a caring manner. As a consequence, opinions about a company's products are often based on the impression the salesperson has left after a meeting with a prospective customer. At no time is the importance of leaving a good impression more true than nowadays when the notion of customer retention is viewed as being as important as the task of seeking out new customers.

The task of selling, of course, differs according to the products or services being marketed. In some situations it might reflect more a position of keeping customers satisfied, and this task will call for more skills of personality and 'caring'. In other situations, contractual negotiations might be the main emphasis of the selling task and here skills of prospecting, negotiating, demonstrating and closing a sale will be crucial elements for success.

In organisational (which includes industrial) marketing in particular, a great reliance is placed upon personal communication. For FMCG products much faith is placed on above and below-the-line communication, but personal selling is the principal method of communication in industrial marketing. Indeed, in organisational selling situations the proportion of selling within the total market budget tends to outweigh all other expenditures.

Personal selling plays a major part in the commercial process of any country. Within the ever-expanding European Union, the place of selling is increasingly important in establishing contact and in bringing about contracts in ever-more competitive market circumstances. Markets are continuously being opened up and barriers to free competition are being broken down. This, of course, is a two-way process so the United Kingdom too is subject to equal competition coming in from other companies within the EU. Thus, in a modern economy, if it was not for selling, business transactions would simply not take place. Indeed, it is effective selling on the part of the international sales people in a country that contributes to a healthy balance of payments in the form of overseas payments for exports.

Where the marketing of products or services involves a more complex decision process, personal selling assumes a critical role. Techniques of negotiation and sales skills plus good knowledge of the product are required to negotiate the sale of major items especially in the industrial marketplace. This can call for highly developed skills of personality as well as of sales technique.

Activity

Think of a product or service that requires the sales skills just referred to. Examine the kinds of skill that the salesperson should possess in this situation.

The purchase of a new computer system for a company involves much negotiation. The buyer, or more appropriately in this case the DMU, demands that salespeople should have an in-depth knowledge of computer systems. This will reduce the perceived risk that members of the DMU might feel before making their purchasing decision. Familiarity will be expected of the seller's own system as well as the systems of competitors. The salesperson should be able to recognise customer requirements in relation to performance of the system and should then be able to focus-in on appropriate arguments when making the sales presentation which might consider such factors as the performance of the system, the likely price ceiling within the DMU, delivery, credit and after-sales service. More to the point, the salesperson should be able to apply appropriate arguments when dealing with different members within the DMU.

Personal selling can be very costly because it does not simply include the salesperson's salary. On top of this must be added the necessary expenses of a motor car, an expense account including hotel accommodation, and support from the head office. Such additional costs are normally larger than the salesperson's salary. More to the point, salespeople are authorised to spend the company's money in achieving sales, so this must be done responsibly.

Marketing effort is designed to achieve long-run satisfaction on the part of customers. Personal selling is about personal communication of information with a view to persuading customers to purchase, so it is a major communications tool. Therefore, how well an organisation manages its sales-force will have a bearing on the ultimate success of the company.

11.2 Benefits of Personal Selling

When compared to the more impersonal methods of other elements in the communications mix, selling has a lot to commend it:

- It is a far more flexible medium in that salespersons can adapt their sales presentations to the individual circumstances of the purchasing situation and respond to the prospect's reactions as the sales interview progresses.
- Each sales presentation can be different and parts of the presentation can be cut out or adapted to suit individual circumstances.
- Perhaps the biggest advantage it has over other forms of promotion is that it usually results in a sale, unlike other elements of promotion which simply move the prospect towards the final sale.

The personal approach afforded by selling is very appropriate in certain circumstances, most of which relate to organisational purchasing situations:

- **Situations of high perceived risk** – which might involve an expensive purchase which carries a certain degree of risk on the part of the purchaser. Good sales presentation can anticipate buyer behaviour and overcome potential fear that the purchaser might feel in relation to a major purchase not being value for money.
- **Technically complex products** – where customers might be confused as they are not necessarily product experts. Careful explanation will be needed on the part of the salesperson so as not to confuse, but at the same time reading the selling situation such that the level of technicality of the potential buyer can be assessed and the sales presentation adjusted accordingly.
- **Commercially-complex negotiations** – which might involve special servicing or training arrangements on the part of the sellers. Such complexity means that the situation might be one of high-risk on the part of the buyer, and again the approach afforded by the personal salesperson can help to alleviate this perception of risk felt on the part of the potential buyer.

11.3 The Broader Task of Selling

All selling jobs are different and this is what makes selling unique, in that 'formula' approaches to the selling task have never been successful in terms of building up long-term relationships. Such formula approaches were a facet of sales orientation, and techniques like 'putting the customer in the position where they can't say "no!"' through the clever use of questions designed to give affirmative reactions, might be alright for short-term transactions, but for long-term customer loyalty it is counterproductive. Indeed, as we move towards a philosophy of customer satisfaction and customer retention as being long-term goals, so the task of selling is becoming more expansive than it was in the past. Salespersons will spend less time on the task of selling and more time acting as liaison between their host organisations and their key clients. To illustrate what is meant by this last statement, let us now consider some of these broader obligations:

Activity

Think about this problem before you move on to the suggested solution. It is designed to make you think and to understand. What do you think these broader obligations of the modern salesperson might be? Can you add any more to the list we have suggested?

- Technical advice in relation to product performance. Arranging an after-sales service visit for a maintenance problem.
- Short-term financial problems that the client might be facing might mean arranging the extension of a credit arrangement.
- Progressing delivery of an order with the manufacturing plant in relation to an order the client needs urgently.
- Following up sales leads that have been given to the salesperson. Although strictly speaking this is a function of every salesperson's job.
- The task of gathering information from the marketplace is now a very important part of a salesperson's broader job remit. As we saw in Chapter 5, the marketing information system inputs market intelligence, and the principal source of such intelligence can come from data gatherers in the field, and what better source than the people in an organisation who work there every day. By the very nature of their work, salespeople have close contact with customers and are well-placed to accumulate information and market intelligence on competitive activity and in relation to the marketplace as a whole. This information can then be used, for instance, in terms of providing strategic advice within the organisation in the areas of forecasting sales and in the area of new product development through providing research and development with information on competitors' products and how these are viewed by buyers.
- Another obvious task of the salesperson is the use of personal communication when liaising with customers. In the past this tended to reply mainly upon face-to-face contact, and the so called 'gift of the gab' was a prime requirement for selling success. However, the modern salesperson has many other means at his or her disposal as a result of advances made in information technology. Here, for instance, laptop computers can be quickly set up and used at the client's office to display diagrams, spreadsheets and reports. There is a whole plethora of other such IT devices that can help to communicate the company's message and image in a modern manner that not only impresses, but builds

confidence on the part of the client in relation to the salesperson and the company being represented.

- This might look like a strange additional duty as marketing is a philosophy that aims to give customers exactly what they require when they require it. However, there are times when raw materials might be in short supply for natural reasons or through human causes like a war, or when an industrial dispute hits a major production component. For whatever reason, the salesperson might then have to consider customer loyalty in the past, and based upon this, assess future potential before giving support in the form of supplying raw material or parts during the period of shortage.

Selling is therefore dynamic and it has acclimatised to its new more professional role in the world today. A number of recent developments can be cited here that reflect this adaptation:

- **Systems selling** which refers to the selling of a total package of related goods and services, and not just the piece of equipment or basic service itself. Companies thus offer solutions to problems rather than attempting to sell individual products.
- **Relationship selling** which stems out of the notion of relationship marketing, whereby selected important customers are singled out for special treatment in terms of developing longer and deeper relationships. This used to be called 'key account selling' whereby important customers were dealt with by a senior salesperson (often the sales manager). However, relationship selling is slightly different in that the persons chosen to do this work are hand-picked salespeople who have the right personality and are able to nurture customers with a view to building up their long-term trust and long-term business commitment.
- **Selling centres or team-selling** has also grown as a result of the development of more professionalism on the part of purchasing people. It is a team of people who are drawn not only from the sales department, but who also represent areas like production, research and development, and finance. The services of non-sales people are called upon as and when required, but the team remains constant. The objective is to meet and demonstrate to customers that they are being visited and serviced 'in depth' with different views being put, rather than just the sales view.

11.4 **Different Types of Selling Task**

The notion of different types of sales task was first put forward by Robert N. McMurry (1961) and this classification still holds good today. He classified selling positions into the following categories which range from the simplistic to the most complicated level of negotiating ability:

- **Mainly delivery** where the job is concerned with the distribution of, say, milk to individual homes, or bread to retail outlets. This type of salesperson will possess little in the way of sales skills and responsibilities, and continued sales are more likely to come from a pleasant attitude and good service. In some situations, like the delivery of branded soft drinks, a small amount of merchandising work might be required such as setting up display material at the point-of-sale.
- **Inside order-taker** is where the task is one of clerical duties and the opportunity to sell is limited at, say, one of the catalogue stores like Argos. Customers have normally made up their minds at this stage, so the process is simply one of processing the order and only occasionally offering advice when the customer asks for it.
- **Outside order-taker** is similar to the above, but here the salesperson goes on a repeat round of regular customers. Most negotiation is conducted at higher levels between, say, the sales manager of a range of grocery products and the purchasing manager of a large chain of food outlets, and it is the task of the salesperson to simply service the account. This task occasionally includes merchandising activity or introducing and demonstrating new products.
- **Missionary selling** is where salespeople are expected to build up goodwill and educate and ultimately influence the actual or potential user rather than simply soliciting orders. Occasional service work can be undertaken as can sales promotional activities.
- **Technical selling** involves the task of explaining the function of a product to a prospect as well as adapting it to individual customers' needs. Such salespeople are often called 'sales engineers', and here the job entails expert knowledge on the part of the salesperson in terms of product capabilities and design, the likelihood being that he or she is going to be negotiating with technically-expert personnel within a decision-making unit.
- **Creative selling** is the final category and this tends to call for the greatest amount of sales skills. Quite often customers do not realise that they have a need for a certain product or service, and it is up to the creative salesperson to communicate with and then demonstrate and convince the buyer of such a need. A good illustration might be a new type of production-line system that will save the company money in terms of the new system having greater speed and less wastage of material.

Activity

In relation to each of the classifications cited, apart from the examples used, think of a product or service example that fits each of the categories.

- Mainly delivery – coal or solid fuel merchant;
- Inside order-taker – a stores person in a builders' merchant's store;

- Outside order-taker – a salesperson who sells products to pet shops;
- Missionary salesperson – somebody who represents a pharmaceutical company;
- Technical selling – a computer salesperson;
- Creative selling – a life insurance salesperson.

11.5 Selling Skills and Qualities

A good salesperson is somebody who is a good listener. Only by listening to customers and recognising their needs and fears can effective points of the goods being offered for sale be put before the customer in the form of a sales presentation. This is really a matter of appreciating and understanding buyer behaviour. Once this has been understood, then the task of selling is much simpler because irrelevant sales points can be discarded. Indeed, one of the most common reasons for customers not purchasing is the fact that they are overwhelmed by information. One of the problems that experienced salespeople face is the fact that they have developed a degree of sophisticated technical expertise, so product points and features which might appear simple to the salesperson may not be clear to the customer. It is only by listening to the customer that the salesperson can assess the level of technical competence and guide the sales discussion accordingly. This, it is felt, is perhaps the most important quality that a salesperson must develop.

There are, however, a number of other qualities that it is felt are needed in order to become a good salesperson. These qualities were the basis of a research exercise, and were first put forward by Geoffrey Lancaster and David Jobber (1997) in their book *Selling and Sales Management*. These are in descending order of importance:

- Communications skills
- Personality
- Determination
- Intelligence
- Motivation and self-motivation
- Product knowledge
- Educational background
- Confidence
- Appearance
- Resilience and tenacity
- Business sense
- Integrity
- Ambition
- Acceptability or personality
- Empathy

- Initiative
- Self-discipline
- Experience
- Adaptability
- Persuasiveness

Interestingly persuasiveness comes last, so the role of the modern sales-person is not seen to be to 'win arguments'. Interpreting these factors into qualities that can be translated into a job specification for the human resource management function, we suggest that the following represents the elements that should be contained in a job specification that relates to an outside sales position:

- **Physical prerequisites** – good speech, presentable appearance that will be acceptable to buyers with whom contact will be made.
- **Attainments** – reasonable education and qualifications that match the degree of knowledge required for understanding the product or service for which representation is sought. Previous experience in the specific product or service area will probably be essential for a senior position as will demonstration of previous success as a salesperson.
- **Qualities and aptitudes** – the ability to communicate effectively and a high degree of personal drive and self-motivation.
- **Disposition** – a mature personality and a strong sense of responsibility in terms of always representing the company's best interests.
- **Interests** – social activities expected that reflect a sociable nature.
- **Personal circumstances** – in terms of family commitments and respon-sibilities. This can be argued in a number of ways so this factor should be looked at in terms of how it suits the particular sales position. If, for instance, family commitments are large and remuneration is based upon some kind of incentive, then the will to earn more will be strong. If, however, the task entails long periods away from home then family life might suffer.

11.6　The Selling Routine

The selling routine, or the sales sequence, is the term used to describe the processes and stages through which a typical presentation to a buyer pro-ceeds. The process now described is clearly too sophisticated for the sale of fast-moving consumer goods to typical customers. In this situation buyers will have made up their minds before they purchase and buying is simply a matter of routinely choosing and paying for the goods. Indeed, in many products that are sold in organisational buying situations the same will apply.

Activity

In which type of organisational buying situation in particular will a simplified purchasing procedure pertain?

In the case of 'routine rebuy' products or services.

It is, therefore, important to realise that the sales routine we are about to describe should be treated flexibly in terms of salespeople being able to adapt it to suit individual purchasing situations, and in some cases miss out certain parts of the sequence. Pre-planning before each sales interview is very important and if the potential customer is known to the salesperson then the interview plan must be tailored and adapted with the customer's needs in mind. Such adaptation also takes place during the sales routine, as the salesperson listens to cues and signals given by the buyer.

Of course, having such a sales routine assumes that the salesperson has a buyer to meet. Before such a meeting can take place 'prospects' must be identified and 'qualified'. These terms are self-explanatory in that a prospect is a potential purchaser and qualified means that the prospect has authority to make a purchase decision. However, the fact that the prospect might not be qualified does not mean that a meeting should not take place; in many organisational purchasing situations the first-ever meeting a salesperson has with a company is not with the actual buyer.

Activity

In a first-time organisational buying meeting, what member of the DMU might the salesperson meet first before meeting the buyer at a subsequent interview?

A 'gatekeeper' who might be a junior purchasing assistant, who will meet the salesperson and then report this meeting to the buyer. If the possibility of doing business exists, the buyer will probably arrange a full presentation at a subsequent interview. In this case the gatekeeper will also have an 'influencer' role to play. It might also be that the salesperson might meet an influencer first, or even a 'decider' (other than the buyer) who could be somebody who has authorisation over specifications (perhaps a designer or somebody from research and development). A later meeting might then be set up with the buyer. In most cases a first meeting with a 'user' would not be appropriate.

Activity

Think for a moment before you go to the answer or make enquiries from friends and colleagues, and then list the means through which you think 'prospects' can be identified with a view to potentially arranging a sales interview.

- Writing to named buyers in trade directories.
- Purchasing a list of named buyers through a database broker and then using a mailing house to canvass them directly.
- Through referrals or sales leads you may have had from colleagues or other market intelligence sources.
- Through potential customer enquiries.
- Through past sales records to identify buyers who might have been dormant for some time.

Figure 11.1 describes the process of the selling routine, and each of the stages referred to is dealt with in more detail in the following sections.

Preparation

At this stage the sales interview has been arranged and the prospect has been qualified. However, long before the interview takes place there are a number of matters in which the sales representative must be versed. Most of this will be information that is known already as part of the salesperson's general knowledge of the marketplace, or it will be information which has been acquired through a formal programme of training. Essential information at this stage is:

Fig 11.1   The selling routine or sales sequence

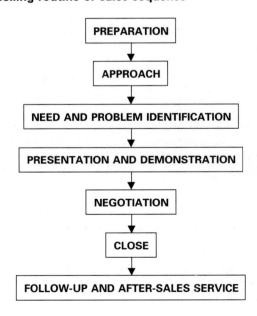

- **Company knowledge** about the latest commercial procedures relating to such matters as price, payment terms, complaints and returned goods.
- **Product knowledge** in relation to technical performance and specifications of current and proposed products and services. This should also include knowledge of the limitations of products in order that false claims will not mistakenly be made.
- **Market knowledge** relates to the activities and product offerings of competitors including the terms and conditions they are giving. In addition, such information should also extend to general sales trends in the marketplace. If a salesperson knows this kind of information, then authority is immediately conferred within any subsequent negotiation procedures. In addition, it is the salesperson's job to find out such information and this all forms part of market intelligence. Such information can usually be gained by talking to buyers in the marketplace during or after a sales interview, so better salespeople will establish a firm and lasting rapport with their buyers and so be in a position to acquire this kind of knowledge during the course of their visits to regular customers.
- **Customer knowledge** relates to knowledge of the customer's organisation, its spending patterns and types and volume of purchases, and personal knowledge in relation to the buyer. A customer record card can be used here which details knowledge of the customer and details of the sales visit. This is usually filled in directly after the sales interview, but not, of course, in the presence of the buyer. It also provides a record for any other member of the company who might have to make a visit to the same buyer, so commercial data like delivery times or price negotiations can be picked up straight away. The information on this record card can relate to general information about the company including any future contracts that the company might be anticipating, or any promises that were made in relation to future orders or contracts. At a personal level, detail in relation to the buyer should also be entered. In any organisational selling situation, if the salesperson has established the appropriate kind or rapport then personal matters might be discussed in addition to business matters, and indeed this is the kind of thing that builds up long-term customer relationships. However, how far this goes is usually a function of the personality of the buyer, some of whom regard personal friendships with salespeople as being a hindrance to successful commercial negotiations.

Activity

What kind of personal data do you think should be recorded in relation to a buyer and why?

Hobbies – does the buyer, say, play golf and at what handicap? Details in relation to family – sons or daughters at school – perhaps about to take examinations. This kind of detail is important to the buyer and it would take a superhuman feat of memory to remember such detail in relation to every buyer visited, so a quick look at the customer record card prior to a sales interview will quickly allow the salesperson to recall the last interview and the personal details that were recounted. Moreover, the salesperson can actually relate to what was said last time and perhaps ask if the golf handicap has been reduced, all of which leaves a good impression of long-term caring and friendship in the mind of the buyer.

- **Aids to selling** include sales literature which describe the company's products or services, current price lists, samples or models. A sales demonstration might utilise spreadsheets or other supporting material delivered through a salesperson's laptop computer and which can be demonstrated in the buyer's office as part of the sales presentation. Anything that supplements the face-to-face verbal part of the sales interview process adds to the variety and quality of the presentation.
- **Journey planning** relates to a plan for calls to regular clients who expect such calls as a matter of course to keep personal lines of communication open between sellers and buyers. A calling cycle should include a variety of 'regular' customers in addition to calls to prospective customers. A method of planning such journeys is what is known as 'differential call frequency', where more important customers deserve more frequent calls than other customers. The system is sometimes referred to as the 'sales journey cycle' and here the normal situation might be to visit most customers once every eight weeks when the cycle will be complete. However, some customers might be visited twice in a cycle and others every other cycle. The kind of organisation involved here is sometimes termed 'cloverleaf', whereby the salesperson covers a closely defined geographical area over a period of time and then another similar area when this has been completed, and so on until the sales journey cycle has been completed – in a cloverleaf type pattern.

  At a more detailed level, each journey should be planned in terms of a definite appointment which will most probably be through some prior telephoned arrangement.
- **Dress and demeanour** include matters of personal hygiene and clothing. Dress and behaviour that suit the client is what is aimed for, but it might not be possible to satisfy all customers if, say, eight are being visited in a single day. In organisational purchasing situations the temptation to over-dress should be avoided as this might upstage the buyer, so the best guide might be to be 'soberly smart' and avoid extremes of behaviour like gushing comments or affectations.

Approach

This is sometimes termed 'the opening' and an inherent skill in selling is the ability to 'size up a situation quickly'. How this initial approach, especially to a new customer, is handled could determine the outcome of the sales interview. Opening remarks are important, and should try to address the circumstances at a very general level, even if it only to comment on the weather. One point worth remembering in the case of a first-time visit to a buyer is to be the first to speak by introducing yourself by your christian name and surname (which should also be cited like this on your visiting card). You will then know very quickly if the buyer is on a 'familiar' or a 'formal'-term basis, as to whether he or she refers to you by your christian name or by your salutation then surname.

Need and problem identification

What the salesperson attempts to do here is to discover purchasing motives or buyer behaviour, especially when it is a call to a new buyer. In the case of organisational purchases overall purchasing motives will tend to revolve around general economic value-for-money criteria, but there might be underlying motives.

Activity

What underlying motives can you think of?

A regular supplier might have let the company down in being unable to meet the quality criteria called for, and they might now be looking for a replacement supplier. Their current supplier might have put prices up to an unacceptable level and they are seeking to change.

A few probing questions, which demand more than straight 'yes' or 'no' answers before the presentation stage, are desirable in order to attempt to determine buyer behaviour. This will clearly affect the course of the presentation as this will then be able to focus on the points that the buyer has made clear are a particular issue. It is also the place where listening skills are particularly appropriate. This indeed is an example of how selling is still important at a face-to-face level in terms of having the ability to be adaptable to individual circumstances.

The presentation and/or demonstration

Effective communication is demanded here and what are known as USP (unique selling proposition) points can be highlighted. These USPs are product or service features which it is felt competitive products do not possess. A common phrase in selling is: 'You don't sell products, you sell benefits', so the benefits that the customer will gain should be communicated efficiently and effectively as part of a logical sequence within the presentation that has been rehearsed in many different ways before the sales interview.

If the presentation can include a demonstration then so much the better because this provides 'hard' evidence, and if the buyer is able to somehow participate in this demonstration (even if it is just to handle the product) then better still because he or she is being seen to empathise with the product and can see its benefits at first hand. Demonstrations of course can be shown on video. Failing this, and indeed as well as this, well-produced brochures showing the merchandise and describing its technical detail will also be very effective.

The presentation should, of course, focus on those points that the buyer regards as being important and this relates to buyer behaviour which should have been assessed by this stage. The level of technicality of the sales presentation should also be adjusted to suit the buying situation. Depending upon whom the presentation is being made to, will depend the nature of the emphasis of the presentation.

Activity

What different kinds of emphasis do you think there can be?

Price – especially in relation to a buyer with an eye for value for money. Quality – especially for somebody who is more concerned with production. Specification – especially for somebody who is concerned more with function and design.

It is also at this stage that testimony can be presented which might include letters from satisfied customers. If guarantees over and above statutory guarantees are available then this too can be mentioned here. Objections from the buyer are possible at this stage, but the experienced salesperson will usually be able to anticipate the nature of these and even forestall them by raising them as part of the sales presentation. A principal objection in organisational purchasing situations is ritualistically one of 'price', so the good salesperson is able to prepare for this in terms of value-for-money points as part of the presentation.

What the salesperson should guard against is over-presentation, and the needs of the prospect should be kept in mind to avoid overwhelming the interview with too much detail. What is looked for at this stage are buying signals, and once these are apparent it is time to bring the presentation and demonstration to a swift conclusion.

Negotiation

The topic of negotiation is a complex process and there are even textbooks devoted to the subject. However, in this context negotiation usually relates to price which is (quite naturally) the final hurdle to be overcome before the final sale is made. But negotiation is not totally about price; it can involve such matters as servicing arrangements, credit terms, penalty clauses in relation to late delivery, plus many more factors. The essential element is that both parties should aim for an accord which benefits them both. In relation to price negotiation, the 'room for manoeuvre' concept which was first put forward by Howard Raiffa (1982) perhaps explains the situation best, and this is illustrated in Figure 11.2.

The concept is that when negotiating price, sellers and buyers have ideas in their minds as to what they would like to receive or pay for their merchandise. Only in very rare cases are these figures the same and indeed market pricing tells us that prices should be set at what the market will bear, so the likelihood is that a higher price will be stated initially with a view to reducing it through negotiation, and indeed it is a philosophy that is at the very centre of market trading. After the sales presentation, matters like credit and delivery will be discussed and agreed as part of negotiation, but price is normally the final item on this part of the agenda. The concept is simple and starts with the supposition that the seller is normally the first person to state the price required (price $S2$). The buyer will counter with the price he or she would like to pay ($B1$). Gradually, negotiation brings the two together and once $B2$ and $S1$ are reached then from both the buyer's and the seller's respective points of view the area of negotiation has been reached, but the buyer will not know $S1$ and the seller will not know $B1$. It

---

Fig 11.2   Room for manoeuvre concept of negotiation

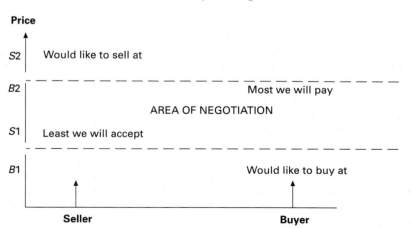

is then a matter of proposal and counter-proposal, coupled perhaps with some concessions on either side before a final price is agreed within this area of negotiation.

Close

The aim of selling is to reach the close stage which will result in an agreement to purchase, and this is the objective of selling. However, it is sometimes the most difficult stage and a number of techniques exist in relation to closing a sale. We have detailed some of the more commonly-used methods:

- **Basic close** is the simplest as it simply consists of filling out an order form, but it presumes that the buyer wishes to buy. If, however, the seller is unsure as to the buyer's purchasing decision at this stage, then this might be a high-risk strategy as it could well frighten the buyer off in the case of a major purchase.
- **Trial close** is perhaps better than basic close because it is an attempt to test the buyer's willingness to purchase by asking an either/or question like: 'If you were to purchase, would you be paying cash or credit?'
- **Alternative choice** is where the salesperson, having received buying signals, attempts to close the sale by offering an alternative choice – 'Would you like it in black or white?'
- **Assumptive close** is another variation which assumes that the purchaser will buy and the salesperson asks questions like: 'Where and when would you like the goods to be delivered?'
- **Puppy dog technique** springs from the idea that if you give a puppy to somebody to look after for, say, two weeks, then they will not want to part with it when you go to collect it. The same philosophy is adopted for tangible goods which might be offered on free trial for a short period.
- **Sharp angle** is a technique that the salesperson uses when the customer asks for information like: 'What is the delivery period?' The salesperson would then respond with something like: 'What delivery are you looking for?' and upon being told, would then say: 'If we can supply it by then will you place the order?'
- **Summary question** is a technique that is used when caution is being exercised on the part of the buyer prior to placing the order. The salesperson will then attempt to isolate the cause of resistance by asking questions like: 'Is it quality?' – 'No!' 'Is it price?' – 'No!' 'Is it delivery?' – 'No!' . . . and so on, until the cause of resistance is isolated. This can then be concentrated upon as part of the sales erosion process in attempting to win the order.
- **Similar situation** is where the salesperson listens to what the purchaser is saying and if this relates to an experience (normally a bad one) relating

to the product for sale, the salesperson then brings in, as part of the conversation, another story that relates to another experience (a good one).

- **Concession close** is normally kept towards the end as the final negotiating and closing ploy. This means keeping a final concession in reserve before agreement is reached in the expectation that this will conclude the sale.

Activity

Apart from those already mentioned, cite an example of a close under each of: trial close; alternative choice; assumptive close; puppy dog technique; sharp angle; similar situation; concession close.

- Trial close – 'If we can offer free servicing for a year will you be interested?'
- Alternative choice – 'Are you thinking of the basic or the de-luxe version?'
- Assumptive close – 'Will it be cash or credit?'
- Puppy dog technique – 'Try this video recorder free for a week'.
- Sharp angle – to buyer's query about colour – 'If we have it in that colour do you want it?'
- Similar situation to buyers who are relating an experience that shows that house contents insurance policies are expensive and a waste of money – 'Mr and Mrs Warrington in the next street were burgled the other week and they didn't have house contents insurance.'
- Concession close – 'I can offer a final 2 per cent discount if you place the order now.'

Follow-up and after-sales service

The order process is not fully completed once the sale has been closed. This final area is becoming more prominent nowadays that customer retention is seen as being a long-term strategy of marketing. The notion of 'customer care' alone is the essence of a number of modern texts. Follow-up can simply mean a telephone call to the buyer to ascertain whether or not the goods were received in a satisfactory condition at the time promised and this kind of thing gives reassurance to the buyer that the sale was in the interests of the customer. After-sales is more than this because it concerns a number of post-sale activities that can be designed to build long-term goodwill on the part of the customer and help to ensure repeat purchases on a long-term basis. Such activity can also reduce what is known as 'cognitive dissonance' which, in the case of a major purchase, is a nagging fear or doubt on the part of the buyer that what has been purchased might not be value for money. A feeling of caring is thus generated through follow-up, and after-sales service can help to reduce these feelings of doubt.

Activity

Give an example of after-sales service.

In the case of a motor car, through the provision of a dealership network that customers know will be able to provide virtually any part from stock anywhere in the country and having the ability to repair or service the car at very short notice.

The selling routine has been a long section. The reason for this is that without selling, and its associated tactics, commerce would not exist. It is important, therefore, that this critical area of marketing has received thorough attention in terms of the techniques involved. The next section now looks at the way this activity is managed through the process of sales management.

11.7 Sales Management

The function of sales management is to devise and implement a sales plan and then evaluate and control it during the course of the planning period. The sales plan is in fact part of the marketing plan and this is dealt with in detail in Chapter 15. The starting point for business planning is the sales forecast which should also be the responsibility of sales management in conjunction with marketing management. The techniques involved in forecasting have been covered in detail in Chapter 5 which examined forecasting in conjunction with marketing information systems. Evaluation and control of the plan are more to do with the tactics in sales management, and the remainder of this section covers these specific areas. Figure 11.3 describes these activities in chronological sequence, and each of the elements in then figure is now discussed as part of the sales management process.

Recruitment

The first consideration here is to establish the size of the sales-force. In any organisation there are competing demands upon the company's funds, so due consideration has to be paid between balancing financial resources against other criteria.

Activity

What do you feel might be the factors that should be taken into consideration when establishing the size of the sales-force?

RECRUITMENT

SELECTION

TRAINING

MOTIVATION

SUPERVISION

EVALUATION

REMUNERATION

Fig 11.3   Responsibilities of sales management

- Numbers of current customers plus number of potential customers.
- The period between calls (for example weekly, monthly, quarterly).
- The number of calls to be made in a typical selling day (for example in certain types of sales task covering a very tight geographical location it might be a lot, whereas in geographically dispersed locations it will probably be less).
- Whether calls are being made to end-users or to distributive intermediaries like wholesalers or distributors.

Prior to recruitment a job description must be written for each sales position and this should then be agreed with and given to human resource management (HRM) who will conduct the initial recruitment and then pass on suitable shortlisted candidates to the sales manager for interview. A typical job description contains a number of elements:

- The job title;
- To whom responsible;
- Duties and responsibilities, including selling tasks which typically include frequency of visits to customers, after-sales service activities and feedback of market intelligence;
- Technical ability in terms of knowledge of products or services and their applications and specific sales abilities;
- Geographical area to be covered;
- Degree of autonomy in terms of reporting to the sales manager and being

responsible for the territory (some sales jobs are tightly controlled and others tend to leave it to the individual salesperson to develop the territory).

Activity

What sources do you feel are most suitable when recruiting field sales-force personnel?

- From inside the company – perhaps certain members of staff who are in the sales office might show an aptitude for selling.
- Sales recruitment agencies – some employ head-hunter services whereby they canvass potential individuals directly.
- From competitive companies – but probably via the recruitment press.
- From recommendations from existing sales personnel.

Selection

At this stage, the human resource management department will have shortlisted appropriate candidates for interview by sales management and sifted out those who do not match the criteria laid down in the job description. This will have been done by asking candidates to fill in an application form which then makes it easier to provide a standardised comparison. However, in some cases candidates are asked to submit a curriculum vitae on the basis that such a CV will demonstrate imagination of the part of the potential candidate and perhaps highlight some areas that a standard application form will not cover.

It is now a matter for sales management to pick an appropriate candidate in an interview situation. There are a number of ways of tackling interviews: one method which tends to be less favoured nowadays is the 'stress' interview whereby an aggressive stance is taken by interviewer and the candidate must 'defend' him or herself and put forward reasons why they should be chosen. This type of interview might be appropriate if the sales task involves high pressure selling – which is, of course, more a facet of sales orientation. However, most interviews nowadays tend to put interviewees at their ease on the basis that what is ultimately needed is a harmonious partnership. There are also two ways in which the interview can be tackled – either on a formal question-and-answer structured basis, or on an unstructured basis whereby the interviewee is encouraged to discuss the position and the interview only interjects occasionally to probe certain points. The qualities that are looked for are some of those listed earlier in this chapter in section 11.5, but most of all what is looked for is somebody who will be an effective member of a team. Research suggests that, for selling, the following factors should be considered during the interview process, bearing in mind the selling job for which the interview is being conducted:

- Demographic and physical attributes;
- Background and experience in selling and in the product or service to be represented;
- Current domestic and financial status and lifestyle;
- Intellectual and perception abilities;
- Interpersonal and presentation skills.

Training

This is an expensive component of the overall marketing budget, coupled to which there is the fact that during training, the salesperson has to be paid whilst not being involved in selling activity. Therefore, sales training should be done competently and professionally in order to gain maximum value for money. Programmes can be done 'in-house' or through outside sales trainers.

In-house programmes can relate to such matters as product knowledge – perhaps in terms of a member of the product development team conducting a session on a new product that is about to be launched, or a modification that is being made to an existing product. In addition to this, an initial training programme might be conducted by the HRM department which will explain the company and its various associations. The marketing manager or director could also input into such a programme in terms of market developments and competitive activities. The sales manager might input training on organisation matters like work routines and preparation and presentation of reports and how these will be used within the company.

External programmes conducted by acknowledged sales trainers can be provided for new staff or through refresher programmes for existing staff. Such training can concentrate on specific sales techniques like closing or dealing with objections, or the sales routine in general. Such a programme can of course be conducted by the sales manager, but this will depend upon the sales manager's skills of delivery and indeed knowledge of modern techniques. Certainly, an in-house programme would be cheaper than one that is conducted at a hotel or conference venue, and what many companies do is to employ a skilled outside trainer to conduct the programme in-house. However, the advantage of sales programmes that are conducted outside and which involve sales personnel from other companies is the breadth of knowledge that is obtained from the training sessions themselves, in addition to the indirect knowledge that is obtained through 'sharing' experiences with salespeople who work in different organisations.

Motivation

Selling is a lonely job. The common misconception of the field salesperson is as a garrulous individual who is shallow thinking and has a joke for every occasion. From what has been explained so far it can be seen that field selling is a very individualistic task often involving long hours' driving and then meeting buyers on a formal basis. Quite often buyers reject the salesperson's offers after the sales presentation and this can be very demotivating. It often means periods away from home, staying in hotels with no colleagues for company. In many selling situations the salesperson looks after an area or territory that is distant from the head office, so this makes personal relationships with colleagues more difficult because a visit to head office might only be once a week to meet and report to the sales manager, or less in many cases.

Motivation is thus of prime importance here in order to ensure that field salespeople do not feel neglected and that they are receiving the appropriate amount of support from head office.

Activity

Think for a moment before reading the suggestions, and then state what factors or activities you feel might be used to motivate members of the field sales-force?

- Accompanied visits to customers by the sales manager or regional manager with the salesperson.
- Financial incentives through commission or some other kind of compensation plan.
- Possibility of some kind of promotional structure within the organisation – although in many cases a good field sales representative does not make a good manager, because of the individualistic, and perhaps selfish, nature of the sales job.
- Job enrichment in terms of praise or recognition through some kind of award. This award might be a prize offered as part of a sales competition which might be based upon a number of different criteria like biggest value or biggest volume of sales in a period, most number of new accounts opened in a period, most promising new salesperson.
- Sales meetings where the opportunity is extended for members of the sales team to meet each other – costly, however, in terms of non-selling time. However, sometimes such meetings can be prefaced with a face-to-face meeting with the sales manager, the prime purpose of which will be to listen to the salesperson's view of the job in terms of points of dissatisfaction and then act upon these.
- Sales conferences which are held periodically and which provide the opportunity for the sales-force to get together, usually in a social setting, to discuss company policies and other matters. Usually, such a conference will have a theme. They are, however, costly to mount, particularly if they are in a hotel or other such venue and include invitations to partners.

- Fringe benefits like using the company car for social reasons, or a holiday sponsored by the company – quite often related to sales performance.

Supervision

It has already been mentioned that selling in the field is an individualistic kind of activity. It also tends to be a geographically dispersed operation. Only in very large companies can there be a structure under a sales manager that divides the country into regions, with a regional manager controlling each region which in turn is split into areas, with an area manager in control of each area with its own field sales representatives. At most, all that can be anticipated under a sales manager is a single tier of either area or regional managers, with groups of field sales representatives reporting directly to each. In most companies the situation is far more modest than this with the country being geographically divided with a single field sales representative in charge of each region reporting directly to the sales manager at head office.

On the subject of individual supervision, this is largely a function of the product or service being sold and the culture of the parent organisation. Clearly, in geographically dispersed markets close supervision will not be possible, or even desirable, for one of the attractions of a field sales position is the amount of freedom it offers in being able to control one's own destiny. It also allows an individual to solve customers' problems in a creative manner, so if close supervision is maintained from the head office then this might do away with any feelings of independence felt by the salesperson.

Performance measures are perhaps the best methods of providing supervision for salespeople who work away from the head office. Such measures can be qualitative ones through such criteria as the quality of sales presentation as assessed by the field sales manager, or the degree of product or market knowledge that the salesperson possesses. This, of course, is assessed by the field sales manager on his or her accompanied visits to customers during the normal course of selling activity, so supervision is also being effected at the same time as an assessment is being made. Quantitative measures are more tangible and these relate to sales volume in general, and, more specifically, to number of orders secured, number of new accounts opened, number of sales and service calls made, or amount of market intelligence gathered.

Evaluation

Evaluating the performance of salespeople is really the result of supervision and this is perhaps the most important aspect of sales management. Performance measures must, of course, be set before evaluation can take place and these measures should be agreed at the appointment stage. Measures of evaluation are obvious ones that relate to such matters as sales volume, number of orders secured and number of calls made. In the case of using these as an incentive, it links into remuneration which is dealt with in the next section.

Remuneration

It has already been mentioned that remuneration is a prime motivator in field selling positions and this is why remuneration is normally linked directly to the volume the salesperson sells. However, it is not necessarily as simple as that in many selling situations. In cases when securing an order is part of a team effort it is then difficult to measure the input of an individual salesperson to the negotiating process, and in such cases a shared commission or a bonus might be more appropriate.

Basically there are three options open when considering compensation plans:

- **Straight salary** is more appropriate when the principal component of the sales task is one of calling on regular customers and customer care, and where retention of existing customers is of prime importance. Quite often such situations call for technical advice being given during sales visits, and it is in this category that we tend to find many sales engineers. A facet of the type of industry in which this is appropriate is in high value/low volume market situations. Straight salary can of course provide security, but such a situation will not attract those whose main motivation is money, and who, because of this very factor, might be more successful individual salespersons. To a certain extent straight salary arrangements can be incentivised through the use of a bonus that in some way is linked to the success or otherwise of the company over the previous period.
- **Straight commission** is the other extreme and here the only incentive is to sell. This too has its drawbacks in that salespeople in this situation will be reluctant to spend time on matters which they do not see as being directly related to sales. They will also be reluctant to spend time away from selling meeting with the sales manager or on sales training programmes. If customer care is one of the company's aims, then this type of system will not encourage such treatment on the part of the sales-force. It is, however, an efficient system from a company's point of view because it is a straight variable cost that only increases as sales increase, but the downside of the argument is that it is often used for these reasons by financially insecure companies.

Activity

Give an example of a product and a service that tends to utilise a straight commission remuneration system?

Home improvements – burglar alarms, double glazing, security screens. Life assurance which attempts to sell a single policy to an individual. In such situations it is also quite common for the salesperson to have another form of employment apart from the selling job.

- **Salary plus commission** attempts to combine the advantages of both systems and this is why it is often termed the 'combined plan' of remuneration. As income is not solely dependent upon commission then management has a greater degree of control over the salesperson's time, yet sales costs are only generated through increased sales revenues. It is a system that will attract ambitious sales persons who wish to combine security with greater earning power through enhanced personal efforts. At its simplest level, payment can be based on a basic salary plus a fixed percentage on all sales. However, in most organisations a more incentive-related system operates which is usually based on what is called an 'escalator', where the commission increases once a certain level of sales has been reached. Another system is the 'sales target' or 'sales quota' system, when commission is only earned after an agreed target or quota has been reached for a specified period. This target is usually for a relatively short period – otherwise if the period is long (say for one year) then if during the course of the year it seems unlikely that the target will be reached, there might be a temptation on the part of the salesperson to stop trying on the basis that the commission level will never be attained. Such a target or quota is agreed with the sales manager beforehand and it normally reflects sales for a period of not longer than three months.

11.8 Summary

Similar to Chapter 7 that related to the product, this has also been a large chapter. Along with products and services, selling is an essential element of the marketing process, for without it products would never reach their intended markets. This chapter has, therefore, covered a large and very important part of the process of marketing.

It has looked at the importance of personal selling within an organisation and how it relates to the communications mix and marketing in particular, as well as to the economy in general. Personal selling has been discussed in terms of its advantages over other elements in the communications mix. Different market situations have been identified, and the types of selling arrangement most suited to each of these has been discussed.

At a more individual level, skills appropriate to selling have been examined which was followed by what is known as the selling (or sales) routine. Each element of the sales routine was examined in detail in terms to techniques that are typically employed.

Good sales management is the most important element of the sales process, and this was examined from the points of view of recruitment, selection, training, motivation, supervision, evaluation and remuneration.

Chapter Review Questions

Selling is part of the communications mix. What are the other elements?
Above-the-line promotion, below-the-line promotion, and public relations as it affects marketing.

In which organisational selling situations is personal selling most appropriate?
Situations of high perceived risk; for technically complex products; in commercially complex negotiations.

What is meant by team selling or selling centres?
People are drawn into a team from other departments like production, research and development and finance and they jointly conduct negotiations with customers.

McMurray quoted a list of sales tasks ranging from the simple to the most complicated. What were these categories?
Mainly delivery; inside order-taker; outside order-taker; missionary selling; technical selling; creative selling.

What elements are contained in the selling routine?
Preparation; approach; need and problem identification; presentation and demonstration; negotiation; close; follow-up and after-sales service.

In sales preparation what information and planning is essential?
Company knowledge; product knowledge; market knowledge; customer knowledge; aids to selling must be organised; the journey plan must be organised; and personal grooming must be appropriate for the purchasing situation.

What is a USP?
A unique selling (or sales) proposition relates to product or service features which your product or service has but which competitive products lack.

List four closing techniques.
Four from: basic close; trial close; alternative choice; assumptive close; puppy dog technique; sharp angle; summary question; similar situation; concession close.

What are the responsibilities of sales management?
Recruitment; selection; training; motivation; supervision; evaluation; remuneration.

What are the three basic forms of field sales remuneration?
Straight salary; straight commission; combination plan.

12 Above and Below-the-line Promotion

12.1 Introduction

In terms of the general public perception of all of the marketing mix elements that a firm may employ, it is perhaps promotion that is the most high profile and prominent 'P' in the '4 Ps'. In fact to most lay people promotion is marketing, as it is the most visible aspect of the marketing process. Promotion is a part of a firm's overall effort to communicate with consumers and others about its product or service offering. Both the company and the consumer have needs which they aim to fulfill – the profit-making company wishes to improve or maintain profits and market-share, and gain a better reputation than its competitors, and the consumer aims to reach his or her personal goals. The total product offering allows each party to move towards these goals, offering a 'bundle of satisfactions' which fulfill needs in an instrumental and a psychological sense. In the United Kingdom the phrase 'marketing communications' is generally preferred to the term promotion, this term often being reserved for a special branch of communications called below-the-line sales promotion.

Promotion or marketing communication?

In a sense all marketing communication activity is a form of promotion that in one way or another is attempting to promote the interest of the brand, product range and/or company. What differentiates above-the-line activity from below-the-line activity is a somewhat arbitrary division; there is no universally accepted definition of either. Below-the-line activity can be defined as non-media advertising. Basically, if a formal piece is submitted to a publication and a commission is paid to feature the piece then this is deemed conventional above-the-line communication. If no commission has been paid, for example in the case of a public relations press release, a trade exhibition or a sponsored sports event, this is referred to as below-the-line communication activity. This distinction is accepted by many and shall therefore be the distinction adopted throughout this chapter.

12.2 **Real and Implied Product Attributes**

The role of marketing communications is to communicate the benefits of the product, service or firm to potential consumers. The same process is undertaken in not-for-profit situations. If we think of the marketing of a political party, for example, the party publicity team (which these days often includes a professional marketing communications firm such as Saatchi and Saatchi who carry out work for the Conservative Party) attempts to convey the benefits of a particular political ideology or even the personality of the party leadership – for example John Major, Tony Blair or Paddy Ashdown in the United Kingdom. Many of the benefits marketing communicators try to convey are 'real'; for example a Jaguar car really can go from 0 to 60 mph in 50 seconds, and so on. But many attributes are implied; they have been created through marketing techniques, particularly marketing communications. For example Perrier water is basically just water, but in the minds of consumers it is much more than this. It is the implied attributes of Perrier that have made the product into a major, global brand. Nike training shoes are another good example. About 70 percent of the people who buy Nike training shoes and other Nike clothes are not actually athletes or even 'sporty'. Most people buy this brand as a fashion product. Young children pursuade their parents to spend up to £120 on a pair of Nike trainers just so that they can be seen wearing the right brand at school and their friends will judge them as 'cool'. Most of the attributes making up the concept of Nike sports products are implied, and created by clever marketing.

Theory of demand describes products and services as a 'total bundle of attributes' which the consumer perceives in a holistic manner. In other words potential consumers see the product or service offering as a unified whole, rather than a bundle of separate component parts such as its price, packaging, shape and so on. In this way, marketing communications convey the meaning of the company's total product offering, helping consumers attain their goals and moving the company closer to its own goals. Many products, particularly in the fast-moving consumer goods (FMCG) category are very similar to other products in their class. For example margarine is basically margarine and no matter what the actual brand selected at the end of the day it is still just margarine. The same goes for soap, toothpaste, jam, polish and a whole host of other everyday products. In times of artificial shortage or deprivation, such as in the war years, most goods were treated as homogenous commodities, basically soap was soap. In less-developed countries the same is true. Many products are perceived by consumers as commodities rather than differentiated branded products with added perceived value.

Let us take two very different products, one from the consumer market sector and one from the industrial sector. The consumer product is a fast-moving consumer good (FMCG) that we have mentioned earlier in a similar context, Perrier water. The industrial product is a heat-treated steel bar used in manufacturing heavy industrial products and produced by the firm Guest, Keen and Nettlefolds (GKN). Even an industrial firm such as GKN tries to use marketing to create a favourable image in the minds of customers, and so the products it produces will have some 'implied attribute' component because the reputation of the firm will to a certain extent be reflected in its products. However, if we look at Figure 12.1 which attempts to compare the two products in terms of the ratio of their real to implied attributes, we see that the FMCG product, Perrier, has a much higher proportion of implied attributes.

Activity

All commercial forms of communication are a form of promotion . . . Discuss.

We can really use the two terms 'promotion' and 'marketing communication' interchangeably. All forms of marketing communication are purposeful communications, designed to achieve a specific commercially relevant effect. Some marketing communications are attempting to bring about an actual sale. For example an advertisement for a certain record company showing a particular album that cannot be purchased in the shops, which invites you to use their freephone number at the end of the advertisement to purchase the record using your credit card, is a form of direct marketing which is trying to elicit a sale. The majority of marketing communications, however, are not of this type and usually have a more intermediate objective such as communicating certain product attributes to the consumer. They are not trying to elicit a sale directly, but are making a contribution to the communication process at the end of which a sale may take place. Whether the communication 'tool' being used is public relations, direct mail, telephone marketing, trade journal advertising, sponsorship or corporate advertising, all of

Fig 12.1   Comparison of the degree of implied attributes making up product concepts in consumer and industrial markets

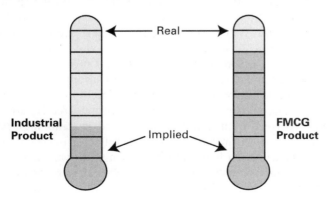

these forms of communication whether direct or indirect are at the end of the day promoting either the product, service or firm. In this sense all forms of commercial marketing communications are varieties of promotion.

12.3 **Needs and Wants**

In the less-developed countries of the world, particularly those areas subject to catastrophes such as drought or famine, a large proportion of the population unfortunately live a precarious existence at, or just above, the level of subsistence. From the moment these people wake up in the morning until the time they go to bed at night, they think largely of survival and how to get sufficient food and water, how to ensure adequate clothing, shelter and safety for themselves and their children. Such places are sometimes politically unstable and can be dangerous. The population not only have to endure poverty undreamed of in the West, but often also constant fear. The famous psychologist Abraham Maslow developed a theory which postulated that mankind's behaviour is governed by what he called a hierarchy of needs. According to Maslow (1954) humans strive to fulfill their most pressing needs first, and only when these have been addressed do they move on up the hierarchy and attempt to satisfy higher-order needs. People with pressing physiological needs such as the need to urgently satisfy hunger or thirst think of nothing else. People with pressing safety needs such as the need for security for their family in a hostile environment will forget all other non-urgent things. Modern marketing with its power to create strong psychological attributes, brand personalities and product differentiation has little relevance in the lives of people forced to live in such conditions. A diagrammatic representation of Maslow's hierarchy of needs is shown in Figure 12.2.

The figure shows that at the bottom of the pyramid physiological needs such as hunger and thirst are of primary concern to the individual, almost to the exclusion of anything else. Marketers can make use of this phenomenon, for example, in advertising and generally promoting soft drinks such as Coca Cola or fast foods such as Burger King, Macdonalds or KFC. Only when these basic, but very important physiological needs are satisfied will the individual turn his or her attention to the next category of need in the hierarchy. When a person is able to meet their most basic physiological needs such as food and drink they start thinking about their safety and that of their family. In primitive times such activity might have taken the form of looking for a more secure cave or making a more effective weapon, or it might have involved organising into groups to try and improve mutual safety. In the modern world, safety needs are reflected in goods and services such as burglar alarms, car locks, double glazing, external lighting, all kinds of insurance, saving schemes and so forth. Marketers use fear in order to market such products.

Fig 12.2 Maslow's hierarchy of needs

Maslow suggested that after a person's basic physiological and safety needs have been met they turn their attention to more loftier concerns. People need to feel part of a group, appreciated by others and to have the opportunity to both give and receive love. In fact science has shown that people who are deprived of these things for any length of time become ill in some way. Fashion items, perfume, supporting the same 'pop' group or football team are all examples of how marketing uses social needs to sell products and services. Esteem-needs can be translated into products and services also. High-status cars, for example, designer clothes or expensive holidays, wines or perfumes all give the consumer self-esteem, recognition and status. Finally we reach the higher-order need to self-actualise. Only wealthier countries can afford to have large sections of their population 'self-actualising'. The best example of this kind of behaviour is probably in California in the United States, especially in cities such as San Francisco where people are indulging in a wide variety of alternative life-styles. Books by self-help gurus, health supplements and exercise videos are all examples of products aimed at the self-actualising consumer.

Activity

Using specific examples distinguish between real and implied product or service attributes.

Products and services can be thought to be made up of two separate but interrelated kinds of attributes – real tangible attributes, and the more intangible 'implied attributes'. Modern marketing, at least in consumer markets, is predominately concerned with implied attributes. Many products and services are intrinsically the same; any differences are relatively small and usually there are far more similarities between competing brands than there are differences. For all intents and purposes many products when stripped of the implied attributes created by marketing activities are homogeneous commodities. Toothpaste is toothpaste and butter is butter, any difference between brands in the real sense of the word is largely superficial. For example Colgate Total brand of toothpaste and Crest are virtually indistinguishable in terms of taste, colour, consistency and actual ingredients. However, both brands make competing claims and are communicated by their respective marketing departments as being radically different, even innovative. It is largely implied attributes that marketing people use to differentiate such similar competing brands in the minds of customers. If we look at services the same principles apply. Any current accounts at the leading high-street banks are basically the same. Financial 'products' are largely intangible, they are given tangibility and differentiated from one another through the creation of implied attributes. A good example of this is the current range of bank accounts on offer from the Midland Bank. Each account is targeted at a particular market segment with a mixture of both real and implied attributes and implied attributes with many of the perceived differences being implied by clever marketing.

12.4 The Marketing Communications Mix

Promotion describes the communications activities of advertising, personal selling, sales promotion and publicity.

- **Advertising** is a non-personal form of mass communication, paid for by an identified sponsor;
- **Personal selling** involves a seller attempting to persuade a potential buyer to make a purchase;
- **Sales promotion** encompasses short-term activities such as giving coupons, free samples and so on which encourage quick action by buyers;
- **Publicity** is another non-personal communication method which reaches a large number of people, but it is not paid for by the company and is usually in the form of news or editorial comment regarding a company's product or service. While a company has control over the previous three variables, it has little over publicity, although it can gain some control over the publicity it receives by the release of news items.

Put together, these promotional activities make up the **promotional mix** with varying emphasis on each element according to the type of product, characteristics of consumers and company resources. Company size, competitive strengths and weaknesses and style of management all influence the promotional mix used.

Other communications elements with which promotion must be coordinated are the product itself, price and distribution channels used. Product communication, including brand name, design of packaging and trademark are all product cues, conveying a subtle message about the total product offering. Price can communicate different things under varying circumstances, for instance conveying 'prestige appeal' for those buyers who perceive that a high price is equal to quality and prestige. The place in which the products are to be found also has notable communications value. Retail stores have 'personalities' which consumers associate with the products they sell. Products receive a **halo effect** from the outlets in which they can be found, and two stores selling similar products can project entirely different product images. For example, a perfume sold through an upmarket store will have a much higher quality image than one sold through discount drug stores and supermarkets.

Promotion is one of a number of activities used by companies to communicate their product offerings. The combination of these variables as perceived by consumers is the **marketing communications mix**.

The marketing communications mix is really a sub-mix of the overall marketing mix. In Figure 12.3 we illustrate the overall marketing budget as a circle. The marketing communications budget is shown as a shaded segment of this circle, and the segment will differ between firms as different amounts or percentages of the overall marketing budget will be devoted to marketing communications.

If we now take the shaded area from Figure 12.3 and enlarge it into into a 360 degree pie-chart as shown in Figure 12.4, then we can show the marketing communications mix as derived from the overall marketing mix. We can see in the pie-chart that each segment shows the proportion of the overall marketing communications budget allocated to each communications 'tool' in the mix. Once again the precise way in which the pie-chart is segmented will differ amongst firms even in the same industry. It will certainly differ between firms in different industries and between firms operating in different market sectors, for example consumer markets and

Fig 12.3   Marketing communications as a proportion of the total marketing budget

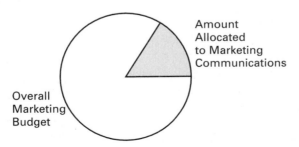

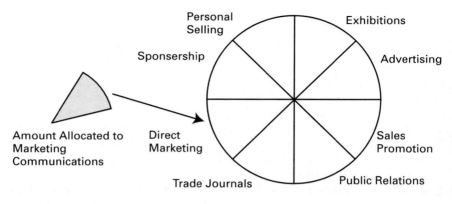

Fig 12.4   Marketing communications mix

industrial markets. Figure 12.4 shows a typical marketing communications mix for a fast-moving consumer good (FMCG) such as a branded packaged grocery product. We can see that the majority of the communications budget is allocated to non-personal forms of communications, especially below-the-line sales promotions and conventional media advertising with relatively little spent on personal forms of communications such as personal selling. This may be contrasted with Figure 12.5 which attempts to show the typical marketing communications mix for an industrial product. This time the majority of the communications budget is allocated to personal selling. Personal selling is the most important communications tool in industrial markets and often represents 90 percent of the marketing communications budget. Trade exhibitions and trade journal advertising is also used extensively in industrial marketing as reflected in the mix shown in Figure 12.5.

Activity

'The marketing communicator is rather like a chef, he/she has a finite array of ingredients at their disposal. It is the creative way in which these ingredients are used to produce the desired outcome that determines the reputation of the chef and the marketing communicator.' Discuss this viewpoint.

The comparison of marketing communicator and chef is an interesting analogy, and in fact the two professions do have many things in common. An imaginative, innovative, original and creative chef will have use of people, willing to pay astonishing prices, eager for a table at his/her restaurant or hotel. Such a chef is able to think of imaginative outcomes, and has the skill to put a complex array of ingredients together in just the right quantities and cooked in just the right way to

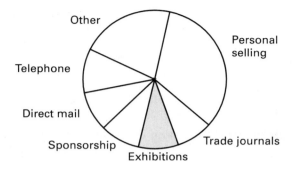

Fig 12.5   Typical marketing communications mix for an industrial product

achieve the desired outcome. The marketing communicator is in a similar situation. He/she has a finite array of marketing communication 'tools' or 'ingredients' at his or her disposal. The gifted marketing communicator is also able to think of imaginative outcomes for a communications strategy which may be for a brand, a corporation or even a political party. In the same way as the chef the gifted marketing communicator will possess the necessary skills to be able to formulate the communications mix in just the right way as to achieve the desired outcomes for the campaign.

12.5 The Marketing Communications Process

Effective communication is the key to effective marketing. The buyer's perception of a market offering is influenced by the amount and type of information they receive and their reaction to that information. Therefore there must be a good flow of information between seller and buyer to help in the decision-making process which precedes a purchase. Marketing communication is the process of execution of marketing decisions, following analysis of market and competitor data by marketers. Decisions are then made as to the optimal organisation and combination of resources and setting up of control systems. It is then that these decisions are implemented in the marketplace, communicating the company's message – the combination of produce, price, place and promotional stimuli – to the consumers, who then interpret these stimuli in their own way. An effective marketing communications system also allows feedback from the consumer to the seller and not just the reverse – it must be remembered that marketing communications is a dialogue between buyer and seller. The basic communications process is shown diagrammatically in Figure 12.6.

In this model the sender is the marketing firm. The firm develops a message and sends this via a particular communication channel to the

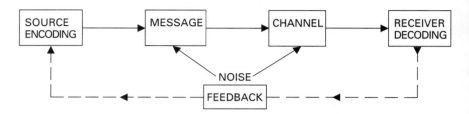

Fig 12.6   Simple model of marketing communications

receiver, in this case the target audience that the marketing firm is trying to reach. We note that the marketing message has been encoded: the marketing firm may have used visual images, comedy, music, guilt and so on to encode the message for maximum effect. When the message reaches the receiver (potential and existing customers) it is decoded. The marketing firm needs to make sure that the message that they have so creatively and carefully encoded is decoded in the way intended, and that the people that the message was aimed at have understood it. In order to find this out and to obtain on-going 'feedback' from the market as to the effectiveness of the communication, some form of post-communication research has to take place. This is shown in Figure 12.6 as a feedback loop.

The 'two-step-flow' model of communications

When a firm is dealing with new products or services the simple model of marketing communications shown in Figure 12.6 may not be appropriate. Another model of communication referred to as the Two-Step-Flow model seems to have some validity in the case of new products. This model of communication was not constructed or developed for marketing, and like so many other theories and models used in marketing it came from an entirely different academic discipline, in this case political science. An American university carried out research into the effects of political communication in the 1948, the research exercise being known as 'The Peoples Choice' (Lazarsfeld, Berelson and Gaude (1948)). The research team found that the majority of voters were not strongly influenced in their choice of political candidate by the political literature, direct mail shots and political broadcasts on the television and radio. We must realise that this form of political marketing communication has been used in the USA for many years, whereas the UK is just starting to get used to extensive, professional political marketing. The majority of voters tended to be influenced by other people, friends, relatives, sports people or actors and singers that they had seen on the television and in the press and for whom they had some respect and took notice of their views. The friends, relatives, personalities and so on that had such a strong leading influence were referred to as opinion

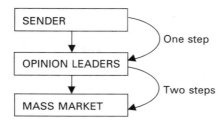

Fig 12.7   The two-step-flow model of communication

leaders. The general idea was that political communication had to be targeted at the opinion leaders if the campaign was to be effective, and they in turn would then pass on their own views and opinions, influenced by the political marketing communication, to the mass of regular voters. In this respect communication to the mass of voters took place in two distinct stages or steps. The key thing for the political communicator was to identify and reach the group of politically-aware people known as the 'opinion leaders'. These people then had to be effectively targeted through media scheduling and planning and the desired message communicated to them. The basic idea of the two-step-flow model of communication is shown in Figure 12.7.

Rogers' diffusion model of communication

The two-step-flow model of communications and the related idea of opinion leaders began to be applied in a marketing context in the launching of new products and services. The two-step-flow model is also related to another important marketing model developed by Everett Rogers in 1965 and known as 'The Diffusion of an Innovation Through a Population'. Because the model has rather a long title we will refer to it as the 'diffusion model'. Rogers' diffusion model is shown in Figure 12.8.

Rogers states that people have a psychological predisposition to buy 'new' products and services which can be modeled using a normal distribution. Certain people derive a great deal of pleasure from acquiring new products and being first in the market. Such people have a low level of perceived risk and in fact they positively like the risk and excitement associated with the purchase of new, innovative products. These people are referred to as 'innovators' and, according to Rogers, account for about 2.5 percent of the population. The next group of people displaying a tendency to buy new products are known as 'early adopters' and account for approximately 13.5 percent of the market. These are still highly adventurous purchasers and the possession of innovative new products gives them a high present value. They still have a low level of perceived risk but are slightly

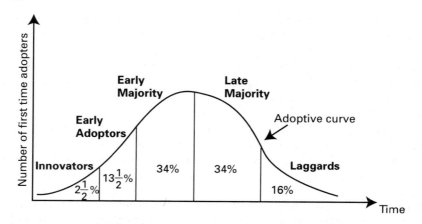

Source: Based on Rogers (1965).
Fig 12.8   The diffusion of an innovation model

more risk adverse than the innovator category. The next two groups, 'early majority' and 'late majority' account for the bulk of the potential market, 64 percent in all. Most people fall into one of these categories. Finally the 'laggards' are people who are not really interested in new product development and tend to purchase products only when their old product is worn out and stops working.

The key question for the marketing communicator is 'are the innovators and early adopters also opinion leaders? If they are then we can apply the two-step-flow concept of communication. The majority of potential customers are too risk-adverse or too disinterested to be first in the market for an innovation; they are largely unaffected by the media communication about the innovation. Instead they are influenced by people that they know who they regard as opinion leaders. Some people may be innovators as early majority types across all products and services. It is more likely however that people will be classified as such for only one or a limited range of products. For example a computer enthusiast may be regarded as a innovator for new computer products. Likewise someone who is interested in photography or cars may be regarded as anopinion leaders in relation to these particular products but not others.

Of course 'new' products actually have different degrees of newness. A new brand of toothpaste containing baking soda is not really that new to people, after all it is still just toothpaste. A vacuum cleaner for your garden is on the other hand quite a radical innovation. These products have recently come onto the market although most people, even keen gardeners, seem a little unsure as to whether they should buy one or not. At present less than 1 percent of households own such a product. If these products are any good then the message will soon circulate by word of mouth and soon virtually every household will own one just as most own a lawn mower or a strimmer; garden strimmers were considered to be a fairly radical innovation only 10 years ago. For new product developments such as these the two-step-flow model and the diffusion model appear to have some application, and may help marketers plan their communication campaigns when dealing with product or service innovations.

These models are usually discussed in the context of consumer products and services. However, they may also have applications in the fields of industrial and business-to-business marketing communications. Larger firms tend to be financially stronger than small ones; they also tend to be technologically more advanced and hence more likely to adopt new innovations related to production equipment or administrative systems and so on. Smaller firms may look up to the Fords, ICIs and Pilkingtons of this world. In other words these larger, well-respected firms may act as opinion leaders to the rest of the market. The implications are obvious, marketers will need to target the innovative and early adoptive firms who may also be viewed as opinion leaders by other firms. There adoption of a product or service will then be taken up or adopted by the mass market in due course as postulated by Rogers.

Activity

What method might you use to encode a message for a political marketing communication?

Whenever you see a party political broadcast on the television or a political advertisement on a poster or in a newspaper, try to analyse it and discover for yourself what encoding techniques the sender of the message has employed. Political messages on television, for example, often use sterling, patriotic music by Handle or Elgar to try and convey the gravity of the message and the fact that the political party concerned is the natural party of Britain. Fear and insecurity, whether about jobs, pensions, health or education are used to try and convey what might happen if the opposition party ever managed to get elected. Pictures, comedy, music and playing on people's fears, aspirations and hopes for the future are all used in political broadcasts in much the same way as they are used in advertisements for products. The only thing that is really any different is the subject matter, that is the message content.

Marketing-related messages

Marketing communications can be defined as the process of:

1 presenting an integrated set of stimuli to a market target with the aim of raising a desired set of responses within that market target; and

2 setting up channels to receive, interpret and act on messages from the market to modify present company messages and identify new communications opportunities.

As both a sender and a receiver of market-related messages, a company can influence customers to buy its brands in order to make profits and at the same time stay in touch with its market so that it can adjust to changing market conditions and take advantage of new communications opportunities.

The source of the message

Receivers of a message are often greatly influenced by the nature of its source. If an audience perceives a communicator as credible, then they will be more likely to accept his or her views. If, on the other hand, the audience believes that the communicator has underlying motives, particularly ones of personal gain, then he or she will be less persuasive than someone the audience perceives as being objective. Some advertisers use 'candid' television interviews with homemakers in order to enhance their credibility and eliminate intent to persuade, sometimes asking consumers to explain why they buy a particular brand or asking them to trade their chosen brand for another.

Another method used by companies to increase credibility is to have the product endorsed by an expert with appropriate education and knowledge on a given subject. This source will be more successful in changing audience opinions. **Specialized sources** of information are often perceived as expert sources, and are successful due to the fact that messages are aimed at selected audiences, for example the use of sports professionals as promoters for brands.

The credibility of a source is also affected by its perceived status or prestige, the higher the perceived status the more persuasive it will be. If a receiver **likes** a source, it will be more persuasive. It is clear that age, sex, dress, mannerisms, accent and voice inflection all affect source credibility and subtly influence the way an audience judges a communicator and his/her message.

A source high in credibility can change the opinion of receivers, but available evidence suggests that this influence disperses in a short time after the message is received. It has also been observed that where an audience initially receives a message from a low-credibility source, their opinion change increases over time in the direction promoted by the source. This is referred to as the **sleeper effect**. Another aspect of this is that when a high-credibility source is reinstated, for example by a repeat advertisement, it has been found that audience agreement with the source is higher after a period of time than if the source had not been reinstated. For a low-credibility source, however, reinstatement results in less agreement with the source than with no reinstatement, that is reinstatement negates the sleeper effect.

Activity

Explain the difference between a need and a want.

Everyone needs certain things. However our genuine needs are fairly basic. We considered the psychological theory of Maslow's hierarchy of needs' earlier in this chapter in which Maslow explained that our real needs are mainly basic physiological needs. For example, none of use can live without water and sufficient food, it is literally a physical impossibility. We need appropriate clothing to keep us warm otherwise we might die of hypothermia. Likewise with shelter, we need somewhere to live and sleep that is dry and warm. The fact is that we need water, literally nothing else, but we want Coca Cola or 7-Up. We need appropriate clothing, but we want Calvin Kline branded clothing. Our needs may be genuine but marketers explore the way that we may satisfy are needs and turn these into wants. It is the way we satisfy our needs through the purchase of goods and services that marketing people are interested in.

12.6 Above-the-line Promotion

Marketing communications can be divided into two broad categories, Above-the-line promotion and Below-the-line promotion. These terms are really only a sort of jargon used in the communications industry. There is no unified generally accepted definition as to what constitutes above or below-the-line promotion activity, and different writers on the subject in both academic articles and books tend to include slightly different things under each of the headings. Generally speaking the term above-the-line refers to paid-for media advertising. If a marketing communications manager buys advertising space in a newspaper, on the television or commercial radio, on a poster site or whatever, the person that sells the space usually earns a commission. If an advertising agency places an advertisement in a Sunday glossy magazine on behalf of a client they usually attract commission. In a sense the marketing firm rents space on the television, newspaper and so on, and whoever buys that space on their behalf or sells them the space directly may be entitled to a commission on the deal. Below-the-line communication, in contrast, is usually defined as non-media advertising. Media are used to communicate a message where no commission is paid, no actual space is rented out to the client as in the case of conventional media advertising. As we mentioned, above-the-line promotion is concerned with conventional media advertising, a subject that we will turn to next.

Media advertising

Media advertising communicates information to a large number of recipients, paid for by a sponsor. It has three main aims:

1 To impart information;
2 To develop attitudes;
3 To induce action beneficial to the advertiser (generally the purchase of a product or service).

An advertisement for a washing powder is paid for by the manufacturer to achieve the end of greater sales of their product; a party political broadcast aims to increase votes. It must be remembered though that advertising is only one element of the communications mix, but it does perform certain parts of the communicating task faster and with greater economy and volume than other means.

How large a part advertising plays depends on the nature of the product and its frequency of purchase. It contributes the greatest part when:

1 Buyer awareness of the product is low;
2 Industry sales are rising rather than remaining stable or declining;
3 The product has features which are not obvious to the buyer;
4 The opportunities for product differentiation are strong;
5 Discretionary incomes are high;
6 A new product or new service idea is being introduced.

12.7 Advertising Models

These have been drawn from several sources, particularly psychology and from advertising practitioners, to explain how advertising works. The stimulus/response formula was used at first, later models taking into consideration the environment in which the decision to buy is made. Daniel Starch said in 1925 'for an advertisement to be successful it must be seen, must be read, must be believed, must be remembered and must be acted upon' (see Majaro, 1970). This model assumed that the advertisement is the main influence on the state of mind of the consumer with respect to the product and made no allowance for the combined or multiple effects of advertisements.

The DAGMAR philosophy

Colley's DAGMAR model (defining advertising goals for measured advertising results – Colley, 1961) allows for the cumulative impact of advertisements and also maps out the states of mind consumers pass through:

1 From unawareness to awareness;
2 to comprehension;
3 to conviction;
4 to action.

This is described as the **marketing communications spectrum**. Advertising, along with promotion, personal selling, publicity, price, packaging and distribution, move the consumer through the various levels of the spectrum as follows:

- **Unawareness/awareness** The advertisement tries to make potential customers aware of the product's existence.
- **Comprehension** The customer recognizes the brand name and trademark and also knows what the product is and what it does; knowledge is gained from the advertisement or from an information search prompted by it.
- **Conviction** The customer has a firm attitude, preferring a particular brand over all others. Preferences may have an emotional rather than rational basis.
- **Action** Some move is made towards purchase, thus the advertisement has been acted upon.

This illustrates the concept that the purpose of advertising is to cause a change of mind leading toward purchase, but it is rare for a single advertisement to have the power to move a prospect from complete unawareness to action. Effectiveness is judged by how far an advertisement moves people along the spectrum.

A study reported by Majaro in 1970 established, by means of questionnaire replies, that companies adopting a systematic **advertising-by-objectives** process had an advantage over others who did not, however it did not prove statistically that an increase in market-share or financial performance follows directly from advertising.

The Lavidge and Steiner (1961) model

This model consists of a hierarchical sequence of events on six levels:

1 Awareness
2 Knowledge
3 Liking
4 Preference
5 Conviction
6 Purchase

These steps divide behaviour into three dimensions: cognitive (the first two), affective (the second two) and motivational (the third pair). Although the two models above differ in the number and nature of stages, there is general agreement that purchase is the result of the persuasion elements, with the assumption that changes in knowledge and attitude towards a product and changes in buying behaviour form a predictable one-way relationship.

Other models

Dissonance theory, however, illustrates a two-way relationship, with behaviour influencing attitudes as well as attitudes influencing behaviour. After making a decision to purchase, the prospect will be involved in cognitive dissonance and will actively seek information to reinforce the decision, focusing on attractive features and filtering out unfavourable data. The major implication of this is that advertising for existing brands in the repeat purchase market should be aimed at existing users to reassure them in the continuation of the buying habit at the expense of the competition.

The **unique selling proposition** was developed by Rosser Reeves (1961), who reported the principles his agency had worked with for 30 years. This states that the consumer remembers one key element of an advertisement – a strong claim or concept. This proposition must be one that the competition does not offer, which will be recalled by the consumer and will result in purchase at the appropriate time.

The **brand-image** school, led by David Ogilvy (1961) focused on non-verbal methods of communication to invest a brand with agreeable connotations aside from its actual properties in use, such as prestige and quality.

It must also be remembered that an advertisement is the channel through which the sponsor communicates their message. The encoded message reaches recipients, through advertising or salesmen, who then decode and absorb it either fully or partly. The quality of the transmission can be distorted by 'noise', occurring because the receiver does not interpret the message in the way the source intended (due perhaps to differences in cultural backgrounds of the two parties), or because of cognitive dissonance which occurs when peoples' receipt of the message does not agree with what they previously believed.

Dissonance may cause a number of different reactions by the receiver:

1 Rejecting the message;
2 Ignoring the message;
3 Altering the previous opinion;
4 Searching for justifications.

The first two reactions are of course negative, and from this feedback the source may change the message or stop communicating altogether with a particular receiver who is not receptive to the source's ideas. It can therefore be seen that advertising does not always convert people into users of a particular product. It can, however, have a positive effect in preventing loss of users, and in increasing their loyalty.

Advertising situations are so varied and unique that it is not possible to generalise about how advertising works. Any potential advertiser should therefore adopt an **advertising-by-objectives** approach which will make clear what they are trying to achieve, how they will achieve it and how they are going to measure its effects.

Setting objectives

Few companies give any detailed scientific thought to exactly what they are trying to achieve through advertising. Clear objectives are needed to aid operational decisions, which include:

- The amount to be spent on a particular campaign;
- The content and presentation of the advertisement;
- The most appropriate media;
- The frequency of display of advertisements or campaigns;
- Any special geographical weighting of effort;
- The best methods of evaluating the effects of the advertising.

Corkindale and Kennedy (1976) found that systematically setting and evaluating objectives provided the following benefits:

1 Marketing management has to consider and define in advance what each element in the programme is expected to accomplish.
2 An information system can be set up to monitor ongoing performance, with the nature of information required clearly defined.
3 Marketing management will learn about the system it is operating from accumulated experience of success (and failure) and can use this knowledge to improve future performance.

Majaro's (1970) major study on objective-setting revealed that most managers saw increasing sales or market-share as their main advertising objective, but in fact this is a total marketing objective and it is unreasonable to expect to achieve this through advertising alone (unless it was the only element of the marketing mix used, as in direct mail and mail order businesses). Majaro's study revealed that methods of evaluation used by most companies were not relevant, and that clear, precise advertising objectives, known to all involved, would rectify this situation. The following advantages of the advertising-by-objectives approach became clear:

1 It helps to integrate the advertising effort with other ingredients of the marketing mix, thus setting a consistent and logical marketing plan;
2 It facilitates the task of the advertising agency in preparing and evaluating creative work and recommending the most suitable media;
3 It assists in determining advertising budgets;
4 It enables marketing executives and top management to appraise the advertising plan realistically;
5 It permits meaningful measurement of advertising results.

Frequently, all the people in a company who have an interest in, and influence on, advertising decisions have different ideas of the purpose of advertising. The chairman may be most concerned with building a corporate image, whilst the advertising manager may see it as an investment directed toward building a brand image and increasing market-share. Marketing objectives have to be separated from advertising objectives. Overall marketing objectives should be defined and the next step is to determine the contribution that advertising can efficiently make to each of these. An advertising objective is one that advertising alone is expected to achieve, and the objectives should be set with the following points in mind:

1 They should fit in with broader corporate objectives;
2 They should be realistic, taking into account internal resources and external opportunities, threats and constraints;
3 They should be universally known within the company, so that everyone can relate them to his or her own work and to the broader corporate objectives;
4 They need to be flexible, since all business decisions have to be made in conditions of partial ignorance;
5 They should be reviewed and adapted from time to time to take account of changing conditions.

Setting advertising objectives should not be undertaken until all relevant information on the product, the market and the consumer is available. Consumer behaviour and motivation must be thoroughly assessed, particularly that of the company's target group of customers. The statement of an advertising objective should then make clear what basic message is intended to be delivered, to what audience, with what intended effects and the specific criteria to be used to measure success.

Corkindale and Kennedy used five key words to summarise the elements of setting advertising objectives:

1 **WHAT** role is advertising expected to fulfill in the total marketing effort?
2 **WHY** is it believed that advertising can achieve this role? (What evidence is there and what assumptions are necessary?)
3 **WHO** should be involved in setting objectives; who should be responsible for agreeing the objectives, coordinating their implementation and subsequent evaluation? Who are the intended audience?
4 **HOW** are the advertising objectives to be put into practice?
5 **WHEN** are various parts of the programme to be implemented? When can response be expected to each stage of the programme?

Activity

Define the term above-the-line promotion.

There is no accepted, unified definition of the term. Generally it is used in the marketing communications profession to denote 'paid-for' space in conventional advertising media for which some form of commission is earned by the person selling the space or placing the order for space on the clients behalf. All conventional media advertising would therefore fall into this category, for example television advertising, newspaper and magazine advertising, cinema and commercial radio advertising and advertising hordings, that is poster advertising. All other non-media advertising would be classified as below-the-line promotion because media space has not been rented and commission has not been awarded by the media owners.

12.8 Below-the-line Promotion

To reiterate, the terms below-the-line promotion or below-the-line communications, refers to forms of non-media communications, some would say non media advertising. Examples are exhibitions, sponsorship activities, public relations and sales promotions such as competitions, branded packs and price promotions. Below-the-line promotions are becoming increasingly important within the marketing communications mix of many companies, not only those involved in fast-moving consumer goods but also for industrial products. For example dealer incentives, exhibitions and sponsorship activities are all growing in popularity. All forms of non-media communications are a form of promotion if we use the word in the broadest sense. A specific form of below-the-line activity is known specifically as below-the-line *sales* promotion. This specific form of promotion is discussed below.

Below-the-line sales promotion

Below the line sales promotions are short-term incentives, largely aimed at consumers but also aimed at the trade – for example wholesalers, retailers, distributors, factors and so on, and company employees, usually the sales force. Over the last 20 years or so there has been greater pressure on marketing budgets and a greater demand on marketing management to achieve marketing communications objectives more efficiently. Hence marketers have been searching for a more cost-effective way to communicate with their target markets than conventional media advertising. A move to below-the-line promotion is one result of this. A good definition of below-the-line sales promotion is given by Hugh Davidson (1997) who describes it as:

> 'An immediate or delayed incentive to purchase expressed in cash or in kind and having only a short term or temporary duration.'

This definition highlights the important characteristic of its short-term nature. Most conventional advertising campaigns are medium to long-term in nature, and some are very long-term indeed lasting for 20 years or more. Below-the-line sales promotions on the other hand are short-term in nature, rarely does such a promotion last for more than six months and the majority last for much shorter periods.

12.9 **The Main Elements of Sales Promotion**

All promotions are variations of one basic type or another, but since the sales promotion is dynamic by nature new types will possibly be developed in the future. Figure 12.9 shows the primary types and their possible uses.

The sphere of sales promotions generally includes the following other marketing elements:

- Display materials (stands, header boards, shelf strips, 'wobblers');
- Packaging (coupons, premium offers, pack flashes);
- Merchandising (demonstrations, auxiliary sales forces, display arrangements);
- Direct mail (coupons, competitions, premiums);
- Exhibitions.

Industrial promotions also include the above elements, but with slight modifications to make them closer in type to those mounted by manufacturers of consumer goods for their retailers, designed to gain large orders over long periods.

Sales promotion planning

A full plan is needed to ensure that each stage of a promotion is reached:

1 Analyse the problem task;
2 Define objectives;
3 Consider and/or set the budget;
4 Examine the types of promotion likely to be of use;
5 Define the support activities (for example advertising, incentives, auxiliaries);
6 Testing (for example a limited store or panel test);
7 Decide measurements required;
8 Plan timetable;
9 Present details to sales force, retailers, and so on;
10 Implement the promotion;
11 Evaluate the result.

Advantages and disadvantages of sales promotions

Advantages:

Fig 12.9 Guide to the effective use of consumer promotions, showing objectives which certain promotions might achieve depending on circumstances

Source: Lancaster and Reynolds (1995) p. 214.

PROMOTION TYPE

OBJECTIVES	Self-liquidating premiums	On-pack premiums	In-pack premiums	With-pack premiums	Container premiums	Continuing premiums	Trade stamps/gyruouchery	Competitions	Personalities	Couponing	Sampling	Reduce price pack	Banded pack	Related Items
Product launch/relaunch							¥			¥	¥	¥	¥	
Induce Trial										¥	¥		¥	
Existing product new usage										¥	¥	¥	¥	¥
Gain new users						¥	¥	¥	¥	¥	¥	¥	¥	¥
Increase frequency of produse						¥	¥							
Upgrade purchasing size		¥	¥	¥	¥							¥		
Increase brand awareness									¥		¥			
Expand distribution									¥	¥		¥	¥	¥
Increase trade stocks				¥								¥	¥	¥
Reduce trade stocks										¥				¥
Expand sales 'off season'								¥		¥		¥	¥	¥
Activate slow moving lines										¥		¥	¥	¥
Gain special featuring in store	¥	¥	¥	¥	¥			¥				¥	¥	¥
Increasing shelf space		¥		¥									¥	¥
Retain existing users						¥	¥					¥	¥	

- Easily measured response;
- Quick achievement of objectives;
- Flexible application;
- Can be extremely cheap;
- Direct support of sales-force.

Disadvantages:

- Price-discounting can cheapen brand image;
- Short-term advantages only;
- Can cause stress with retailers;
- Difficulty in communicating brand message.

The importance of sales promotion

It is often difficult to know which marketing expenditures can be attributed to sales promotion. For example price reduction can cause confusion – 3p off a packet of biscuits is a sales promotion, but what about price discounting by manufacturers? The most widely quoted source of sales promotion expenditure data is that provided annually by Harris International Marketing (HIM) which comes from an analysis of the quarterly Harris *International Sales Promotion Intelligence Reports* (*HISPI*). These indicate that sales promotion is increasing in importance every year in the UK.

Activity

Define the term below-the-line sales promotions, and use specific examples to compare and contrast it with conventional media advertising.

Below-the-line sales promotions can be defined as immediate or delayed incentives to purchase, expressed in cash or in kind and having only a temporary or short-term duration. The key phrase here is 'short-term duration'. There are two important factors that distinguish below-the-line sales promotions from above-the-line conventional media advertising. Firstly, unlike conventional media advertising, no space is actually bought in the media – for example television, newspapers, magazines and so on – and no commission is paid by the marketing firm or earnt by the person selling the advertising space or placing the client's order for advertising. Secondly, conventional media advertising tends to be at least medium-term and often long-term in both its effects and its duration. For example, if we take the alcoholic drink Guinness as an example: the Guinness advertising campaign tends to be on the same theme for 1 to 2 years, there are small variations between advertisements but the underlying theme of the campaign is the same. We can compare this with a Guiness below-the-line sales promotion such as a competition (duration about six months) or 'extra product' promotions, for example at one point Guinness offered 13.5% more 'product' for the same money and this offer was 'flashed' across the can for extra impact; this lasted for about two months.

Telephone marketing

Telemarketing can be defined as 'any measurable activity that creates and exploits a direct relationship between supplier and customer by the interactive use of the telephone'. The American Telephone and Telegraph Company define it as 'the marketing of telecommunications technology and **direct marketing** [our emphasis] techniques'.

Telephone marketing can take the form of both 'in-coming call' and 'out-going call'. In-coming call telephone marketing usually makes use of special numbers such as the 0800 number or 0345 number, which enables the caller to call freephone. Other numbers enable callers to call from anywhere in the country, or even overseas, for the price of a local call. In-coming call telephone marketing campaigns are usually used in conjunction with other marketing communications tools.

Direct mail

What it is
Direct mailing is the use of the postal service to distribute promotional material directly to a particular person, household or firm. The most familiar users of this technique in the UK today are probably *Readers Digest* and the Automobile Association.

What it is not
Direct mail is often confused with the following related activities, which all fall under the general heading of direct marketing.

1 **Direct advertising**   One of the oldest methods of reaching the consumer, with printed matter being sent directly to the prospect by the advertiser, often by mail but sometimes by personal delivery, handing out to passers-by or left under the windscreen wiper of a car. **Direct mail advertising** uses the postal service, and this **is** a form of direct mail.
2 **Mail order**   Mail order advertising aims to persuade recipients to purchase a product or service by return post, with deliveries being made through the mail, by carrier or through a local agent. Thus it is a special form of direct mail, seeking to complete the sale entirely by mail and therefore being a complete plan in itself. Mail order is therefore a type of direct mail, but not all direct mail is mail order.
3 **Direct response advertising**   This is a strategy of using specially designed advertisements, usually in magazines or newspapers, to invoke a direct response, such as the **coupon-response press advertisement**, which the reader uses to order the advertised product or request further information. Other variants offer money-off coupons and incentives to visit the retail outlet immediately. This is only one of many ways of using direct mail.

The growth of direct mail in UK marketing

The usage and acceptance of direct mail increases annually according to Post Office statistics, and one reason for this is that the media has become increasingly fragmented, with two commercial TV channels along with cable channels and the rapid growth of 'freesheets' and special interest magazines. This means that advertisers have to either spend more money to reach their audience, or spread the same maount of money over a wider range of media. Improvements in the quality of large mailshots have attracted an increasing number of large advertisers. Direct mail, with increasing use of computerisation, enables advertisers to segment and target their markets with flexibility, selectivity and personal contact.

Uses of direct mail

Direct mail can be used to sell a wide range of products or services, and its uses are also varied. To help define direct mail more fully it is appropriate to deal with direct mail to consumers and businesses separately.

Consumer direct mail

Some of the most common uses of consumer-targeted direct mail are:

1 **Selling direct** Direct mail is a good medium for selling a product directly to the customer by a company that has a convincing sales message. It provides a facility for describing the product or service fully and for an order to be sent straight back, cutting out middlemen.
2 **Sales lead generation** A product such as fitted kitchens or central heating requires a meeting between the customer and a specialised salesperson, and direct mail can be used to acquire good, qualified leads. A mailshot that has been well thought out can reveal the very best prospects and rank other leads in terms of potential, enabling interested responses to be followed up by a salesperson. An invitation can be made for the customer to view the product in a retail outlet, showroom or exhibition. **'Cordial-contact' mailings** create a receptive atmosphere for salespeople by building on the reputation of the company, creating a good impression, which can be converted into buying action by a later mailing.
3 **Sales promotion** Promotional messages such as special offers will reach specific targets through direct mail, in the same way prospects can be encouraged to visit showrooms or exhibitions.
4 **Clubs** The most popular users of direct mail in this category are book clubs and companies marketing 'collectibles', presenting a convenient method of communication and dealings between club and members.
5 **Mail order** Direct selling and recruitment of new customers and agents are possible through direct mail.
6 **Fundraising** It is easy through direct mail to communicate personally with an individual, and therefore it is an excellent method of raising

money for charitable organisations. Large amounts of information can be included to induce the recipient to make a donation.

7 **Dealer mailings** Dealers or agents can use direct mail to reach prospects in their own areas.
8 **Follow-up mailings** These help to keep the company's name before the customer following a sale, for example checking that the customer is satisfied with a purchase. New developments, products and services can also be communicated or invitations issued, thus maintaining contact and increasing repeat sales.

Business direct mail
Direct mail is more effective than mass advertising for identifying different market sectors and communicating to each an appropriate message. Some of the more common uses are:

1 **Product launch** Direct mail is able to target the small but significant number of people who influence buying decisions.
2 **Sales lead generation** Direct mail provides qualified sales leads, as well as doing some initial selling.
3 **Dealer support** Dealers, retail outlets, franchise holders and so on can be kept fully informed of marketing promotions and plans.
4 **Conferences** Potential delegates in specific business sections can be issued with invitations through direct mail.
5 **Follow-up mailing using the customer base** Mailing existing customers regularly encourages repeat sales.
6 **Market research/product testing** Market research, especially amongst existing customers, is possible through direct mail, using questionnaires as part of a regular communication programme. Small-scale test mailings give an accurate picture of market reaction, with low risk, and a successful product can later be mailed to the full list.

Direct mail as part of the promotional mix
When direct mail is added to, say, a television or press campaign, then the effectiveness of the overall campaign can be significantly raised. The media reach a broad audience and raise general awareness of the company and its products, while the direct mail campaign is targeted specifically at the groups of people or companies most likely to buy. Mailing lists of respondents to couponed press advertisements or television or radio commercials with a phone-in number can be used for direct mail approaches.

Activity

Briefly outline some of the major benefits of using direct mail as part of an integrated marketing communications campaign.

An important part of the above sentence is 'integrated marketing communications campaign'. Direct mail, or any other marketing communications tool, is rarely used by a marketing firm in total isolation. They usually form part of a multi-media mix which is usually made up of both above and below-the-line promotional tools. There are examples of marketing companies using predominantly one communication tool: for example Cornhill Insurance uses predominately sports sponsorship (cricket sponsorship) but also uses direct mail and media advertising. In terms of direct mail perhaps the most prolific user of the medium is the publishing company *Readers Digest*. This company not only markets its own magazine by direct mail and attempt to get people to sign up for a subscription, but they also use this technique to market related products such as gardening books, DIY manuals, cooking books and language courses. There direct mail material is often linked with below-the-line sales promotion activity. Many of their direct mail shots contain promotional material, usually some form of competition where you can win a new car or a fabulous amount of money if only you will buy their latest set of language teaching tapes or whatever. Direct mail can be personalised and hence sent to a specific individual. Direct mail is a very flexible medium, and the company can put as much or as little in to the envelope as they wish. It is controllable, therefore, in terms of the amount and types of material included. It is also very flexible in terms of time and can be coordinated with telephone marketing and conventional media advertising campaigns and so on. Direct mail is relatively cheap when compared to other media, and response rates are such as to make this form of marketing communications a highly effective tool which has grown in importance and popularity over the last 20 years and continues to grow in terms of sophistication and applications.

Exhibitions

Exhibitions are another form of below-the-line promotional activity. As with many other methods exhibitions are growing in use and popularity. They come in three basic forms: there are exhibitions aimed at the consumer, those aimed solely at the trade, and those aimed at and open to both. The third category is the most common. Most exhibitions start off as trade exhibitions and then after the first week or so when all of the trade business has been conducted they are usually opened to the public. The public usually pays an entry fee which brings in revenue for the exhibition organiser and helps to pay for the costs of actually staging the exhibition. The general public may have an actual interest in the products and services being exhibited, for example the Clothes Show, Motor Show and Ideal Home Exhibition. Sometime the actual products and services are off little direct interest to the general public, that is they are highly unlikely to actually buy any of the products on show, but nevertheless attendence at the exhibition makes for a good day out and the public is prepared to pay for the privilage of visiting the exhibition. The best example of this situation is probably the Royal Agricultural Show held at Stoneleigh between Coventry and Warwick each year. It is mainly concerned with livestock, feedstuffs and agricultural equipment and so on, but is nonetheless very popular with the general public.

Audience quality

Trade exhibitions tend to attract a high-quality audience, for example managing directors and company chairmen will often attend an important trade exhibition. Hence trade exhibitions offer the marketing firm the opportunity to come in personal contact with high-status decision-making-unit (DMU) members. Exhibitions attract a wide range of decision-makers and influencers ranging from technical staff such as engineers and purchasers to senior management. Generally the more prestigious the exhibition venue the higher the status of the visitors. Exhibiting is now an international business and there are major exhibition sites in most countries of the world.

Sponsorship

Sponsorship is the final below-the-line promotional activity we shall consider in this chapter. Like all other activites mentioned it is growing in popularity. In some ways sponsorship achieves many of the functions of exhibitions discussed above especially in terms of audience quality. We have already established that in business-to-business marketing environments, high-status decision-making-unit members are notoriously difficult to contact on a personal basis. The firm sponsoring an event can invite important members of a prospective customer company's DMU to the event thereby enabling personal contact to be made.

12.10 **Summary**

The marketing communications mix is made up of personal selling, a range of conventional advertising media and an equally impressive range of non-media communication tools. The conventional media tools, which involve renting space on television, newspapers, posters, radio and so on, are referred to as above-the-line promotional techniques. Other marketing communications techniques, such as sales promotion, sponsorship and exhibitions do not involve the commissioning of space or air-time in or on conventional media. These techniques are referred to in the industry as below-the-line techniques. Marketing effectiveness dependss significantly on communications effectiveness: the market is activated through information flows. The way a potential buyer perceives the seller's market offering is heavily influenced by the amount and kind of information he or she has about the product offering , and the reaction to that information. Marketing therefore relies heavily upon information flows between the seller and the prospective buyer. To many people marketing communications, such as television advertising, direct mail and poster advertising is marketing. They can be forgiven for thinking that way because marketing communications is certainly the most highly visible aspect of marketing activity and it impacts every day on every person's life. You know from reading this book that marketing communications, whether above or below-the-line activity, is collectively just one of the conventional '4Ps' of the marketing mix. However, it is a very important part. No matter how good a firm's product or service offering is, the benefits to the consumer needs to be communicated effectively. Marketing communications, in the form of above and below-the-line promotion, lies at the very center of any marketing plan.

Chapter Review Questions

Explain how both above and below-the-line promotional tools can be used in such a way as to result in a truly integrated marketing communications programme.
Some communications tools are long-term in nature, such as conventional media advertising, corporate image, product brands and so on, and some are short-term, for example below-the-line sales promotions such as competitions, branded packs and price reductions. Some tools are direct such as telephone marketing, direct selling (for example Avon Cosmetics) and direct mail (for example *Readers Digest*), and some are indirect as with conventional television or radio advertising. Each communication 'tool' in the mix has specific strengths and qualities: each element has a specific part to play in the overall scheme of things, and builds on and interacts with each other element. The effectiveness of any given marketing communications mix is derived from how successfully all of these mix elements mesh and reinforce one another in achieving the overall marketing communication objective of the firm.

How are the below-the-line communication tools of exhibitions and sponsorship similar in terms of attracting a high audience quality and facilitating personal contact with important prospects?
In business-to-business markets buying decisions are usually made by groups of people that marketer's call the decision-making unit, or DMU for short. The DMU is made up of various people within the purchasing organisation and these people will have different roles, different vested interests and different levels of seniority. Very senior people such as managing directors and the chairmen of companies often play an important role in the purchasing decision-making process for a wide range of products and services. However, it is very difficult for the marketing firm to arrange personal contact with such important, high-status DMU members. Such people rarely, if ever, see a salesperson. Exhibitions and sponsored events, whether concerned with sport such as golf or the arts, may often attract such high-status people and thus provide an opportunity for the marketing firm's team to at least make personal contact with them.

How does 'marketing' differ from 'marketing communications'?
Some texts argue that the marketing mix is really a communications mix. The rationale for this position is that virtually everything in the marketing mix, whether it be price, distribution (place), product (or service) as well as of course promotion all communicate something. Other texts differentiate between marketing and marketing communications by considering marketing communications as one of the later stages of marketing within the overall marketing process.

What does marketing communications communicate?
'Communications' is the process of establishing a commonness of thought between a sender and a receiver. It is therefore a process, and as such has elements

and interrelationships which can be modelled and examined in a structured manner. There must also be a commonness of thought developed between sender and receiver if communication is to occur in a true sense. Commonness of thought implies that a sharing relationship must exist. In its simplest form the process can be modelled as a simple flow diagram such as that shown in Figure 12.6. The sender designs a commercial message using encoding techniques; this is then sent via a channel to a receiver who decodes the message; and research is need to ensure that the message is being decoded (understood) in the way intended by the sender. Marketing messages are purposeful and are intended to effect some form of response or change in thinking in the receiver.

13 Public Relations

13.1 **Introduction**

Public relations is an extremely important and versatile marketing communications tool, and can be employed both within and outside the organisation. Most lay people think public relations is merely an external marketing tool, with the marketing firm attempting to communicate with a wide range of external 'publics' in order to cast the organisation in a favourable light in peoples' minds. This way of thinking is very limited and fails to appreciate the great value of public relations as an internal marketing communications tool. Good internal marketing, that is achieving the right internal organisational culture and getting everyone 'pulling' in the same direction in terms of marketing effort, is a vital prerequisite to effective external marketing strategies, particularly those based on the concepts of long-term relationship marketing principles. Public relations has a vital role to play and contribution to make to the creation of an effective internal marketing culture within an organisation. In this sense public relations has seen a dramatic increase in its importance as a strategic internal marketing communication tool.

Public relations is a very versatile communications tool and is today used by just about every type of organisation whether it be a charity, a university, the civil service, a political party or a commercial organisation. It is concerned with the strategic management of information in such a way that certain publicity objectives are achieved. It is not always the case that positive publicity is the outcome of a managed public relations campaign, because it is often impossible to achieve a net positive outcome. For example, public relations has a particularly important role to play in crisis management scenarios. Where a catastrophe has occurred, especially where people have been injured or even lost their lives – for example a ferry or aircraft disaster – it is often a case of containing the situation, putting a fair and balanced account of events forward to the general public, and mitigating the adverse affects of the disaster to the organisation concerned.

A brief history of public relations

Public relations (PR) is not as new as some people might expect. Its modern-day origins in the United States can be traced as far back as 1807 with President Jefferson's address to congress, though evidence suggests that even the ancient Greeks and Romans gave much attention to influencing public opinion. Public relations in Britain began as a government information and propaganda machine during the First-World War and was used even more extensively for this purpose in World War Two. Industry seemed to show little interest in public relations as a commercial communications tool until after 1945, when its use increased exponentially over the next 30 years in a sort of PR explosion. Public relations' relatively poor reputation over these 30 years was a result of poor, amateur practitioners, and by the 1960s the whole public relations profession was referred to by derogatory names such as the 'gin and tonic brigade'. The people who made up this brigade were usually public school educated and members of the right gentleman's club. They often carried considerable social influence and were able to 'open doors' because they had the right connections; their main function seemed to be the wining and dining of important clients. The situation has changed a great deal in the 1990s and, generally, public relations professionals come from a much wider background and are often trained in the art of communications management with some having degrees in journalism or even public relations itself. Unfortunately the profession still operates under the shadow of its 'gin and tonic' postwar image.

After its initial success had been demonstrated, public relations began to spread slowly throughout industry and commerce. At first staff appointments in industry were less common than the use of the services of a management consultancy, market research firm or advertising agency. Because of this slow internal adoption of professional public relations practitioners internally by industry and commerce, external public relations firms developed at an enormous rate, many of them lacking skilled staff of sufficient expertise but merely taking advantage of and exploiting the boom in the public relation profession. This phenomenon is quite common, it happened at the end of the 1980s when 'total quality management' (TQM) was the latest business fad, and every man and his dog somehow became experts in the art of TQM virtually overnight. Consequently, because of the hasty expansion of public relations firms, particularly in London, the poor reputation of public relations among journalists, businessmen, politicians and even the general public that persists to some extent today, can be traced back to this period of uncontrolled and unthinking growth. In the last 20 years many agencies have built reputations for highly marketing-orientated public relations, most notably companies such as Shandwick which is quoted on the stock market. In more recent years some have even built a reputation for strong relationship marketing-orientated public relations.

Some of these firms tend to specialise in consumer PR, trade relations, corporate PR, financial, industrial, service and technical PR. A growing number of firms are offering services in public relations for not-for-profit organisations such as tax-exempt charities, and even in the dark arts of political public relations.

Activity

Examine the position that professional public relations is just as valuable employed within marketing organisations as outside them.

Public relations is concerned with communicating desirable information to a wide variety of 'publics' and not just customers.

One important group would be the employees of the organisation.

In order for the management of an organisation to be able to create a genuine 'marketing orientation' within the firm they must have the full cooperation and assistance of all people working within the firm. After all a commercial organisation is simply made up of the people that work within it.

Many progressive marketing orientated firms today follow what has come to be known as a relationship-marketing strategy, where the emphasis is on customer-retention rather than acquisition, and on building long-term, profitable relationships with customers.

Public relations employed internally can assist management in achieving the right internal culture and cooperation that is really a prerequisite for genuine external relationship-marketing behaviour towards customers.

Recent developments

From the mid-1970s onwards a change developed in the role and perceived value of public relations, leading to a growth in this form of marketing communications which has continued right up to 1997 and is all set to continue into the next century. Explanations for this upsurge are many and varied. Many in the industry identify the late 1970s recession as a major turning point, when companies were desperate to reduce costs in order to stay in business. As often happens in times of economic downturn the managers of many firms look to marketing budgets as a 'first strike', regarding marketing expenditure as a luxury and a cost rather than a necessary investment. Many managers found that public relations, with a much broader base and cost-effectiveness, was preferable to maintaining the conventional advertising budget.

The cost-saving aspect of public relations is certainly one of the major reasons for the growth in the popularity of this form of marketing communications among the management of marketing firms. Other factors may include the increasing complexity of the business world which has produced a need for more complex communications to get the commercial or corporate message across. Another possible factor is the growth of fast-developing new business sectors such as information technology, financial services, travel and leisure which has lad to a new breed of marketing manager who is fully conversant and appreciates the value of public relations as a marketing communication tool. A further factor is a recognition by management, especially those working in business-to-business marketing firms, of the importance of creating and maintaining relationships with a wide range of people and groups. There has been recognition for a number of years that in industrial and organisational marketing situations there are complex buyer–seller interactions involved in the marketing process. Some of these take place amongst the 'official' marketing channels of communications – for example between the salesperson and the official buyer, or at least the purchasing team or committee within the buying organisation. However, interactions were thought to also take place on a less formal basis, amongst technical personal from both the marketing and buying firms, for example. It was recognised that these informal buyer–seller interactions were just as important as the more formal contacts and that these too had to be managed and not left to chance. The recognition that organisational or business-to-business marketing involved an often complex web of formal and informal, but no less important, commercial interactions become known as the 'interactive approach', and was basically the precursor to what today is often referred to as the relationship marketing approach. Of course, throughout its development as a marketing communications tool, public relations has always been first and foremost an instrument for establishing, crystallising, cementing and maintaining mutually beneficial relationships with various groups of people or 'publics'. It is therefore no surprise that as the recognition of the importance of the interactive and relationship-driven nature of modern marketing practice became accepted and practised by firms, the adoption of public relations as a key marketing communications tool also grew in stature and importance, particularly in the area of corporate communications. The role of public relations in achieving sound relationship-marketing practices as well as its contribution to achieving good internal marketing is examined later in this chapter.

13.2 The Role and Nature of Public Relations

Defining public relations

The task of defining the exact nature of public relations (PR) is not an easy one. A plethora of definitions currently exist, each one emphasising a slightly different approach and each attempting to arrive at a simple, brief and accurate form of words. The difficulty in developing a single acceptable definition reflects the complexity and diversity of the profession. For the

purposes of this discussion we will look at two of the more useful definitions. Firstly, that of the Institute of Public Relations (IPR) in the UK
(Lancaster and Reynolds, 1995) p. 216:

> 'Public Relations practice is the deliberate, planned and sustained effort to
> establish and maintain mutual understanding between an organisation and its
> public.'

The essential features of this definition are firstly that PR practice should be
deliberate, planned and sustained, not haphazard; and secondly that mutual
understanding is necessary in order to ensure that the communication
between the organisation and 'its public' is clear, that is the receiver perceives the same meaning as the sender intends.

An alternative definition is provided by the late Frank Jefkins (1988) p.
185, one of the United Kingdom's most prolific writers on the subject, who
states:

> 'Public Relations consists of all forms of planned communication, outward and
> inwards, between an organisation and its publics for the purpose of achieving
> specific objectives concerning mutual understanding.'

This definition is basically a modified version of the Institute of Public
Relations' definition and provides two new elements:

1 'Public' becomes 'publics', since PR addresses a number of audiences;
2 The inclusion of 'specific objectives', making PR a tangible activity.

Achieving a marketing orientation

In the marketing literature we read a lot about how it is vitally important for
an organisation to become 'marketing-orientated', 'customer-focused' and
to adopt the 'marketing concept'. In fact achieving a truly marketing orientated organisation is easier said than done. It does not simply occur by
magic, nor will it happen by simply altering people's titles and calling them
marketing executives instead of sales personnel, or whatever. For a firm to
be truly marketing oriented all the staff working for it have to be so. There
is a saying adapted from Buddhist philosophy that states 'for a forest to be
green each tree has to be green'. This principle also applies to the marketing
orientation of the firm. In a sense, achieving a marketing orientation
amongst all of the workforce within an organisation is in many way similar
to achieving a religious conversion. If we use Christianity as an example,
just because someone carries a bible around with them and goes to church
on a regular basis does not make them a Christian necessarily, at least in the
true sense of the word. The concept of being a Christian comes from within,
not from attending a particular building or reading a particular book. Likewise true marketing orientation has to come from within also: from within

the minds of the people making up the organisation. But how does senior management achieve this change in attitude and bring about the right customer-focused spirit within their organisation? Well no one is saying that internal public relations techniques on their own can achieve this, but they can certainly make a significant contribution.

Communications and public relations

Communications is central to public relations. The purpose of PR is to establish a two-way communication to resolve conflicts of interest by seeking common ground or areas of mutual interest. If we accept that this is the primary function of PR, then we must also accept a further implication. Public relations 'exists', whether implicitly or explicitly, whether an organisation likes it or not. Simply by carrying out its day-to-day operations, an organisation necessarily communicates certain messages to those who, for whatever reason, interact with the company, who will then form an opinion about it and its activities. The need for PR is to orchestrate, as far as possible, the behaviour of the organisation and the messages that result from such behaviour, in order to help develop a corporate identity or personality.

Public relations is not paid for like, say, advertising, although of course the marketing firm will have to pay fees if it employs a public relations consultant, or a salary if they have an internal specialist. Because public relations is not perceived by various publics as a paid-for type of communication, it tends to have greater source credibility. That is because the write-ups in the press or business journal, television or radio programme and so on are seen as emanating from an independent third party rather than a commissioned advertising agency. It is often said that the mark of good public relations is that the receiver of the message does not realise public relations has been employed. If it is obvious that the message has been cooked up by spin-doctors or PR gurus, then the message loses much, or indeed all, of its intended effect. In a sense good public relations are in some ways analogous to good security. If a firm, a film star or a politician are employing security personnel to look after them, one of the key criteria for success in this line of work is that no one knows or is even remotely suspicious that they are anything to do with security. They simply blend into the background and are indistinguishable from other members of the public. It is this anonymity that makes them so effective and such a powerful deterrent. The role of public relations within the overall marketing communication mix is shown in Figure 13.1.

Corporate identity

The concept of corporate identity or 'personality' is inextricably linked to public relations. All PR activities must be carried out within the framework

Fig 13.1   The role of public relations within the overall marketing communications mix

of an agreed and understood corporate personality. This personality must develop to reflect the style of the top management, since they control the organisation's policy and activities. A corporate personality can become a tangible asset if managed properly and consistently. However it cannot be assumed that all managers will consider the role of corporate personality when they make decisions. Therefore the PR executive needs to be placed so that he is aware of all the issues, policies, attitudes and opinions that exist within the organisation, and that have a bearing on how it is perceived by outsiders.

The use of the term 'personality', rather than the more oft used 'image' is deliberate. An image is a refection, an impression which may be a little too polished, a little too perfect. True PR is more than skin deep. This is important because in common parlance, a 'PR job' implies that somehow the truth is being hidden behind a glossy and even false facade. But properly conducted public relations emphasises the need for truth and full information. The PR executive, as a manager of corporate personality, can only sustain in the long run an identity which is based on reality. Corporate public relations is concerned with image, very often group image if the organisation is a diversified company, and this image is based on a long-term, carefully-planned programme designed to achieve maximum recognition and understanding for the company's objectives and performance in keeping with realistic expectations.

International public relations

Many firms are now involved, in various degrees, in international business of some kind even if it is only importing raw materials or exporting a proportion of their finished goods. In the same way that public relations can assist the marketing effort in the home country, so can similar techniques provide aid to exporters in their efforts to enlarge the scope of their overseas marketing activities. Public relations in international markets can be targeted at various levels. For example an individual country such as Great Britain has a vested interest in projecting a favourable image overseas. Even the royal yacht *Britannia'* is used to entertain foreign trade delegations and boost British trade and trade relations. There has been a certain amount of controversy in Britain around a replacement for *Britannia*, with many of the more enlightened speakers on this issue in the House of Commons and the Lords seeing the public relations value of such a vessel from a purely hard-headed commercial point of view as being well worth the cost involved.

Public relations is also employed overseas to represent a particular industry. At the present time the British Meat Federation are representing the interests of the British beef farmer overseas, and representatives of this body give papers at conferences, speak on behalf of the beef industry at the European parliament and design general press releases for the European press. The British wine, cheese and defence industries, to name but a few, are all actively involved in international public relations trying to build good commercial relationships overseas.

Activity

Examine the position that good communications is absolutely central to effective public relations.

- Public relations is a form of marketing communications and hence forms an intrinsic part or component of the marketing communications mix.
- The purpose of public relations is to establish a two-way effective communications link with a whole range of publics including internal publics, that is those working for the organisation.
- An organisation carries out activities that result in publicity; this publicity may be good or bad.
- The role of public relations is to engineer events, as far as possible, so that the resulting publicity is good and to effectively communicate this 'good publicity' to various groups of publics in an appropriate manner.
- Hence public relations is basically concerned with communications, and good communications lies at the very heart of effective public relations.

13.3 **What PR is Not**

Misunderstanding and ignorance as to the nature of public relations has led to its being confused with other disciplines and activities. It is appropriate at this point to clarify certain distinctions:

Public relations is not 'free' advertising

1 Advertising emphasises selling, whereas public relations is informative, educational and creates understanding through knowledge.
2 Public relations is not free. It is time-consuming and therefore costs in terms of management time and expertise.
3 Editorial space and broadcasting time are unbiased and therefore have more credibility than advertisements.
4 Every organisation necessarily has PR.
5 Public relations involves communications with many groups and audiences, not just consumers.

Public relations is not propaganda

Propaganda is designed to indoctrinate in order to attract followers. It does not necessarily call for an ethical content, so facts are often distorted or falsified for self-interest. Public relations on the other hand seeks to persuade by securing the willing acceptance of attitudes and ideas. The former Soviet Union authorities lied to their own people; they showed them totally untypical and biased pictures of the West to try and make the population believe that the Soviet system was superior to democracy and capitalism. They exaggerated the claims made for the output of their economy and progress in equality and health. All of these 'official' communications were blatant propaganda designed to deceive the people.

PR is not the same as publicity

Publicity is a result of information being made known. The result may be uncontrollable and either good or bad. Public relations is concerned with the behaviour of the organisation, product or individual that leads to publicity. It will obviously seek to control behaviour, if this is possible, in such a way that publicity is good. Some times the actions or events that lead to adverse publicity are outside the control of the organisation, and the role of public relations in such circumstances is to mitigate the effect of possible adverse publicity. For example the firm Eurotunnel unfortunately had to deal with a serious fire in the channel tunnel in 1996. Thankfully no one was seriously injured although the poor people involved were very frightened and thought they were going to die. A quite damming report into the incident was published in May 1997 highlighting serious weaknesses in the company's safety procedures. Eurotunnel now has an upward struggle convincing a wide range of publics including the press, government, banks and potential and actual customers, that the firm behaved in a responsible manner and that such an incident is highly unlikely to happen again. Many holiday-makers have been put off crossing the channel by tunnel as a result of this fire.

A further example of this type of situation is in the UK's beef industry. The adverse publicity associated with independent scientific tests on BSE or 'mad cow' disease as it has come to be called has resulted in a virtual worldwide ban on British beef and associated products by the European Community (EC) authorities. This ban, which shows no sign of being lifted at the time of writing, has potentially catastrophic consequences for many groups of people – farmers, slaughterers, butchers, meat processors, super-markets and so on – within the United Kingdom and poses grave economic problems for the UK government. Even when the ban is eventually lifted the British Meat Federation and other similar professional bodies within the UK, and overseas where British beef is exported, will face a tremendous task of convincing former consumers of British beef that it is now entirely safe. Ordinary advertising messages and sales promotion techniques are unlikely to have much effect. Public relations is likely to be the most promising marketing communications tool in such circumstances and is in fact already being employed to try and get public opinion and political opinion in Europe behind the idea of lifting the worldwide export ban on British beef and beef products.

Activity

How might the receivers of messages created as a result of public relations activity regard these messages with a greater degree of 'source credibility' than other forms of commercial messages?

As we mentioned earlier in this chapter, the mark of good public relations is that it is in a sense 'invisible' to the various groups, individuals or publics to which it is directed. If it is obvious to all and sundry that a particular commercial or corporate message is a public relation concoction, then the message immediately loses all or at least some of its impact and effect.

The behaviour, events and resulting publicity and messages resulting from public relations activity are all the more powerful because they appear to the receivers to be completely unsolicited. The favourable mention of a firm on a financial television programme, or a favourable piece on the future commercial prospects of an organisation in the business press, or maybe coverage of a charity event sponsored by an organisation on the local radio news, should all appear to have been delivered entirely by disinterested third parties, who had no particular vested interest in the nature or the content of the message being delivered and were simply doing their job as journalists, television programme editors or whatever.

It is this impression of spontaneous, unsolicited messages delivered by unre-lated and commercially-independent and disinterested parties that give public relations its unique qualities and its extraordinary power as a marketing commu-nications tool.

13.4 **The Need for Public Relations**

As public relations is essentially a process of communication, it is needed most when conditions are such that normal communications are strained and some people are left uninformed. In a modern industrial economy commercial organisations have a genuine need for sophisticated communications which can be accurately tailored and targeted at specific groups of people. In a very real sense, especially in areas such as political campaigning, communications itself has become a twentieth century skill. With the development of communications there has been a parallel development in the sophistication of the audience. Generally people are better educated and hence are better able to make objective judgements about the messages they receive. The very word communications is a current buzz-word, and the terms 'effective communications' and 'inadequate communications' are almost post-modernist. The subject of communications is worried over by managers in commercial and non-commercial organisations, by trade union leaders, by political spin-doctors and even media advisors to the Royal Family, and with very good reason. Failure to communicate can be identified as part of the cause, even the main cause of many industrial, commercial and non-commercial organisational problems. Public relations is by no means a universal answer for every situation, but at least it is a formal system of communications and as such employs the concepts of analysis, action, review and control which can provide structure and a way forward in many situations.

Changing social attitudes have forced a new responsiveness and a sense of responsibility in official and commercial life. The average man or woman's belief that they are entitled to be told is gradually becoming matched by a sense of accountability which was largely missing as little as 30 years ago. For example, boards of directors can no longer dispose of the ordinary shareholder's money, or pay themselves huge amounts of money and other benefits such as share options, without adequate explanation. It is in this social climate that an appreciation of public relations as a management and advisory function is being recognised.

13.5 **Publics**

Public relations encompasses all attempts by the company to anticipate, track, review and where possible influence or control the type of publicity communicated to various sections of the public via the media. In doing this the organisation hopes to be able to cultivate and maintain a positive corporate image. In fact the strategic management of publicity through the employment of public relations is often referred to as **corporate communications**. Public relations is concerned with communicating to a wide range of publics and not just to the organisation's customers or clients.

The public relations practitioner has to conduct activities which concern every public with which the organisation has contact. This is because in order to exist, succeed and survive an organisation depends on many individuals and groups of people. Even in the distribution of products, for example, a manufacturer must communicate with sales people, delivery staff, servicing staff, wholesalers, mail order houses, agents, importers, exporters, overseas agents and often many different kinds of retailer including chain stores, co-operatives, department stores supermarkets and smaller independently-owned shops. There are many other people or groups of people that may affect the success or failure of a commercial enterprise. These would include printers, package manufacturers, transport contractors, media owners and advertising agents. To these we can add others such as journalists who may write about our products or company, television producers of consumer affairs programmes and technical innovation programmes such as Tomorrow's World and so on. Business analysts, professional bodies, trade associations, government departments and other organisations are also important publics.

The publics of an organisation are those groups of people with whom it needs to communicate. Obviously the exact nature of these groups and individuals will vary to some extent from organisation to organisation. However, the following eight are adapted from the seven basic publics identified by the late Frank Jefkins.

1 **The community**
2 **Employees**
3 **Government**
4 **The financial community**
5 **Distributors**
6 **Consumers**
7 **Opinion leaders**
8 **Educational world**

Let us now look at the above categories in a little more detail.

The community

Good community relations are important for every organisation. An organisation can and should act as if it were a member of the community and not abuse its power. It should behave as a responsible 'citizen' just like any private member of the community. The situation is one of interdependence: industry needs the support of the community, and the community must understand industry. It is important for an organisation, through its public relations function, to establish a community-relations programme that both deals with complaints and involves itself in community activities. This may include local press relations, special visits to the workplace, open days, sponsorship, community projects and so on.

One a wider scale, companies such as Levi Strauss have a voluntary committee in every factory which involves itself in local charities. British Petroleum (BP) sends 1 percent of its workforce out on community projects. Other firms like Citybank and Marks and Spencer are involved in local business, employment and housing creation. The general public tends to judge commercial organisations by the way they conduct themselves in the same way that individuals form a good or bad impression of the people that they come in contact with. Commercial projects such as the building of new plant or the processing or storage of waste materials, may affect or even interfere with local conditions and amenities, and care should be taken by the firm to anticipate and mitigate such resentment and to placate it as far as possible. An increasingly important aspect of community relations is the subject of pollution particularly with the rise of environmentalism and 'green politics' over recent years all over the world. Increasingly firms are having to take environmental management issues into account when planning their commercial operations. It has become politically and socially unacceptable and hence commercially less profitable to disregard aspects such as pollution. This greener, cleaner marketing movement has had a big impact on the public relations industry. The first task of public relations is to help industry itself become aware of environmental issues and the potential long-term consequences for the environment, public opinion and hence the commercial consequences of their actions. The second is to persuade both management and the public to see the whole problem in perspective and to recognise that environmental problems such a pollution can be avoided. The third responsibility of public relations is to make industry and its customers recognise that the firm is conducting its business in an environmentally responsible and socially ethical manner.

Employees

Internal or employee public relations is often a neglected area in the study of public relations. Britain is still a somewhat class-ridden society despite the greater equality and meritocracy of the last quarter of a century. Worker–management relations are still often 'them and us' and highly confrontational, in fact they often tend towards the 'man-machine' attitude of Taylorism. The late Frank Jefkins, a very prolific writer on the subject of public relations, sees poor industrial relations as basically a public relations problem of poor communications within the firm. As Jefkins sees it, the solution to such problems lies in involving employees in all areas of decision-making, in setting organisational goals and establishing 'mutual understanding' amongst all parties. Appropriate objectives for management to set for public relations in the area of employee relations could include increasing awareness of company policy, improving safety standards and determining the cause of (and helping to reduce) high staff turnover. High turnover of staff is symptomatic of problems within the organisation and deep unhappiness amongst the workforce. A discontented and disaffected workforce can be disastrous for an organisation. Marketing orientation within firms requires the cooperation of all staff. It is virtually impossible to achieve marketing orientation with a disaffected workforce. The public relations role, here, is of paramount strategic importance.

Internal public relations embraces everything which encourages employees to make their maximum contribution to productivity and the prosperity of the organisation. It overlaps with personal welfare, industrial relations, education, staff development and marketing orientation and it should be fully integrated with these facets of management. Public relations can contribute to the creation of an atmosphere in which people will work more effectively. It can initiate a suggestion scheme, a safety campaign, it can lessen waste, carelessness, absenteeism and so on, and it can enable management to communicate more effectively with employees at all levels.

Government

Perhaps the biggest growth and development in public relations over recent years has been in the areas of government relations and political lobbying. This form of public relations activities has two main purposes, first to keep companies informed of legislative changes that may affect their business and secondly to attempt to influence the government or local government in favour of their industries. Political public relations is often misunderstood, particularly with the recent examples of 'cash for questions' in the House of Commons and other allegations of corruption and sleaze in government. The success of some businesses depend heavily on decisions made in parliament which is the reason for the existence of certain pressure groups. Some companies have politicians as directors. Such people keep management abreast with political ideas and they can often put forward a case for the company or the industry in which the company is operating, in political circles if the need arises.

Personal contact is always the best way of establishing mutual respect, and many organisations invite members of all political parties to informal meetings where matters of interest can be discussed.

The financial community

The spate of take-overs and mergers in British industry over the last 20 years illustrates very aptly the need for financial public relations. There is a need for commercial organisations to communicate with a diverse range of interested parties such as investors, both private and city institutions such as pension funds, share analysts, financial journalists and so on. Effective financial relations will produce certain benefits to the firm. Those companies that have established reputations will have less difficulty in raising the additional capital that may be needed for future investments. Many companies rely for their very existence on the support of banks. Such organisations are highly 'geared' and much of their capital structure is made up of bank debt. The bank finance supporting this capital structure is often of a short-term or medium-term nature, and financing arrangements are continually under review. Short-term loans are repaid and a further set of loans are often negotiated. Good relations with the major banks is absolutely fundamental to an organisation's financing strategy. Holding companies often hold shares in their own subsidiary companies, which are often offered as collateral in support of bank loans. Obviously the holding company has a strong interest in keeping the price of such shares at an appropriate level otherwise the value of their collateral on which their loan finance is based falls in value. Public relations is used to communicate the commercial health of an organisation and the favourable future prospects that investors can expect over the medium term. This information is aimed at key groups with the intention of helping to support market sentiment for the company and hence support the share price, and to assuage any doubts potential lenders may have about the commercial robustness of the firm.

Distributors

Distributors are those who handle goods between producer and consumer. They include a diverse array of businesses, wholesalers, retailers, dealerships, agencies and factors. It is essential that these marketing intermediaries are both informed and educated about the company's products, services and methods of carrying out their business. The more the staff working for marketing intermediaries know about the manufacturing company and its products and services the greater will be their confidence and expertise in marketing its product or service offering. After all, marketing intermediaries are often independent businesses with their own distinct set of commercial needs and wants. The manufacturing or service firm who markets through a distribution network is relying on these marketing intermediaries to achieve their own commercial goals. There are many public relations techniques that can be applied to create greater knowledge and understanding amongst the staff of marketing intermediaries – videos, talks, training courses and works visits to name a few.

A manufacturer can be vitally affected by the behaviour and efficiency of marketing intermediaries, and assessing and influencing their attitudes is thus of paramount importance. There are many instances where the goodwill of the dealer or distributor can make the difference between success or failure for a manufacturer. Much activity on advertising, sales promotion, merchandising and packaging can be wasted if the wrong relationships exist at the point of sale. For many commercial enterprises the affective use of marketing intermediaries is a key factor in the success of their business. Public relations can play a key role in creating and maintaining long-term commercial relationships which are so important to success.

Consumers

Consumer relations is thought by many people to be the only public which concerns public relations. As we have seen from the list of various publics in this section this is simply not the case. However, it is an area of considerable importance because at the end of the day although other groups of publics are important, actual customers are especially important. The whole purpose of the profit-making firm is the generation of satisfactory returns by the satisfaction of customers' needs and wants more effectively and efficiently than competitors. If other groups are discontented or lack sufficient communication from the marketing firm this may cause problems. If customers are disaffected and decide to buy from another supplier you have no business left to worry about.

It is perhaps the large retailers who have the most dealings with customers, and this group of traders has done much in the way of public relations activity aimed towards this important group. Stores are conveniently laid out, service is good and products represent fair value for money. Littlewoods distribute a small brochure to members of staff to show them how to improve the image of their store as well as creating better customer relations. They like to show that they are a 'live organisation' constantly listening and responding to customers' views and opinions. Other firms such as C & A and Kwik Fit operate ongoing staff training schemes to inculcate proper customer awareness amongst staff.

A major aspect of customer relations is the subject of complaints and returns. This subject is probably especially applicable to mail order firms more so than other retailers, where purchasing is carried out 'at a distance'. Since the organisation is not actually physically seen, in the sense that a customer can visit a shop, office or whatever, then it is essential that the subject of complaints and returns be treated by such marketing firms particularly carefully. Operators of mail order catalogue businesses such as Kay's, Gratten's and Littlewoods all pay particular attention to this aspect of business.

Public relations can be used for many aspects of product and service support. It can help to educate the market before and during a product launch through extensive press involvement via conferences, demonstrations and interviews with key personnel. Public relations can also maintain consumer interest by publishing case history articles describing the use of a particular product or service.

Opinion leaders

An opinion leader, as the name suggests, is a person or group of people who may have a particularly special or strong influence on the opinions of others. Such people or groups are often held in high esteem by the wider public for a variety of reasons. From an individual product point of view consumer affairs programmes and consumer magazines such as *Which* are held in high esteem by the general public who believe them to produce fair and unbiased views on various products, services and organisations and to act in the best interests of the consumer. Marketing firms attempt to achieve favourable reports from such programmes and publications as they know that positive messages will be more readily accepted and believed by the market as a whole. Other opinion leaders may include professional bodies, trade associations, pressure groups and government.

The concept of opinion leaders has been discussed earlier in Chapter 12, and a diagram illustrating the two-step-flow model of marketing communications which incorporates the idea of opinion leaders was shown in Figure 12.7. It is shown again in Figure 13.2 in a slightly altered form and expressed in the context of public relations specifically.

Looking at the model in Figure 13.2 we can see that the firm's public relations message is targeted at individuals or groups – for example trade associations that have been identified as opinion leaders. These opinion leaders then diffuse the message to wider groups of publics which contain the categories listed in this section.

Educational world

Many companies pay considerable attention to this area of activity in the hope of aiding recruitment, particularly graduate recruitment, and improving general community relations as well as general corporate image. For example, the main high-street banks place great importance in exhibiting at colleges and universities at the beginning of the academic year with a view to persuading new students to open an account with them. They usually offer a number of special benefits such as loans and so on, as well as giving

Fig 13.2   The two-step-flow model of marketing communications applied in the context of public relations

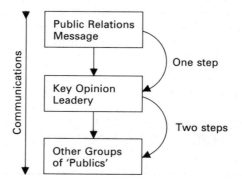

away T-shirts and other merchandise. At one time Skol lager sponsored a free-beer (actually it was free Skol lager) night at the student unions of all the leading universities during 'freshers' week. The idea was to cast Skol in a good light in the minds of students. Many students were drinking alcohol for the first time during that particular week, and if their first drink was Skol lager they might stay with the brand throughout their student career. A further example is the chemical producer ICI who issue charts and diagrams to schools and colleges on how their compounds are made from basic raw materials, and how they are made up into everyday products such as paint, fertilisers, solvents and other products. Various companies invite parties of schoolchildren and students to visit their plants or factories to see how things are made. A good example is the Cadburys company at Bournville near Birmingham. Schoolchildren visit the plant and see how all their favourite chocolates are made and they are also given a special commemorative box of chocolates to take away with them. The box is actually made of tin and many of these children use the tin as a pencil case even into their student years. Some people keep these tins for the rest of their lives.

Activity

When considering the various groups of 'publics' that public relations activity is concerned with, why do many practitioners consider that customers are a particularly important, possibly the most important group?

Public relations, as we have seen throughout this chapter, can be applied by organisations in many different contexts which require communications to various groups of publics. These are not just profit-making organisations. For example, a charity requires donors and the general support of the general public as well as government. A political party requires votes in order for its candidates to be elected as members of parliament and to form a government. A museum or art gallery requires visitors in order to prove to grant-awarding bodies that they are worthy of being supported with public funds. They also require benefactors and patrons to donate large sums of money in order for them to acquire works of art or other historical artefacts and to prevent them being sold abroad. All of these organisations make use of public relations targeted at various key groups in order to help them achieve their objectives.

In a profit-making organisation, the retention and acquisition of customers is a necessary requirement for survival. All other areas of a business might be running smoothly, for example purchasing, personnel, production and so on, and public relations may be being used with considerable effect on other key groups such as the government, the financial community or the local community. However, if the firm has no customers none of these other things really matter because before long the firm will find itself placed into liquidation. All groups of publics are important but as far as the profit-making firm is concerned customers are paramount.

13.6 **Media Used in Public Relations**

Personal communication

Personal communication is the strongest and most persuasive means of putting across a message. The message is aided by the force of the personality of the communicator who can adapt both content and manner of delivery to the reactions of his or her audience. A polished speaker can do much to enhance the image of the company, particularly at press conferences. The job of the public relations officer is not necessarily to appear on the platform himself, but to organise events so that an appropriate representative of the organisation can address the audience.

Printed communication

- **Direct mail** This is a very versatile medium which is suitable for a variety of purposes including direct marketing, general advertising and public relations. Direct mail can be used to send copies of press releases to interested parties, and can be used to dispatch house magazines to employees, customers, distributors, agents and others. This medium is also used to send invitations to sponsored events, exhibitions, conferences, demonstrations, film shows and so forth.
- **Literature** Literature is obviously related to direct mail above which often targets certain pieces of literature to the desired target audience. Literature for direct mail purposes usually consists of leaflets, folders, booklets, books and other pieces of print including wall charts, diaries, postcards and pictures for exhibiting and framing. Public relations literature tends to be explanatory and educational, providing information or telling a story rather than trying to persuade or sell something. Literature can be usefully distributed to visitors, customers, dealers and members of the local community, while hand-outs and press kits are used at conferences. Public relations efforts of this nature can inspire confidence and trust in an organisation which in turn can result in many long-term commercial benefits.
- **The press** The press-release is probably regarded as the most important form of public relations by practitioners. Two important factors in press relations are timing and distribution, choosing the correct moment to release news and seeing that it reaches the right people. The aim of press relations is to gain maximum publication or broadcasting of public relations information through newspapers, magazines, radio and television, in order to achieve specific communications objectives with clearly defined target audiences. The most common method of achieving this is the press release sent to relevant journalists.

Visual communications

- **Photography**   Good photographs have an impact and an appeal that is lacking in printed media. To actually see a photograph of some event that has happened lends further credence to the report as it provides 'proof' in the audiences mind that what has been reported has actually happened. Photographs are rarely used in isolation but normally in conjunction with a press release, the one form of public relations supporting and augmenting the other.
- **Films**   Films were once the province of the larger organisation because they were relatively expensive to make. Even today professional film-making is still a costly business. If the film is to be distributed overseas or in cinemas then it obviously needs to be produced to a very high standard otherwise it will give the wrong impression about the organisation and in that sense will be counterproductive. The development of camcorder machines has meant that a film can be produced by amateurs relatively cheaply and is suitable for certain public relations purposes. For example, prospective students and their parents may visit a college on open days and may be shown a video of the college campus and its facilities; it may even include glowing testimonials from present and past students in order to bring home the message. The camcorder is suitable for this form of activity but if the visual communication is going to get a much wider audience it needs to be of a higher quality and professionally produced.
- **Television**   Television is a medium of high visual impact: not only can points be explained verbally but products can also be shown. Sometimes footage of a company's participation in a sponsored event or some other organised public relations event is shown on television programmes, although the BBC's official policy is not to mention company or brand names. However, the increase in sponsored events by commercial firms both in sport and in the arts has increased dramatically over the last 20 years or so, and it is now virtually impossible not to mention the sponsoring company's name or show a shot of a company or brand name when reporting events such as motor racing, football and so on. The BBC also show science and technology programmes, the best known probably being Tomorrow's World which shows new products, and representatives from the company that has developed the product are also on the programme discussing various details. There is a growing demand for company personalities to appear on television programmes and to give interviews on radio, especially with the dramatic increase in local radio. There has also been a dramatic increase in the interest with anything to do with 'business'. There are now many programmes on the BBC and all of the commercial channels to do with business and money, which offers many opportunities for firms to capitalise on the public relations oppor-

tunities offered from this increasingly popular, important and sophisticated medium.

- **Exhibitions**   There has always been a strong public relations dimension to exhibitions. They offer marketing communicators a rare opportunity to come into face-to-face contact with high-status decision-making-unit (DMU) members. Many visitors to exhibitions go to view the market offering in its entirety, in a short space of time and under one roof. Visitors treat the exhibition as a shop window and an opportunity to gather technical information; often products are available for inspection along with working models and films of the company and its products. There is often a strong entertainment component to exhibitions with stands offering complementary drinks and sometimes even food to serious potential clients. Networking is achieved by lunch and dinner engagements and if the exhibition is overseas or in London, firms often give complementary tours or tickets to local events such as the opera or a concert. All of the media listed above can be used in exhibitions including personal contact, literature, films and the event itself may also be reported on the radio in the financial and business press and of course on television.

- **Sponsorship**   Sponsorship has already been mentioned in a public relations context. We are not saying that public relations and sponsorship are one and the same thing, rather that sponsorship has a strong public relations component to it. Firms can use sponsorship in a variety of ways. Being associated with the arts for example, gives a strong sense of supporting and being part of the fabric of society. It also has a strong entertainment value. Important clients and other key individuals form other important groups of publics can be invited to artistic events such as concerts, plays or the opera. Afterwards they can mix with important artists such as conductors and opera singers over drinks or over dinner. In this way key individuals are contacted, entertained and long-term relationships are built and maintained. Some firms sponsor worthy causes such as an archaeological dig or a local brass band.

Activity

Explain the contribution direct mail can play when marketing management is planning an integrated public relations programme.

Direct mail is a very versatile marketing communications tool, and it is also very precise. With the exception of personal contact and perhaps telephone marketing, which are also very precise marketing communications 'tools' from a targeting and delivery point of view, direct mail offers an unparalleled degree of precision.

Like sponsorship we are not saying that direct mail and public relations are one and the same thing, far from it. But, like sponsorship, direct mail has many public relations applications and specific contributions to make.

Direct mail messages can be highly personalised and can be made to fit individual communication requirements. Direct mail can contain product, service or corporate literature, invitations to sponsored events, conferences and exhibitions.

Generally the imaginative use of direct mail and database marketing techniques can make a valuable contribution to an integrated public relations programme.

13.7 **Internal and Relationship Marketing**

We have mentioned many times the concepts of internal and relationship marketing. The term 'internal marketing' is the process of applying the general principles of marketing to the staff and workforce of the organisation. We read very often that marketing as a business philosophy is all about achieving the right internal company culture that will result in that company becoming what we might call marketing-orientated.

The process of internal marketing involves much more than simply the application of public relations inside firms. In fact internal marketing operates at the interface between marketing and human resource management and involves both of these management disciplines. However, as we have discussed earlier, the application of internal public relations certainly has a salient role to play in the overall process of achieving a good internal marketing culture. The most common means of achieving internal public relations objectives in many companies is via company publications. However if these are to be effective, they must be much more than paternalistic house journals; they must provide a forum for open, two-way discussion on company issues. Whatever methods are employed, the important requirement is that they represent a genuine desire to communicate on behalf of both workers and management. This reinforces the point that public relations can only reflect reality. The contribution of both internal and external public relations to relationship marketing practices is discussed below. Figure 13.3 shows the relationship between public relations and internal and relationship marketing.

Relationship marketing is based on the premise that existing customers are the most valuable asset a firm has and must be cultivated and looked after properly. Relationship marketing applies to some firms more than others, but many firms are now adopting a more long-term relationship-marketing approach. This philosophy of marketing looks way beyond the next sale or transaction, and in fact views customers as a stream of potential income stretching over their potential lifetime. The true capital value of a customer is the net present value of a discounted stream of revenue attributable to the customer over their lifetime. In fact some consultancy firms specialising in relationship marketing, notably Bain & Co., based in Boston, USA (Corperate head quarters at 2 Copley Place, Boston), use investment-appraisal techniques such as discounted cash flow to value a

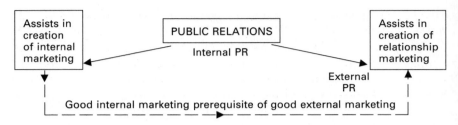

Fig 13.3   The relationship between public relations and internal and relationship marketing

customer portfolio. Bain and others also hold the position that it costs five times as much to acquire a new customer than it does to retain an existing customer, and that generally speaking existing customers allow for higher margins, need less marketing resources and are therefore more profitable.

Relationship marketing is about forging long-term relationships based on customer satisfaction, exceeding expectations and trust. For this to happen everyone working in the marketing firm must adopt a relationship-marketing mentality or stance or it simply will not work in practice. Good internal marketing is in a way a prerequisite for effective relationship marketing, and as we have already discussed internal public relations can make a salient contribution to the achievement of the right internal marketing culture. Therefore it stands to reason that indirectly, internal public relations contributes to relationship marketing. External public relations aimed at customers, marketing intermediaries and other important groups makes a direct contribution to fostering good long-term, commercially beneficial relationships, which is what we now call relationship marketing.

13.8 **Summary**

Public relations is a very important and very versatile marketing communications tool. It is rarely used in isolation but instead forms an intrinsic part of the organisation's integrated marketing communications mix. There is a public relations application to most of the marketing communications variables used by the modern firm, whether this is personal selling, sponsorship, exhibitions, direct mail, telephone marketing or indeed any other form of communication.

Public relations can be applied both within and without the organisation. Good internal marketing, the process of achieving a true marketing orientation within organisations, is a vital prerequisite to effective external marketing strategies, particularly those based on relationship marketing principles. Public relations has a vital role to play and contribution to make to the creation of an effective internal marketing culture within an organisation and to creating, fostering, nurturing and maintaining mutually beneficial long-term relationships with customers and other key groups of people. In this respect public relations has seen a dramatic increase in prominence and importance as both a strategic internal and external marketing communications tool.

Public relations is defined by the Institute of Public Relations as 'the deliberate, planned and sustained effort to establish and maintain mutual understanding between an organisation and its publics. Each element in the firm's communications mix, for example advertising, sponsorship, direct mail, exhibitions, below-the-line sales promotions and so on, has a specific part to play in the marketing firm's marketing communications strategy. Likewise, public relations has a specific role to play in the overall scheme of things; its role is to help build an understanding of a company and a number of publics with whom the marketing firm is communicating or may wish to communicate. This has the effect of augmenting and increasing the source credibility of marketing messages from other elements in the communications mix by improving the image and reputation of both the company and its product and services. An organisation is judged by its behaviour, and public relations is about goodwill and reputation. At its very best, public relations can be the discipline that really determines the content of the messages companies send to their customers and other target audiences.

Whether consciously achieved or not, the firm's customers and other publics will hold a particular point of view about the company and its products and/or services. Everything about the company, its products, employees and actions will communicate something. Company image and corporate identity is of vital importance to the marketing effort. What is communicated by the marketing organisation should not simply be left to chance but should be planned and managed by the professional application of the art of public relations.

14 International Marketing

14.1 International Marketing Definitions

There is much uncertainty between the terms multinational marketing, international marketing and exporting.

- **Multinational marketing** refers to a number of very large companies whose business interests, manufacturing plant and offices are spread throughout the world. Although their strategic headquarters might be based in the original parent country, they tend to operate autonomously in individual countries. Multinational companies can also be exporters and importers, but the main point is that they actually produce and market goods within the countries in which they have chosen to develop.
- **International marketing** is the term commonly used to describe all international activity and indeed it is the term used to describe this chapter for this precise reason. However, strictly speaking it is a term used to describe companies whose overseas sales account for more than 20 per cent of their total turnover, and where a strategic decision has been taken to enter foreign markets and where product mix and communications mix adaptations are considered when supplying goods or services for a particular overseas market.
- **Exporting** is the term commonly used to describe the commercial activity involved when international transactions take place. However, in an international marketing sense it refers to those companies who consider overseas business as being marginal to their main activities. In such circumstances they simply accept export orders, rather than engage in active manipulation of their marketing mixes to suit the needs of customers in specifically targeted countries.

14.2 The Significance of International Marketing

The economic theory of comparative advantage states that each country should specialise in the production of those goods it can most efficiently

provide, which should encourage unrestricted trade, international specialisation and increased global efficiency.

This is perhaps a commonsense yet idealistic view, since individual countries for a variety of political and economic reasons erect barriers to the free
movement of goods and services between them. Agreements are formed
which encourage free trade within defined geographical regions, but which
tend to erect barriers against those who are not in this 'club'.

World trading blocks

The biggest of these clubs is the so-called Common Market or the European
Union (EU), which was formerly known as the European Community (EC)
and before that the European Economic Community (EEC). Its latest title
of EU perhaps reflects the change that has taken place since the initial
phases when it was termed the EEC. In the early days it was seen as a
trading block – hence its title – whereas the current title reflects its trading
and political role as a kind of United States of Europe. Indeed this is an
issue which currently rages among member nations of the EU in terms of
those wishing for more federal control from Brussels (the headquarters)
and those wishing to keep their autonomy. Currently the membership of the
EU is as follows:

> Belgium, France, Germany, Netherlands, Luxembourg, Italy, Ireland, United
> Kingdom, Denmark, Greece, Spain, Portugal, Finland, Sweden and Austria.

Other similar organisations exist throughout the world, but they are not
as politically integrated as the EU. These organisations are:

- North American Free Trade Association (NAFTA), comprising the
  USA, Canada and Mexico.
- Organisation for Petroleum Exporting Countries (OPEC), comprising
  Saudi Arabia, Kuwait, United Arab Emirates, Qatar, Iran, Iraq, Libya,
  Algeria, Nigeria, Venezuela and Indonesia.
- Association of South-East Asian Nations (ASEAN), comprising
  Singapore, Thailand, Malaysia, the Philippines, Indonesia and Brunei.
- European Free Trade Association (EFTA) has lost most of its member-
  ship to the EU, but those remaining in this trading block are Norway,
  Switzerland and Iceland.

However, international business continues to rise on a worldwide basis
as barriers to trade slowly come down. This has been principally due to
the incremental agreements being sought by the General Agreement on
Tariffs and Trade (GATT), now the respensilierty of the World Trade
Organisation, which was formed to develop fair trading practices amongst
its members who now total over 100 individual countries.

Reasons for international trading between companies

Amongst individual companies there is an increasing need for them to expand their markets into the international arena for a number of reasons, namely:

- To increase the overall level of total profits;
- Because the home market might be saturated;
- To take advantage of an innovative-to-the-world product or service;
- To satisfy the goals of corporate management who might wish as a general matter of policy that the company should be committed to international operations;
- To enjoy the corporate tax advantages offered in overseas countries;
- To enjoy the funding benefits from setting up manufacturing and assembly bases in certain overseas countries which might also offer access to the trading block to which that country belongs;
- To obtain economies of larger-scale operations;
- Freer trade in general as a result of GATT accords.

However, against these positive factors and advantages there are a number of negative factors, namely:

- The reason why a company might wish to enter the international arena is to escape competition in the home market. One of the principal reasons that has spurred a number of UK companies to unwillingly enter EU markets is because UK markets have now been legitimately opened up to other Europeans countries
- To dispose of surplus production or to utilise surplus manufacturing capacity. This is a negative factor, but a number of companies dispose of their surplus production overseas at cost, or even below cost, rather than cut their prices on the domestic market. In the case of selling below cost there is an international law under 'Anti-dumping and countervailing measures' which prohibits dumping as it constitutes unfair competition against domestic manufacturers. The USA in particular is very sensitive to products being dumped in the USA and will enact this legislation whenever it is appropriate to do so
- Import tariffs which impose a percentage duty on the cost of landed products pose a negative factor to exporting as do import quotas which impose a numerical value on the numbers of products that can be imported. Sometimes import licences are required which demand a licence to import certain goods or services and in most cases the foreign government has to be paid for such licences
- Political unrest is a factor which negates against companies wishing to trade in a foreign country. Quite often it stems from political unrest, but in certain cases an overseas government might stop payment for goods or services that have been provided on the basis that it seeks to preserve its

foreign exchanges. In the UK an organisation exists called the Export Credits Guarantee Department (ECGD) which is set up to insure companies against such risks, and indeed insurance is available to insure against non-payment by individual overseas companies. However, the negative side is that such services cost money, and this all adds to the costs of trading competitively on an international basis.

14.3 **A Macro-overview of International Trade**

Foreign exchange is important to a country in order to pay for the goods and services it imports. As a country it is vital that we export to pay for essential imports, because we are not self-sufficient in food or raw materials and a lot of manufactured goods. However, we are also a free trading nation and traditionally we have put up few barriers to those countries who have wished to market their goods and services here.

The gap between a country's total exports and its total imports is known as the balance of trade, and in payment terms it is known as the balance of payments. If a country imports more than it exports in value terms then the balance of payments will be in deficit, but if exports are higher than imports then the balance of payments will be in surplus.

Help for exporters

A number of organisations exist to help UK companies to engage in international trade, and many companies belong to trade associations which reflect the corporate views of their subscribing members. Such trade associations often provide significant advice in relation to export markets. Many public libraries now offer special sections devoted to information relating to the export trade. However, the most significant of the organisations that gives export advice is the British Overseas Trade Board (BOTB) which is a branch of the Department of Trade and Industry (DTI). The BOTB helps exporters by providing financial support to individual companies who are working with a recognised agency like a Chamber of Commerce in a number of ways:

- Financial support when exhibiting at overseas trade fairs or exhibitions.
- Subsidies to air travel and accommodation expenses when travelling as part of an overseas trade delegation to a specific part of the world.
- Low-interest loans for a substantial amount of the costs involved in entering new export markets on the basis that if the venture is unsuccessful the loss is shared.
- Help in general in terms of putting exporters in touch with markets (for example Computerised Export Intelligence which is a subsidised scheme through which companies receive regular updated reports in relation to

export opportunities). It also engages in export intelligence gathering in a more general way in terms of investigating the commercial viability of doing business in certain countries and making this information available to the business community.

- Help through contacts with British embassies in overseas countries. In recent years such embassies have become far more commercially proactive in terms of helping the interests of British overseas businesses. Services provided by such consular offices can include the preparation of shortlists of potential agents or distributors of a company's products.

Stages of economic development

In relation to individual countries an international classification exists to denote the stage in terms of development status in which such countries are placed. This classification is as follows:

- **Undeveloped countries** (sometimes termed subsistence economies) which have subsistence living and engage in barter trade for the exchange of goods largely in central markets. There is no specialisation and no modern marketing activity.
- **Less-developed countries** have more of a self-sufficiency philosophy with a predominance of small-scale cottage industry. Agriculture and manufacturing is labour-intensive. Producers tend to be marketers (production orientation).
- **Developing countries** are sometimes referred to as 'newly industrialising countries' (NICs) and they have specialisation of labour and manufacturing. There is a separation of production from the marketing function.
- **Developed countries** (sometimes termed industrialised countries) engage in regional, national and international marketing. There is specialisation of manufacture and mass distribution.
- **Affluent countries** is a further category that is sometime used and this relates to countries who have reached developed country status, but additionally its population demands high quality, sophisticated consumer goods.

Activity

Think of a country that fits each of the categories just listed.

- Undeveloped countries – Ethiopia
- Less-developed countries – Uganda
- Developing countries – Malaysia
- Developed countries – Greece
- Affluent countries – Sweden

14.4 **The Four Ps of the International Marketing Mix**

It makes sense to institute a marketing policy for international markets developed on the basis of an integrated marketing mix rather than simply selling products designed for the domestic market on an international scale. Marketing mix elements for international operations are no different to those used for domestic marketing, the principal difference being in the range of options. It is up to the marketing manager, or the manager designated to look after international operations – perhaps the international marketing or sales manager – to decide, on the basis of what marketing research indicates, how the marketing mix should be adapted for each target area in which the company markets or is considering entering.

Each of the marketing mix elements, which includes the important aspect of selling that is considered separately from promotion, are now considered from the viewpoint of examining the issues that are at stake when considering them in the context of international marketing.

Product

Due regard must be given to whether to market the entire product range or part of the range, and whether to modify these products to suit local demand, standards and regulations that might pertain in the overseas market. This might mean high modification costs, packaging, labelling and product or brand-name considerations.

A policy of standardisation ('we sell what we make') is typical for a passive company who has found itself in international trade by accident. This is akin, perhaps, to simple exporting in terms of fulfilling unsolicited export orders. Such orders might come from an advertisement in a domestic journal that has some circulation overseas, but the company's philosophy tends to be that it will export if it has surplus stocks or production capacity. When selling to countries with a similar culture to that of the United Kingdom (for example Ireland, Canada, Australia, New Zealand and the USA) there will be few problems because of the similarities in terms of culture and language.

Some companies adapt their products to as to promote sales in particular countries ('we make what we can sell') and engage in market segmentation. Instead of simply attempting to sell domestic product overseas, attempts are made to adapt product in terms of their design, their function and their size.

Where a company is committed to continuous, rather than *ad hoc*, overseas sales and takes on the notion of international marketing activity as being central to its very existence, then it can be regarded more truly as an international marketing company ('ecological approach').

From what has been said it is clear that international marketing decision-making must consider the organisation's resources and its corporate objectives, and if the company is to seriously consider the international marketing route (the ecological approach) then it should have the backing of the board of directors and the active support of top strategic-level management.

Price

Price considerations

Depending upon whether the company pursues a strategy of differentiated, undifferentiated or concentrated marketing in relation to its chosen market segments, will depend upon the price levels to be charged overseas. Considerations relating to chosen market segments will affect the decision as to whether to adopt a skimming or penetration approach to pricing. In the end analysis, the method of pricing international sales, will very largely depend upon how important the overseas price will be in the overall marketing mix.

An extra factor in terms of costs which has to be considered in pricing decision concerns as tariffs and logistics costs. In addition to this there is the added uncertainty of extending credit for goods supplied to an overseas customer whom the company does not know as well as an equivalent domestic customer. However, this latter need not be such a problem as part of the sales agreement can include payment through a letter of credit or an irrevocable letter of credit, which means that the buyer's and the seller's banks exchange agreed funds at a certain point in the export delivery cycle.

Consideration should also be given as to the currency in which payment is to be made. Most export order arrangements stipulate 'hard' currency payments in US dollars or pounds sterling. However, there are circumstances in which the order can only be received if payment is made in the local currency. Here, consideration should be given to the strength of the currency and the fact that it might devalue by the time the contract is paid. In such a case, what might have originally looked like a reasonably lucrative contract might end up as a loss-making venture. For some export contracts to less-developed countries, the government of that country might insist on some kind of barter deal, whereby in return for a company's products some other products of that country must be taken as payment thus saving the country valuable foreign exchange. Added to this is the probability that in order to be competitive, margins on products destined for overseas markets will carry less profit that those manufactured for home consumption. With such added costs, and potential uncertainties, this is precisely the reason why a number of manufacturers prefer to remain with the domestic market rather than becoming involved internationally.

In meeting pricing objectives, both cost and market considerations are important together with the very practical issue of 'Is it worth it?' Clearly, if the company is simply breaking even to achieve volume in its international activities, then serious consideration should be give to only engaging in domestic sales.

Price quotations

At a more practical level, price will have to consider the extra costs for packing and freight charges. As a result, quotations in export markets sometime include freight charges and sometime it is the ex-factory cost. The principal quotations used include:

- **Ex-works** which means that the purchaser has to bear all of the costs of packing and freightage and insurance, plus other liabilities like import duties after they have left the supplier's factory.
- **Free alongside ship (FAS)** means that the exporter is responsible for transporting the goods to the point where they are being loaded onto the ship.
- **Free on board (FOB)** extends the responsibility to the exporter until the goods have been loaded on the ship. The ship's master will then give the goods a 'clean bill of lading' which means that they have been accepted as being in good condition for the sea journey. If the goods are not received in good condition by the ship's master a 'foul bill of lading' will be issued which is not to say that the goods are damaged, but that the way they are packed might be not sturdy enough to stand the sea journey, in which case any insurance claims will be problematical. Assuming a clean bill of lading, from there the importer pays the costs of carriage insurance and freight.
- **Carriage insurance and freight (CIF)** means that as well as placing the goods on board the ship the exporter is also responsible for the freight to the end-port destination plus any freight insurance charges. A variation of this quotation is 'Cost and freight' (C&F) which is similar, but the importer pays the insurance premium.
- **Free delivered**, or 'franco rendu' as it is sometimes called, means that the exporter has responsibility for all the costs of freightage right to the customer's premises which will include payment of any import duties, obtaining import licences where appropriate plus all other administrative details right up to organising foreign exchange where necessary. Clearly, this option is the most complicated one for the seller and the least complicated for the buyer. However, companies that engage in regular international marketing have departments specifically established to deal with these kinds of transactions so the problem becomes one of routine.

Activity

The types of quotation that have been considered range from very simple to quite complicated on the part of the supplying company. Which price quotation will best suit a small supplier and which would suit a large supplier?

- Small supplier – ex-works or perhaps FOB.
- Large supplier – any, but certainly a complex quotation like free delivered should not pose a problem.

Transfer pricing

There is one further important consideration in relation to international pricing decisions that is of particular benefit to multinational companies, although it is of equal value to international marketing companies with overseas manufacturing or assembly bases. This is the subject of transfer pricing which is applicable to companies that transfer components and finished products between their plants in different manufacturing countries.

The basis of transfer pricing is that prices of components and finished products moving between manufacturing or assembly locations can be manipulated in order to minimise import duties or corporation tax to the benefit of the enterprise as a whole. It works as follows:

- Component parts or completed products can be transferred into a high-duty country in which the company has a manufacturing/assembly base at an artificially low transfer price to minimise duties payable
- Components or finished products can be transferred into high corporation tax countries at high transfer prices so that profits in this country are minimised
- Components or finished products can be transferred at high prices into a country from which dividend repatriation is restricted or subject to additional government taxes

It is, of course, more complicated than it seems and there are yet further considerations that can be made. For example, in countries with high inflation rates, where devaluation of the currency is feared, it will be possible through transfer pricing to avoid the accumulation of funds in that country, and thus largely avoid the effects of any devaluation. The corollary is that national governments are also interested in the possible abuse of such arrangements. Naturally, the government of the exporting country will want to see that the transfer price is not artificially low, and it will endeavour to see that appropriate profits are made and fair levels of taxes are paid. In the importing country, the government will want to see that goods are not being transferred at unreasonably high prices which will reduce local profits and corporation tax liability. At the same time customs and excise might well investigate to see that artificially low transfer prices might be seen as an attempt to minimise duty liabilities.

Promotion

The company has a number of courses open to it in terms of promoting itself internationally which includes media advertising, point-of-sale promotion, trade exhibitions, trade fairs, brochures and direct mail. The avail-

Table 14.1   **Adapted from Keegan's five strategies for international marketing**

Strategy	Promotion	Product
1	Same	Same
2	Same	Different
3	Different	Same
4	Different	Different
5	Invention	

Source: Keegan (1993).

ability and the relative quality of such media is, of course, an important consideration as are factors like costs and foreign language considerations for translations of promotional literature. Of course promotion as an element of the marketing mix involves selling, and in the international marketing context the principal concern here is the type of representation that will be adopted. In these circumstances selling takes on a wider remit than it does in a domestic marketing situation. It also includes the type of distribution to be employed, because in most instances of international selling the seller also plays a critical part in the distribution and often the stocking of the goods. This aspect is considered in the next section under 'place'.

The most important aspect of international promotion is the policy that will be adopted in relation to standardisation. Warren J. Keegan (1993) has put forward five strategies for international marketing in terms of both Promotion and Products. His idea has been adapted and is shown in Table 14.1.

Activity

Think of a product or service that best fits each of the strategies listed in Table 14.1.

1 Famous brands of cola (this is termed **straight extension**).
2 Famous brands of petrol using an international logo and advertising theme, but adapting the product to suit different climatic conditions (this is termed **product adaptation**).
3 Bicycles – a leisure promotion in western countries and a means of transportation promotion in less developed countries (this is termed **communications adaptation**).
4 Clothing – different clothing to suit different tastes and different promotions to reflect fashion in certain countries and functionality in others (this is termed **dual adaptation**).
5 In some countries **product invention** might be necessary in order to meet customer needs at affordable prices. The example Keegan cites is a hand-cranked manual washing machine for subsistence-level countries.

Place (or distribution)

This is probably the most critical decision for the international marketer and the principal choice is between direct representation from the company or through some kind of commission agent or distributor. If the decision is to use direct representation from the company, then this can be very expensive in terms of costs and expenses, especially if the representative is required to live permanently in the overseas country. There is also the problem of culture, and indeed in some countries it would not be possible for a foreigner to conclude negotiations single-handedly and some kind of local intermediary would be required. Many local companies offer their services as commission agents working simply on commission for the goods they sell and leaving the commercial transactions to the supplying company and the customers they sell to. At the other extreme there are distributors who purchase and stock the products and then resell them in the overseas market in addition to providing service facilities.

This aspect of international marketing is a very important part of the organisation's representational and selling arrangements, and it is considered separately in the next section under 'sales channels'.

Place, of course, has a logistics implication and here the process is far more complicated than for domestic marketing. Goods must be packed in appropriate packaging for seafreight if they are bulky and cannot be transported in containers. Containerisation has, in recent years, made the task of international trade much easier and cheaper, because an individual company's goods can often go in a container that is shared with other companies exporting to the same destination. The shipping company or a shipping agent organises logistics, so it is not a matter of the company having to locate another company to share a container load. Air freight is a possibility and here packing costs are much cheaper as packing does not have to be at a standard to withstand a lengthy sea journey. Freight insurance charges by air are also much cheaper as there is less likelihood of damage than with sea transport. Air freight is still considerably more expensive than sea, but it is a rapidly growing international transport medium that is particularly suited to perishable goods and goods that have a high value in relation to their weight, since they can be in the hands of the customer in a matter of days rather than weeks by seafreight.

14.5 Sales Channels

Before a company establishes its marketing arrangement in an overseas country it should research appropriate distribution possibilities and its export marketing research will suggest the best distribution arrangement among the following alternatives.

Direct exporting

The company that chooses this route, rather than marketing through an independent distributor, has a number of choices open to it in this respect:

- Set up an **overseas branch** or a **subsidiary company**   This has the advantage of offering the fewest organisational changes, allows management to think in more global terms of its responsibilities and commitments, and gives it more control over its selling and marketing efforts.

    However, the downside is the high cost and greater risk, plus the fact that in such circumstances the physical distance between the overseas branch and head office is greater and this might lead to possibilities for misunderstanding and misinterpretation of policies put forward by the head office and a general feeling of 'isolation' which can lead to motivational problems.

- A **joint venture** can take the form of an overseas arrangement with an indigenous firm, and in some markets this is the only way in which the exporting company can legitimately do business. In other instances the joint venture might be between two or more companies with complementary products or services forming a joint venture to collectively enter an overseas market.

    The advantage here is particularly to small manufacturers who can defray some of the costs of performing such a venture on their own. In the case of a joint venture with a local company, entry to the overseas market is often made a lot easier because of a knowledge of trading and ways of doing business in that marketplace. It can be particularly attractive when the manufacturer sees such a partner as becoming a potential assembler or stockholder who will tend to be more firmly committed to the success of the venture than, say, a distributor, who would also distribute other manufacturers' products as well as those of the exporting company with a correspondingly lower degree of commitment.

    Against these advantages there is the possibility that the partner to the joint venture might eventually become a competitor with indeed, the possibility of friction between the parties in relation to matters of financing, profit-sharing and control.

Licensing

These arrangements can take a number of forms. A company may negotiate a licence for a foreign company to produce and market its products overseas or simply to market the goods. Alternatively, the company might grant a franchise to an overseas company which will involve the granting of rights to sell certain goods or services in defined markets using methods agreed by the supplier.

The advantages offered by licensing is that it is a low-risk option with low investment costs and speedy entry to the overseas market.

Disadvantages lie in the fact that it will be less profitable in the long term than direct exporting, and the company's international reputation may suffer if the licensee produces products which don't meet expectations. Legal processes for such arrangements are often complex, lengthy and costly.

Use of intermediaries

A number of possibilities exist for this kind of arrangement and it is the means through which the majority of trade by small and medium-sized companies is done. These are now examined separately under their respective categories:

- **Export houses** are export merchants who are based in the home country and who buy goods from the home producer and sell to their clients overseas. In this type of arrangement risks are reduced, but there is no control over exports.
- **Confirming houses** are similar to export houses, but here they act on behalf of overseas buyers of goods, finding sources of supply in return for a commission from the buyer.
- **Buying offices** are used by a number of large overseas companies and their specific function is to arrange initial contacts between overseas companies and prospective suppliers. They will then see through any contract that might result to its completion, right up to export documentation and final settlement if necessary.
- **Agents** are probably the most popular type of intermediary used in international marketing. A commission agent acts on behalf of a principal (the exporting company). The agent then secures orders, and receives an agreed percentage commission on these orders.

    How far the agent becomes involved in the actual distribution of the goods depends upon the agency agreement. In some cases the agent receives the goods directly and then forwards these to the customer, but in other cases the agent's responsibility ends when the contract has been agreed. In other instances the agent might be on an agreed retainer as well as a percentage commission on orders obtained. In the event of this latter arrangement, it is probable that the agent might act exclusively only for the principal's organisation in relation to their particular goods or services. Agents will probably carry complementary lines and in some cases competing lines from other manufacturers. In such circumstances there would be a danger of competing lines, and not the principal's lines, being 'pushed' in the marketplace.

    Agents are thus a convenient way of doing business at relatively low cost through an intermediary who knows the local market and local conditions of trading. However, the principal loses a certain amount of control in terms of how the company's goods are marketed. If the agent is carrying other complementary lines then the commitment to market the principal's product lines will not be as urgent as would be the case if only the principal's products were being represented.

- **Distributors** are the final category and they represent the most complicated end of the continuum which starts with the simple commission agent. They actually purchase goods from the manufacturer and then market these, in some cases also carrying out functions like packaging and producing promotional material plus follow-up duties like the provision of service facilities and ensuring spare parts availability.

The main disadvantage for the principal here is lack of control in terms of how the product is being marketed. In addition, such an arrangement is likely to be done on tighter profit margins, as the distributor is doing far more than an agent would do in terms of providing payment when the goods are received (if this forms part of the contract) and then carrying out additional warehousing and service functions. However, the right distribution arrangement in one country might mean that the manufacturer will have more time and resources to concentrate on other world markets.

14.6 **Cultural and Environment Factors**

This final section attempts to address a number of extra matters to which due deliberation should be granted when a company becomes involved in international marketing. These are considered under a number of separate headings:

- **Language** should be considered from the point of view of both the written and spoken language in terms of sales literature and sales presentation. There might also be a language hierarchy in the country, and in some countries it is not expected that translations will be made from English – the major international language – into the local language.
- **Attitudes and values** may be different in some countries in relation to matters such as timekeeping and appointments. In some societies it would be deemed exceptionally discourteous to be late for an appointment, yet in other cultures lateness is the norm. In some societies there is a strong feeling of kinship between members of the population and particularly towards the individual's family, where in some cases it would be extremely disrespectful to question the word of the head of the family.
- **Religion** is a very important consideration in terms of the observance of such matters as prayer times, religious rituals, sacred objects, sacred taboos and religious holidays.

- **Aesthetic considerations** cover matters like what is regarded as beautiful or good taste, which then includes design criteria like colours and shapes and even brand-name considerations. Many international brand names have been coined which sometimes have unfortunate connotations in certain languages.
- **Education** in a country is important, for if goods are to be marketed there, levels of understanding and literacy must be considered when compiling instructions for use in respect of more complicated products.
- **Law and politics** should be considered particularly in the case of there being a potential dispute in relation to the products being supplied. Does the home country law take precedence over the supplier country's law, or does international law apply? Here, consideration must be given to drawing up a sound contract of sale.
- **Internal organisation** of the country is important in terms of its commercial infrastructure which can range from the way business is conducted to the state of the road and general transport systems.

14.7 **Summary**

International marketing is a very broad subject and many individual textbooks are devoted solely to this topic. In this chapter we have considered its importance to a country and to individual companies. We have examined the broader aspects of international trade in terms of difficulties encountered when trading internationally, including how countries are structured in terms of their economic development and some of the world's trading blocks. Practical problems have also been considered from a company's standpoint and in this respect each of the elements of the marketing mix has been considered in turn in the context of how it should be manipulated when marketing internationally.

Chapter Review Questions

Explain the difference between multinational marketing and international marketing.
Multinational marketing generally refers to organisations whose manufacturing and business activities are scattered throughout the world and they tend to function autonomously from their areas of operation. International marketing describes companies who have made a strategic decision to enter foreign markets and they adapt maretking mixes to suit the marketplace in their chosen areas of operation.

What is the theory of comparative advantage?
Each country should specialise in the production of those goods it can most efficiently provide which should encourage unrestricted trade, international specialisation and increased global efficiency.

Name six member states of the EU.
The United Kingdom, France, Netherlands, Italy, Denmark, Finland.

What is NAFTA?
North American Free Trade Association.

Give four reasons for trading internationally.
Because the home market might be saturated; because top management has made a policy decision to enter international markets; to enjoy better corporate tax advantages offered in an overseas country; to obtain economies of larger-scale operations.

Which UK organisation is the main provider of assistance to exporters?
The British Overseas Trade Board (BOTB) which is a sub-division of the Department of Trade and Industry (DTI).

Cite the classification system used to denote the stages of development that countries have reached.
Undeveloped countries (subsistence economies); less-developed countries; developing countries (newly-industrialising countries or NICs); developed countries; affluent countries.

What are the three different product policies that a company might adaptat in relation to its overseas activities?
Standardisation – we sell what we make; adoption – we make what we can sell; ecological approach.

Name four different price quotations in relation to different responsibility levels for delivery.
Ex-works; free on board (FOB); cost and freight (C&F); free delivered.

What is transfer pricing?
Where prices of components and finished goods can be manipulated between manufacturing/assembly plants in different countries to take advantage of the different customs and excise duty or corporation tax rates in different countries.

Explain Keegan's five strategies for international marketing.
Permutations of 'same' and 'different' against 'promotion' and 'product' gives four, and the fifth is 'invention'.

Which form of international transport offers the most economical rate for the insurance of goods being transported – air or seafreight?
Airfreight.

Overall, which form of transport is cheapest – air or sea?
Generally sea, but in the case of high value/low weight goods the cheapest might be air because the goods will be in the hands of the importer much quicker which then means quicker payment which can be used to fund more export work that much move quickly.

Name two options that a company has available to it when engaging in direct exporting.
An overseas branch/subsidiary company; a joint venture.

What is licensing?
Where a company negotiates to licence an overseas company to produce and/or market the goods.

Name three methods of exporting through the use of intermediaries.
Export houses; agents; distributors.

Cite four factors that should be considered under 'cultural factors' when marketing internationally.
Language; religion; education; aesthetic values.

15 Marketing Planning

15.1 **Marketing Planning in the Context of Corporate Planning**

Corporate planning or strategic company planning comprises the following sequential steps:

- **Mission statement** (or defining the company mission) has an influence on all planning throughout the organisation, for it is a statement of the company's overall business philosophy. It is normally a set of guidelines, rather than something that is stated in hard and fast quantitative terms.
- **Situational analysis** means evaluating external and internal factors that will affect the planning process and asks the question 'Where are we now?' This means researching and analysing all information that might have a bearing on the organisation and its operations, from internal factors like individual departmental company resources, to external factors like current political events that might impinge on the activities of the company.
- **Set organisational objectives** requires company management to put forward guidance as to how the company should fulfil its mission and this clarifies where the company wants to be. These, unlike the mission statement, should be expressed in achievable quantitative terms.
- **Choose strategies to achieve these objectives** which are the concrete ideas that set about achieving company objectives and they relate to how the mission will be accomplished.

It is from this latter point that we can then start to plan strategically and tactically for marketing, as can other major divisions of the organisation which include: finance, production, human resource management and distribution. The function entrusted with bringing all of these separate planning functions together is termed corporate planning, and it is up to the person entrusted with corporate planning to ensure that one department's plans are in harmony with other departments' plans, and that they all work towards achieving the overall organisational objectives.

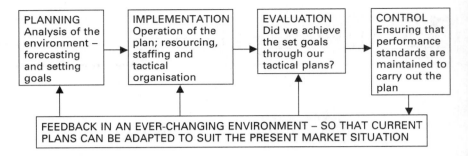

Fig 15.1   An overview of corporate planning

Activity

Think up an appropriate mission statement for your organisation.

Pepsi Cola's mission statement is: to be an outstanding company by exceeding customer expectations through empowering people guided by shared values.

In forward-thinking organisations it is the managing director or chief executive who is the corporate planner, and in such an event strategic planning is seen to be at the core of managerial activity for it is this activity, that drives the organisation.

However, all too often it is the case that as strategic planning concerns the longer-term future, it can be put to one side in the interests of dealing with everyday tactical matters. To this extent, in larger organisations, corporate planning is often set up as a separate function reporting directly to top management, with the specific remit of bringing together and synergising all individual departmental plans into the final corporate plan. It is placed directly under top management in what is called a 'staff' relationship, but is not a 'line' relationship, that is, in the line of command of the company from the board of directors downwards (for example, it is not alongside marketing management in terms of the hierarchical structure).

Figure 15.1 provides a more practical idea of how the corporate planning process works out in reality.

In terms of how planning works, Figure 15.2 demonstrates how general strategic plans are formulated by top management and these progress to more practical levels as they are implemented throughout the management hierarchy.

At top management levels, these plans for the longer term can be anything from one year to five or ten or even more years, depending upon the

Fig 15.2 Planning hierarchy

---

planning horizons in the particular industry. It is also at this level that strategic business units (SBU) are created with a view to these SBUs carrying out the general plans that have been decided by top management. An SBU is a group or unit within an organisation that comprises separately identified products or market divisions with a specific market focus. A manager in charge of an SBU has the responsibility for integrating all of that SBU's functions into a marketing programme so it can then be measured in terms of its success at the end of an accounting period.

Plans thus become more practical, and shorter-term in nature, as they are translated into tactical action plans further down the organisational hierarchy. Planning horizons at a functional level tend to be for one year, and during that year plans are spelt out on a periodic basis through the year – usually on a month-by-month or quarter-by-quarter basis. Figure 15.2, therefore, shows how marketing plans become more practical and tangible moving from the corporate level towards sales and advertising.

15.2 **An Overview of Marketing Planning**

Strategic marketing planning is the application of a number of logical steps in the planning process. There is no one clear formula that must always be applied, and indeed one specific model would not suit every marketing planning situation. Different textbooks also cite slightly different models that are variations on a similar general theme.

Figure 15.3, which is a relatively comprehensive model, gives an overview of the strategic and tactical marketing planning process. The early part of this model shows how it fits into the corporate planning framework, and from there more detailed activities take place that result in an implementable marketing plan.

This marketing planning framework forms the structure of the remainder of this chapter.

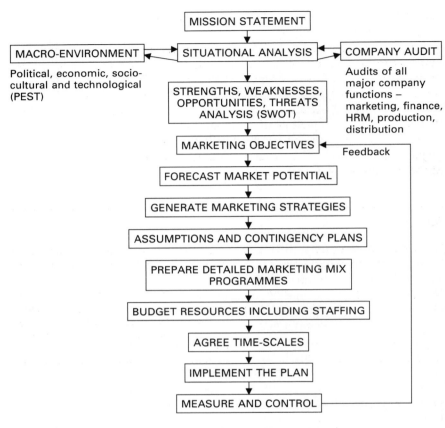

Fig 15.3 Summary of the strategic marketing planning process

Situational analysis

The mission statement has already been explained, but the next stage that relates to an analysis of the current situation is now explained for it has two inputs. The first input relates to the organisation's macro-environment and these are factors over which the company has little or no control. They are listed under four separate headings – political, economic, socio-cultural and technological – and are known by the acronym PEST. Added to these factors, some marketing planners also add 'legal' (the acronym then being SLEPT) and some add 'competition' if these are felt to be specific issues. This is the external audit part of what is called the company audit. From this external audit a number of very short statements are made in respect of each of the PEST + C + L subdivisions. The statements do not have to be justified, as they are mere observations that will help formulate more detailed plans at a later stage.

The next part concerns what is called the company audit or, in corporate planning terms, the internal audit. This looks at the individual capabilities of the company, SBU by SBU, and department by department, and again short statements or observations are made that do not have to be justified. These two actions are what is called the corporate auditing process and they develop to form the situational analysis. Marketing's part of this total corporate auditing procedure is termed the 'marketing audit', and it is included here as part of marketing planning because it forms the beginning of the marketing planning process.

Activity

Think of the kind of questions relating to marketing that could be asked as part of the marketing audit process under 'situation analysis procedure' relating to macro-environmental factors and company-specific factors.

Economic factors like inflation, unemployment levels and taxation. Socio-cultural factors like eduction, environment and consumer life-styles. At a company level factors like reviewing marketing activity like pricing and discounts and the range and quality of products or services that the company markets.

SWOT analysis

The SWOT analysis (strengths, weaknesses, opportunities, threats) is an attempt to translate company-specific factors from the company audit into company strengths and weaknesses plus external environmental factors (from the PEST analysis) into external opportunities and threats. As was the case with the PEST analysis, no attempt should be made to justify the points being placed in each of the categories as it is meant as a mere statement which will assist marketing planning in the later stages.

In terms of its presentation, the SWOT analysis is normally put into a four-box-matrix with internal strengths and weaknesses being listed in the top two boxes and external opportunities and threats in the lower two boxes. Experience has shown that for most companies, ranging from the very large to the very small, the number of strengths and weaknesses is around 10–15 each, and the number of opportunities and threats is about 5–12 each. Any less, normally indicates that the SWOT is not complete, and any more indicates that a number of points are being repeated in a different form of words.

Marketing objectives

Objectives are concerned with what is to be achieved, unlike strategies that are the means of achieving objectives. These objectives are obtained from corporate level strategies and such objectives should be very specific. An acronym used in this context is that marketing objectives should be SMART – which stands for specific, measurable, achievable, realistic and timely. An objective must, therefore, have some kind of measurable characteristic which might relate to a standard of performance like a percentage level of profit or a situation that has to be achieved like penetrating a specific market.

Activity

Think of a marketing objective for a service organisation of your choice.

A large insurance company might decide to enter the annuities market and achieve a 5 per cent share of this market by the end of the year.

Forecast market potential

This is a stage that a lot of marketing planning texts seem to miss. It is illogical really, for without a forecast of the market potential a company does not really know for what it should be making its plans. In fact, as was shown in Chapter 5, forecasting is at the very basis of all company planning. The techniques involved in forecasting have already been covered in Chapter 5 and it is for medium and long-term planning horizons that medium and long-term sales forecasts are needed.

Generate marketing strategies

Strategies are of course the means through which marketing objectives can be achieved; they are meant to detail selected approaches that the company will use to achieve its objectives. Determining strategies leads to a series of action statements that are clear sets of steps to be followed to achieve the objectives. Operational decisions then spill out of these marketing strategies and these form the tactical foundations of the detailed marketing-mix programmes.

Assumptions and contingency plans

Assumptions relate to external factors over which the company has little control. These should be stated as a series of points that relate to, and which preface, the make-up of the detailed marketing-mix plans in the next stage. Assumptions should be as few as possible and if they are not needed then they should not be introduced. For each assumption a directional contingency plan should be formulated, so in the case of an assumption being wrong the appropriate contingency plan can be brought in. At this stage, contingency plans should not be detailed. They will probably only consist of a sentence or two that are merely directional plans to be implemented if assumptions are incorrect in practice.

Detailed marketing-mix programmes

This part of the plan enables the organisation to satisfy the needs of its target markets and to achieve its marketing objectives. This indeed is what comprises the bulk of an organisation's marketing efforts. The first part of this programme is to determine the marketing mix, and here detailed consideration must be give to each of the areas of the 'four Ps', plus customer considerations in terms of segmentation, targeting and positioning. All of the ingredients of the marketing mix must be combined in an optimum way so that they work together to achieve company objectives. This part of the plan is concerned with who will do what, and how it will be done. In this way responsibility, accountability and action over a specific time period can be planned, scheduled, implemented and reviewed.

As this is an action plan, the time period must be realistic. Most plans are for a period of one year which is the conventional planning period, and, as we saw in Chapter 5 that related to forecasting, one year is regarded as a medium-term planning horizon. A plan must also contain time scales which detail marketing activities normally on a month-by-month or a quarter-by-quarter basis, and indeed timing is addressed in the plan after the resourcing section.

This is not to say that marketing planning should not be for longer than one year, and indeed it is normally the case that long-term issues are also addressed in the marketing plan. Long-term will, of course, have different meanings for different industries. In the case of modern electronics long-term is probably not longer than three years, whereas in steel production long-term can mean 10 years or more.

When long-term planning is addressed as part of a marketing plan, then all that can be realistically put forward is a directional plan, because to plan in terms of month-by-month expectations for say five years hence would cause the plan to be spuriously unrealistic, and when reality proved the plan to be hopelessly incorrect then confidence might well be lost in the planning process. Many companies do, however, have rolling plans that are modified in the light of what actually happened. As one planning period finishes (one month, one quarter, one year) the rolling plan will be modified in the light of what has happened, and a further planning period will be added on to the end of the plan.

Activity

What criteria do you feel should be considered in relation to 'products' when designing a detailed marketing mix programme?

Quality; features; style and design; services and warranty; packaging; range of products in terms of width and depth; new product development.

In addition to the above, planning tools like the matrices put forward in Chapter 7 are appropriate to use here for analytical purposes.

Activity

Consider what planning tools relating to products might be appropriate in this context?

BCG matrix; GE matrix; Shell directional policy matrix; Ansoff's matrix.

An area of marketing planning that deserves specific attention here is that of attaining the sales revenues that have been forecast as part of the planning process. Put in practical terms, the sales-forecast has predicted the amount of sales that are possible, and budgeting (dealt with in the next section) will determine the expenditure available towards achieving this forecast. It does not, therefore, follow that the forecasted sales are intended to be achieved in practice. Individual members of the field sales-force will each have been given sales targets or quotas to reach, and the summation of all of these targets or quotas should equate to the budgeted-for sales that each salesperson must achieve towards reaching the planned-for sales. This is why many sales personnel refer to their sales target or quota as their sales budget, which is not an expenditure limit as the description might infer, but it is a reference to the amount they must sell in order to satisfy the sales volume requirements of the marketing plan.

We have, of course, only considered product in these activities, so clearly similar considerations need to be made in relation to other elements of the marketing mix. Indeed, this part of the marketing plan is the largest section, and in many cases this section, plus its various marketing-mix sub-sections, is bigger than the rest of the plan put together.

Budget resources and staffing

Now that detailed decisions have been made in relation to the different elements of the marketing mix, the next stage of the programme is to budget. Organisations have many demands on their limited resources, and it is this final balancing act that will be the responsibility of corporate planning. Budgeting covers not only general marketing expenditure, but also salaries and expenses for staffing. If the plan calls for an increase in sales and market-share, then this will normally have resource implications for the marketing department, perhaps in terms of more representation or increased advertising costs.

It is at this budgeting stage that plans are sometimes modified in the light of reality, and the initial marketing objectives might well have to be modified as a result. Practical financial considerations might well cause the organisation to tone down its original marketing objectives.

Time scales

This normally takes the form of what is termed a Gantt chart. A Gantt chart places time along the top of the chart and activities down the side and an example is illustrated in Figure 15.4.

Implement the plan

This is precisely what the heading says. The plan is now put into action within the predetermined budget and resource parameters, and along the time-scale that has been agreed. More importantly, those who will carry out the plan should be informed of its details and know the part they must play within its implementation to ensure its success. In fact this section would not really be addressed in a planning document as it is self-evident, but it is here as this is the 'doing' part of the planning process.

Measure and control

A marketing plan cannot be operated without some means to monitor, measure and control its progress. A system of controls should be estab-

Fig 15.4   Gantt chart showing time scales in a marketing plan

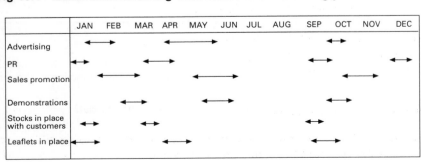

lished whereby the plan is reviewed on a regular and controlled basis and then updated as circumstances change. Such controls can address the tactics in terms of sales analyses which will commence with a comparison of budgeted sales revenue against actual sales revenue. Variations might be due to volume or price variances – perhaps an unfavourable variance being due to having to cut prices to match the tactical actions of competitors.

The marketing information system provides essential inputs to the marketing planning system as was shown in Chapter 5. This information comes from market intelligence, marketing research and the organisation's own internal accounting system. This information then inputs into the marketing plan. It is a control mechanism as well, because customer reactions are also fed into this marketing information system from market intelligence through the field sales-force or from marketing research studies. Information on sales analyses is also fed into the system so assessments can be made as to whether forecasted sales are being achieved or not.

As the planning horizon unfolds and plans do not go exactly as anticipated, action can then be taken as required, and this is the reason behind the feedback loop in Figure 15.3. These measures of performance thus allow the planner an opportunity to adjust and fine-tune plans as necessary during the planning period.

15.3 Summary

In any well-ordered modern company, managers have a duty to plan, organise, direct and control the activities of those for whom they have taken responsibility. In this chapter we have investigated the meaning and relevance of strategic and tactical marketing planning in an ordered framework of structures. This has shown that planning is a very practical activity that should be approached in a professional manner, as such plans will give guidance not only to top management, but also to those whose task it is to carry out such plans. More to the point, an ordered system of planning will give more security to an organisation in terms of its vision and the image it presents to both its internal employees and to the outside world.

Chapter Review Questions

What are the sequential steps in the strategic corporate planning process?
Mission statement; situational analysis; set organisational objectives; choose strategies to achieve these objectives

What are the stages in a strategic corporate planning model?
Planning; implementation; evaluation; control.

How does the planning hierarchy work from the top downwards?
Corporate planning; functional planning; sub-functional planning.

What are the stages in a typical marketing planning framework?
Mission statement; situational analysis; SWOT; marketing objectives; forecast market potential; generate marketing strategies; assumptions and contingency plans; detailed marketing mix programmes; budget resources and staffing; agree time-scales; implement the plan; measure and control the plan.

What are PEST factors?
Political; economic; socio-cultural; technological.

References

American Marketing Association (1961) *Report of the Definitions Committee of the American Marketing Association* (Chicago: American Marketing Association).

Ansoff, I. (1957) 'Strategies for Diversification', *Harvard Business Review*, September/October, p. 114.

Burbridge, J. Jr (1987) 'The Implementation of a Distribution Plan – a Case Study', *International Journal of Physical Distribution and Materials*, 17(1), pp. 28–38.

Cespedes, F. V. and Corley, E. R. (1990) 'Managing Multiple Channels', *Business Horizons*, July/August, pp. 67–77.

Colley, R. H. (1961) *Defining Advertising Goals for Measured Advertising Results (DAGMAR)* (New York: Association of National Advertisers), p. 17.

Corkindale, D. R. and Kennedy, S. H. (1976) *The Process of Advertising* (Bradford: MCB Publications), p. 61.

Davidson, H. (1997) *Even More Offensive Marketing* (London: Penguin).

Day, J. and Reynolds, P. (1996) 'Considering the Marketing Entrepreneurship Interface: Approach and Directions 1987–1985', American Marketing Association, University of Illinois Research Symposium, Stockholm, 14 June 1996 proceedings.

Drucker, P. (1973) *Management Tasks, Responsibilities and Practices* (New York: Harper & Row).

Herzberg (1966) *Work and the Nature of Man* (Cleveland: William Collins).

Jefkins, F. (1988) *Public Relations*, 3rd edn (London: Pitman).

Keegan, W. J. (1993) *Global Marketing Management* (Englewood Cliffs, N.J.: Prentice-Hall).

Kotler, P. (1997) *Marketing Management: Analysis, Planning, Implementation and Control*, 9th edn (Englewood Cliffs, N.J.: Prentice-Hall).

Lancaster, G. and Jobber, D. (1997) *Selling and Sales Management*, 4th edn (London: Pitman).

Lancaster, G. and Massingham, L. C. (1993) *Essentials of Marketing* (Maidenhead: McGraw-Hill).

Lancaster, G. and Reynolds, P. (1995) *Marketing* (London: Butterworth-Heinemann).

Lavidge, R. J. and Steiner, G. A. (1961) 'A Model for Predictive Measurements of Advertising Effectiveness', *Journal of Marketing*, October.

Lazersfeld, P. F., Berelson, B. and Gaude, H. (1948) *The People's Choice: How the Voter Makes up his Mind in a Presidential Election* (New York: Columbia University Press).

Ledbetter, W. W. and Cox, J. F. (1977) 'Operations Research in Production Management and Investigation of Past and Present Utilisation', *Production and Inventory Management*, 18, pp. 84–92.

Majaro, S. (1970) 'Advertising by Objectives', *Management Today*, January.

Maslow, A. (1954) *Motivation and Personality* (New York: Harper & Row).

McMarry, R. N. (1961) 'The Mystique of Sufer-Salermunship', *Harvard Business Review*, March–April.

Ogilvy, D. (1961) *Confessions of an Advertising Man* (New York: Atheneum).

Porter, M. E. (1980) *Competitive Strategy: Techniques for Analysing Your Business and Competitors* (New York: Free Press).

—— (1985) *Competitive Advantage: Creating and Sustaining Superior Performance* (New York: Free Press).

Raiffa, H. (1982) *The Art and Science of Negotiation* (Cambridge, Mass.: Harvard University Press).

Reeves, R. (1961) *Reality of Advertising* (New York: Alfred Knopf).

Robinson, P. J., Faris, C. and Wind Y. (1967) *Industrial Buying and Creative Marketing* (Boston: Allyn & Bacon).

Rogers, E. (1962) *Diffusion of Innovations* (New York: Free Press).

Schlussberg, H. (1980) 'Simulated versus Traditional Test Marketing', *Marketing News*, no. 23, October.

Shapiro, B. P. and Bonoma, T. V. (1984) 'How to Segment Industrial Markets', *Harvard Business Review*, May–June, pp. 104–10.

Shell Chemicals (1978) in S. Q. J. Robinson *et al.*, 'The Directional Policy Matrix Tool for Strategic Planning', *Long-Range Planning*, June, pp. 8–15.

Strong, E. K. (1925) *The Psychology of Selling* (New York: Harper & Row).

Webster, F. E. Jr and Wind, Y. (1972) *Organizational Buying Behaviour* (Englewood Cliffs, N.J.: Prentice-Hall).

Wind, Y. (1978) 'The Boundaries of Buying Decision Clusters', *Journal of Purchasing and Materials Management*, no. 14, Summer.

Index

A

above-the-line   209, 235–55
accessories: raw materials   120
accountant's approach   150, 156–9
achievement (buyer behaviour)   49, 239
ACORN (segmentation)   34
action planning   313–14
adaptive forecasting   98
adoption process   56–9, 134–6
advertising   240, 250–5
advertising by objectives   252–5
aesthetics (international marketing)   304
affluent countries   204
after sales   225–6
age (segmentation)   30
agents   302–3
AIDA   54
air freight   300
alternative choice   224
analysis of variance   82
analytical marketing system (MkIS)   81–2
ANOVA   106
Ansoff matrix   122–3
Anti-dumping   292
approach (sales)   221
Arhur D. Little matrix   144
ASEAN   291
aspirers (segmentation)   36
assortment (product)   127
assumptions (planning)   312–13
assumptive close (selling)   224
attitudes (buyer behaviour)   53
attitudes (international marketing)   303
attraction (buyer behaviour)   63

automatic vending   188
awareness (adoption process)   57

B

Barksdale & Harris matrix   144–6
basic close (selling)   224
batch production   4
behavioural segmentation   35–6
below-the-line   209, 255–64
benefit segmentation   36, 37
blind test   112
Booz, Allen & Hamilton   126
Boston Consulting (BCG) matrix   137–9
brand (life cycle)   130
brand image/name   149, 252–3
brand loyalty (segmentation)   35–6
brand management   122, 160
brand positioning   40–1
break even quantity (BEQ)   157–9
British Overseas Trade Board   293
bundle of satisfactions   118, 192, 200
business analysis (product)   125
business format franchising   187–8
business planning   16
business to business marketing   261, 269
buyer behaviour   16, 42–69
buyer decision process/model   54–6
buyers   67
buying offices   302
buying situations (organisational)   66
buy-response model   113

C

C&F   297
Cable TV   177

cafeteria question   110
capital transfer tax   7–8
cash cows   137, 145
cash dogs   145
catalogue (mail)   188–9
category (life cycle)   130
causal models (forecasting)   93
channel arrangements   178–9, 300–3
channel choice   175–83
channel conflict/cooperation   183
channel coordination   181–3
channel of distribution   14, 168–90
checklists   110
chi square   82
CIF   297
close (selling)   224–5
clubs (sales)   260
coercive (buyer behaviour)   63
cognitive dissonance   57
combined plan   233
commercialisation (product)   126
commission   232
commission agent   300
communicability (product)   135
communications mix   209, 233, 235, 240–3, 262, 271
communications process   243–9
community (of PR)   277–8
company knowledge (selling)   219
compatibility (product)   58, 135
competitions   256
competitive environment   21
complexity (buyer behaviour)   58, 135
components   120
concentrated marketing   41
concession close   225
conclusive research   106–7
conferences (sales)   230
confirmation (buyer behaviour)   57
confirming houses   302
conflict (channel)   179–81
conglomerate diversification   123
consistency (product)   127
consumer goods   120–2
consumer protection   9
consumers (and PR)   281
containerisation   300
contingency planing   312–13
control (planning)   315
convenience goods   121
Co-operative Societies   177, 185
cordial contact mailing   260
corporate identity   271–2, 276
corporate planning   307–9

cost leadership (Porter)   141
cost plus pricing   156–7
cost trade-off model   205
coupons   256
creative selling   214
critical success factors   126
cultural influences (buyer behaviour)   42–53, 303–4
custom marketing   41
customer care/focus   170, 225
customer knowledge (selling)   219
customer size/type (segmentation)   37
customer use projection   92
cyclical effect   82

D
DAGMAR   250–1
data collection (forecasting)   88
dealer mailings   261
death duties   7–8
decay curve (product)   126
deciders   67
decision making unit (DMU)   39, 67–8, 210, 217, 263
decline (life cycle)   133
decline (Porter)   142
delivery selling   214
demand curve   153
demand orientated pricing   159
demographic segmentation   30–5
demonstration (sales)   221–2, 256
dependent variables   106
depreciation   157
depth (product mix)   127
depth interviews   78, 104, 108
descriptive research   105
desk research (forecasting)   88
developing countries   294
development (life cycle)   130–1
development (product)   125
dichotomous question   110
differentiated marketing   40
differentiation (Porter)   141
diffusion of innovations   59, 134–6, 245–7
diminishing returns   208
direct exporting   301
direct mail   256, 259, 260–2, 284
direct marketing   173, 189, 259
direct response (advertising/selling)   259, 260
direct segmentation   35–6
discounts   165–6
display materials   256

dissonance theory 252
distribution mix/channels 14, 168–90, 197–200, 300–3
distribution research 114
distributive environment 20
distributors 280, 300, 303
diversification 123
divisibility (product) 135
DMU 39, 67–8, 210, 217, 263
dodos 146
dogs 138, 145
door-to-door selling 188
double moving average 95–7
dress (for selling) 220
DTI 293

E
early adopters 59, 134, 246
early majority 59, 135, 246
ECGD 293
economic environment 22–3
economic order quantity (EOQ) 205–6
economist's approach (pricing) 150, 152–6
economy lines 186
education (and PR) 282–4
education (international marketing) 304
education (segmentation) 32
EFTA 291
ego 48
elasticity 152–4, 203–4
electro-mechanical devices 112–13
emerging industry (Porter) 142
employees (in PR) 278–9
entrepreneurship 2
EPOS 113
escalator commission 233
EU, EC and EEC 291
European Union (EU) 210, 275, 291, 292
evaluation (adoption) 57
evaluation (product) 125, 126
evaluation (sales) 231–2
exclusive distribution 175
executive opinion 91
exhibition 256, 262, 286
experimentation (marketing research) 80–1, 106
expert (buyer behaviour) 63
exploratory research 78, 104–5
exponential (life cycle) 131–2
exponential smoothing 97–8

exporting 290, 302
extended user test 112
ex-works 297

F
factor 171
fad (product) 128–9
family life cycle 32, 45–6
family size (segmentation) 32
FAS 297
fashion (product) 129
fast moving consumer goods (FMCG) 20, 122, 154, 171, 184, 209, 236–8, 242
field experiments (marketing research) 80–1
fifth P (people) 14, 15
films (and PR) 285
financial community (in PR) 279–80
fixed costs 157–8
flow (distribution) 173–4
flow production 4–6
FOB 297
focus (Porter) 141
focus groups 108
follow-up 161, 225–6
forecasting (sales) 16, 82, 86–98, 312
forecasting error 98
form (life cycle) 130
formula approach to selling 212
four Cs 151
four Ps 11, 13–14, 15, 40, 169, 194, 202, 295–300, 313
franchising 187–8
franco rendu 297
free delivered 297
freesheets 260
Freud, S. 48
fringe benefits 231
fundraising 260–1

G
Gantt chart 315
gatekeepers 67
GATT 291–2
General Electric (GE) matrix 139–40
geographic segmentation 30, 37
geometrically weighted moving average 98
global marketing 301
goal related behaviour 48
going rate pricing 160
Government (and PR) 279

group discussion   78, 104, 108
growth (life cycle)   131–2

H
halo effect   241
hard core loyals   35
hard sell   9
header boards   256
Herzberg, F.   51–2
hierarchy of effects/needs   59–60,
   238–9
historical perspective (of marketing)
   1–3
horizontal conflict   180
hygiene factors   51–2
hypothesis testing   82

I
id   48
idea generation   125
image (corporate)   272
imitative products   123–4
'in' supplier   67
income (segmentation)   31, 44
independents (retail)   177
industrial buying   60
industrial channels   178–9
industrial goods   119–20, 242–3
industrial marketing   209
industrial revolution   1–2, 3, 4
industry/market evolution model   140
inelasticity   152–4
infants   145
influencers   67
information (adoption)   57
information audit (MkIS)   83
innovative products   123
innovators   59, 134, 245–6
inside order taker   214
installations   120
insurance (export)   300
intensive distribution   175
interactive approach   269
interest (adoption)   57
internal accounting system (MkIS)
   73–5, 316
internal data (forecasting)   88–91
internal marketing   266, 287–8
international marketing   290–306
international marketing mix   295–300
international PR   272–3
Internet   173, 176–7, 189
intertype conflict   181–2
interview (for sales post)   228–9

interviews (marketing research)   78–9
introduction (life cycle)   131
inventory   198, 204–6
inverse demand curve   165

J
JICTAR   89
job enrichment (sales)   230
job production   4
job specification (selling)   216, 227–8
jobber   178
joint venture   301
journey planning   220
jury method   91
just-in-time   16, 68, 195–6, 198

K
Keegan's five strategies   299
kinked demand curve   155–6
knowledge (buyer behaviour)   57–8

L
laboratory experiments (marketing
   research)   80
laggards   59, 135, 246
language (international marketing)
   303
late majority   59, 135, 246
Lavidge & Steiner model   251
law (international marketing)   304
law of supply and demand   153
lead generation (sales)   260
lean manufacturing   68
learning (buyer behaviour)   53
legal environment   22
less-developed countries   294
licensing   301–2
lifestyle segmentation   36
linear moving average   95–7
literature (PR)   284
Little (A.D.) matrix   144
logistics   14, 191–208, 300
long-term planning   313
loyalty (segmentation)   37

M
macro environment   21–6
mail order   188–9, 259, 260
mainstreamers (segmentation)   36
Majaro (advertising)   253–4
management by objectives (MBO)   51
management science   81
marginal analysis (MkIS)   85–6
market diversification   122–3

market intelligence (MkIS)   75–6, 316
market intensification   122
market knowledge (selling)   219
market leaders   160
market research   261
market space   189
marketer's approach (price)   150,
    159–65
marketing communications research
    115–16, 261
marketing concept   1–12, 101, 169–70
marketing definitions   11, 192
marketing experiment   112
marketing information system (MkIS)
    15, 70–86, 102–4, 316
marketing mix   11, 13, 29, 118, 149,
    194, 241, 295–300, 313
marketing models   15
marketing objectives   312–13
marketing organisation   17–18
marketing orientation   2, 11, 16, 17,
    270
marketing philosophy   1, 13
marketing planning   307–17
marketing planning process   310–16
marketing research   101–17
marketing research process   107–8
marketing research system (MkIS)
    76–81
Maslow, A.   49–50
materials handling   191
maturity (life cycle)   132–3
McKinsey & Co. (critical success
    factors)   126–7
McKinsey/GE matrix   139–40
measurement (planning)   315–16
media advertising   249–50
medium-term planning   313
merchandising   256
message (source)   248
mission statement   307
missionary selling   214
MkIS definition   71
modern era (manufacture)   3–9
modification (product)   129
modified rebuy   66
monopoly   154
mosaic (segmentation)   34
motivation (buyer behaviour)   48–52
motivation (sales)   230–1
motivational research   108–9
motivation-hygiene theory   51–2
moving averages   93–7
multi-level marketing (MLM)   172

multinational marketing   290
multiple choice question   110
multiples   177, 185–6

N
NAFTA   291
nationalisation   6–7
nationality (segmentation)   32
need identification (selling)   221
negotiation (sales)   223–4
neighbourhood dwelling
    (segmentation)   34
nested segmentation   38
network marketing   172
new products   123–7
new task (buying)   66
NICs   294
noise (communications)   116
non-price competition   154
non-probability sampling   109
not-for-profit marketing   101, 149, 268

O
objections (sales)   222
objective forecasting   87, 92–8
objectives (organisational)   307
observability (buyer behaviour)   58
observation (marketing research)   79,
    112–13
occasions (segmentation)   36
odd/even pricing   165
oligopoly   154–6
one stop shopping   186–7
OPEC   291
open ended question   110
open ended question   111–12
opening (sales)   221
opinion leaders   45, 281–2
opportunity cost   198
optimisation   81–2
order processing   198
organisation chart   18
organisational buying   60–9, 209
organisational objectives   307
'out' supplier   67
outside order taker   214
overseas branch   301
own label brands   186

P
pack flashes   256
packaging   146–7, 256, 300
party plan   188
PDM   191, 194, 195, 196, 198–9, 200–7

penetration pricing   162–3
people   14
perception (buyer behaviour)   52–3
perfect competition   154
performance (sales)   231
personal communication (in PR)   284
personality (buyer behaviour)   47–8
personality (corporate)   272
persuasion (buyer behaviour)   57–8
PEST   21, 26, 310, 311
pets   138
photography (and PR)   285
physical distribution   169, 191
physiological needs   49, 239
pile it high philosophy   185, 186
pilot testing   109–10
PIMS   137
place   13–14, 192, 300
political (segmentation)   32
political environment   22, 304
Porter's generic strategies   140–1
portfolio (product)   136–46
positioning   27, 30, 40–1
post-adoption   57
PR (definition)   270
predictive research   105–6
premium offers   256
preparation (sales)   218–20
presentation (sales)   221–2
press (and PR)   284
prestige pricing   165
price   13, 149–67, 296–8
price leaders   160
price lining   165
pricing concepts   152–65
pricing perspectives   150
pricing research   113
primary data   78–81
problem children   137–8, 145
problem identification (selling)   221
problem solving (buyer behaviour)   42
product   13, 118–48, 295–6
product adoption   134–6
product categories   119–22
product development   123, 125
product diffusion   134–6
product diversification   123
product flow   173–5
product knowledge (selling)   219
product life cycle   128–33, 162, 164
product line   126
product management   122–3, 160
product mix   127
product positioning   40–1

product research/testing   113, 261
production orientation   10
promotion   13–14, 235, 240, 261, 298–9
propaganda   267
proximate macro-environment   19
psychographic segmentation   36
public relations (PR)   209, 266–89
publicity   240, 274–5
publics (of PR)   269, 276–83
pull promotion   168
puppy dog technique   224
purchasing procedures (segmentation)
   37–8
purposeful sample   109
push promotion   168

Q
qualities for selling   215–16, 228–9
quantitative forecasting   87
question marks   137–8
questionnaires   79–80, 106, 110–12
quota   233, 314

R
rationing   6
recruitment (sales)   226–8
reference groups   45
reformers (segmentation)   36
relationship marketing   68, 267–8,
   287–8
relative advantage   58, 135
relaunched products   124
religion (international marketing)   303
remuneration (sales)   232–3
replacement products   123
resale price maintenance (RPM)   184
research process   107–8
respect (buyer behaviour)   49
retail audit   79, 113, 114
retailing   183–9
reverse marketing   68
reward (buyer behaviour)   63
room for manoeuvre concept   223–4
RORO   200
routine rebuy   217

S
safety needs   49, 239
SAGACITY (segmentation)   32–3
salary (sales)   232
sales aids   220
sales budget   233, 314
sales commission   232
sales conferences   230

sales forecasting   16, 82, 86–98, 191, 314
sales management   226–34
sales meetings   230
sales orientation   10–11
sales promotion   240, 256–8, 260
sales quota   233, 314
sales routine/sequence   216–26
sales skills   215–16
sales target   233, 314
satellite TV   177
saturation (life cycle)   132–3
SBU   136, 137, 138, 139, 143, 161, 311
scrambled merchandising   181, 187
screening   125
secondary data   76–8, 88
segmentation (consumer)   29–37
segmentation (industrial)   37–9
segmentation   16, 27–41
selection (sales)   228–9
selective distribution   175
self-actualisation   49, 239
self-concept (buyer behaviour)   47–8
self-esteem (buyer behaviour)   49, 239
selling (benefits)   211
selling   19, 209–34, 240
selling centres   213
selling tasks   211–15
sensitivity panels   108–9
service levels   193, 200, 204
sex (segmentation)   30
sharp angle   224
shelf strips   256
Shell directional policy matrix   143
shifting loyals   35
shopping goods   121
silent revolution   8–9, 31
similar situation (selling)   224–5
simple moving average   94
simulation   81–2
situational (segmentation)   38
situational analysis   307, 310
skills (selling)   215–16
skimming (price)   163–4
sleeper effect   248
SLEPT   310
smoothing coefficient   97–8
social class   31, 44
social influences (buyer behaviour)   42–53
social needs   49, 239
socio-cultural environment   23
soft core loyals   35
spin doctor   271, 276

sponsorship   263, 286
stars   137, 145
status (buyer behaviour)   63
STEP   21, 26
step cost   158
stockholding   198, 204–6
storage   191
straight rebuy   66
straight salary (sales)   232
strategic business unit (SBU)   136, 137, 138, 139, 143, 161, 311
strategy   307
structured interviews   78
subjective forecasting   87, 91–2
subsidiary (overseas)   301
succeeders (segmentation)   36
summary question (selling)   224
superego   48
supervision (sales)   231
supplier environment   20
supplier's market   10
supplies (product)   120
supply chain integration (SCI)   151
supply curve   153
surveys (marketing research)   79–80, 109–10
switchers   36
SWOT   311
synergistic dividend   182–3
systems analysis   83, 88–9, 200–2
systems selling   213

T
tactics   307, 316
target   233, 314
target marketing   27, 28–9, 30, 101
target pricing   156–7
task environment   170
taxation   7–8
team selling   213
technical selling   214
technological environment   24
telephone marketing   259
television (and PR)   285–6
test market   80–1, 125–6
theory X and Y (McGregor)   50–1
thermometer question   110
time series   92–3
timing (planning)   315
total business logistics   191, 197, 208
total product offering   192
total quality management (TQM)   267
tracking study   79

training (sales)   229
transfer pricing   298
transition to maturity (Porter)   142
transportation   199–200
trend fitting   82
trial close   224
trialability (buyer behaviour)   58
two-step flow model   244–5, 282

U
unaided recall question   110
undeveloped countries   294
undifferentiated marketing   40
unique selling proposition (USP)
    221–2, 252
usage status (segmentation)   35, 37
users   67

V
values (international marketing)   303
variable costs   157
variation (planning)   316

vending   188
venture team   124
vertical conflict   180–1
virtual value chain   189
voluntary group   185

W
war horses   145–6
warehousing   191, 198, 199
wealth (redistribution)   8
weighted moving average   94–5
welfare state   8
wholesaler   171, 177, 185
width (product)   127
wildcats   137–7, 145
Wind, Y. (buyer behaviour)   62–4
wobblers   256
word-of mouth communication   247

Z
Zakon's matrix   136–7